SOLUTIONS TO POLITICAL POLARIZATION IN AMERICA

Political polarization dominates discussions of contemporary American politics. Despite widespread agreement that the dysfunction in the political system can be attributed to political polarization, commentators cannot come to a consensus on what that means. The coarseness of our political discourse, the ideological distance between opposing partisans, and, most of all, an inability to pass much-needed and widely supported policies all stem from the polarization in our politics.

This volume assembles several of the nation's top analysts of American politics to focus on solutions to polarization. The proposals range from constitutional change to good-government reforms to measures to strengthen political parties. Each tackles one or more aspects of America's polarization problem. This book begins a serious dialogue about reform proposals to address the obstacles that polarization poses for contemporary governance.

Nathaniel Persily is the James B. McClatchy Professor of Law at Stanford Law School. He is an award-winning teacher and a nationally recognized constitutional law expert who focuses on the law of democracy, addressing issues such as voting rights, political parties, campaign finance, and redistricting. He has been appointed as a special master or court-appointed nonpartisan expert to draw redistricting plans for several states, including New York, Maryland, Georgia, and Connecticut. In 2014, he served as the senior research director for the bipartisan Presidential Commission on Election Administration.

D1603857

Solutions to Political Polarization in America

Edited by
NATHANIEL PERSILY
Stanford Law School

CAMBRIDGE
UNIVERSITY PRESS

CAMBRIDGE
UNIVERSITY PRESS

32 Avenue of the Americas, New York NY 10013-2473, USA

Cambridge University Press is part of the University of Cambridge.

It furthers the University's mission by disseminating knowledge in the pursuit of education, learning and research at the highest international levels of excellence.

www.cambridge.org
Information on this title: www.cambridge.org/9781107451919

© Cambridge University Press 2015

First published 2015

A catalogue record for this publication is available from the British Library

Library of Congress Cataloguing in Publication data
Solutions to political polarization in America / edited by Nathaniel Persily.
    pages cm
Includes bibliographical references and index.
ISBN 978-1-107-08711-8 (hardback)
1. Polarization (Social sciences) – United States.   2. United States – Politics and government.
3. Social conflict – United States.   4. Right and left (Political science) – United States.
I. Persily, Nathaniel.
JK1726
320.973–dc23   2014035265

ISBN 978-1-107-08711-8 Hardback
ISBN 978-1-107-45191-9 Paperback

For my wife, Andrea Persily

Contents

Contributors

Nathaniel Persily
James B. McClatchy Professor of Law, Stanford Law School

Alan I. Abramowitz
Alben W. Barkley Professor of Political Science
Emory University

Michael J. Barber
Assistant Professor of Political Science
Brigham Young University

Sarah A. Binder
Professor of Political Science
George Washington University
Senior Fellow
Brookings Institution

Adam Bonica
Assistant Professor of Political Science
Stanford University

Bruce Cain
Charles Louis Ducommun Professor in Humanities and Sciences and
    Professor of Political Science
Stanford University

George C. Edwards III
University Distinguished Professor of Political Science
Texas A&M University

Jacob S. Hacker
Director of the Institution for Social and Policy Studies, and Stanley B. Resor
    Professor of Political Science
Yale University

Gary C. Jacobson
Distinguished Professor of Political Science
University of California, San Diego

Elaine C. Kamarck
Lecturer in Public Policy, John F. Kennedy School of Government
Harvard University
Senior Fellow, Brookings Institution

David Karol
Professor of Government and Politics
University of Maryland

Frances E. Lee
Professor of Government and Politics
University of Maryland

Arend Lijphart
Professor Emeritus of Political Science
University of California, San Diego

Jane Mansbridge
Adams Professor of Political Leadership and Democratic Values
John F. Kennedy School of Government
Harvard University

Nolan McCarty
Susan Dod Brown Professor of Politics and Public Affairs
Woodrow Wilson School
Princeton University

Russell Muirhead
Robert Clements Professor of Democracy and Politics and Associate Professor
    of Government
Dartmouth College

Paul Pierson
John Gross Professor of Political Science
University of California, Berkeley

Richard H. Pildes
Sudler Family Professor of Constitutional Law
New York University School of Law

Markus Prior
Associate Professor of Politics and Public Affairs
Woodrow Wilson School
Princeton University

Jonathan Rodden
Professor of Political Science
Stanford University

Steven S. Smith
Kate M. Gregg Distinguished Professor of Social Science
Washington University

Natalie Jomini Stroud
Associate Professor of Communication Studies
University of Texas at Austin

Introductory Chapters

1

Introduction

Nathaniel Persily

The topic of political polarization dominates discussions of contemporary American politics. Commentators may mean different things by the term, but widespread agreement exists that much of the dysfunction in the U.S. political system can be blamed on or explained by polarization. The coarseness of our political discourse, the ideological distance between opposing partisans, and most of all, an inability to pass much-needed and widely supported policies all stem from the polarization in our politics.

This volume assembles several of the nation's top analysts of polarization in American politics. However, unlike the many other volumes written on this subject, this book focuses on solutions to polarization. As such, it necessarily takes these authors, who more often analyze causes and consequences than propose remedies, out of their comfort zone. Debunking conventional wisdom and warning of unintended consequences tend to be more valuable coins in the realm of political science. The professional risks usually exceed the rewards of sticking out one's neck to suggest, with admittedly incomplete information, reforms that might address the most serious policy challenges of the day. We are, therefore, very thankful for the Hewlett Foundation, which helped alter the cost-benefit calculus and supported a conference that produced the chapters for this volume.

The proposals are intentionally brief, readable, and at times, tentative. But each suggests a direction for the country to address the widely maligned claim of polarization in our politics. They range from the mundane (e.g., tweaks to campaign finance laws) to the overly ambitious (e.g., compulsory voting, proportional representation, elimination of primary elections). Recognizing that the U.S. separation-of-powers system is uniquely threatened by polarization, several authors suggest (sometimes fancifully) constitutional change. However, most of the proposals take the basics of our constitutional structure as a given. Still, much can be done short of a constitutional amendment or convention to address the many facets of America's polarization problem.

DEFINING POLARIZATION

Before turning to solutions it is important to define the problem. Polarization, like "corruption," is quickly becoming a catchall for whatever ails American politics. For purposes of this book, three separate but interacting phenomena fall within the ambit of "polarization." The first is ideological convergence within parties and divergence between parties – what we might call "hyperpartisanship." The second, often characterized as "gridlock," refers to the inability of the system to perform basic policy-making functions due to obstructionist tactics. Third, when we speak of polarization we often mean something beyond government dysfunction: a larger cultural phenomenon of "incivility," namely the erosion of norms that historically constrained the discourse and actions of political actors or the mass public.

These phenomena interrelate, but every solution to polarization does not address all three of its manifestations. Lowering the bar for policy making by eliminating or limiting the filibuster, for example, has not brought the parties closer together or made them more civil. Similarly, changes in the electoral system aimed at increasing the number of moderate legislators will only affect the potential for gridlock if party leaders allow votes to take place in which moderates might be peeled away from the party's position. And changing the tenor of media coverage of politics – were it even possible – would not necessarily result in a kumbaya moment leading to negotiation among elites with fixed views on the size of government. A comprehensive solution to polarization may require addressing these three different manifestations, but some may be more amenable to policy intervention than others.

Hyperpartisanship

As many have argued, the current state of high ideological definition of the parties stands as an example of "be careful what you wish for" for political scientists. For decades, political scientists decried the "irresponsible" party government that characterized the parties in Congress. In particular, the Democratic coalition, consisting as it did of Southern Dixiecrats and Northern urban liberals (among others), failed to exhibit the coherence that political scientists envied about European parties in parliamentary systems, particularly Great Britain. If only the parties could be more disciplined and ideologically defined, the argument went, then they would be more accountable to voters and perhaps more likely to pass popular legislation that otherwise could not break through the "Conservative Coalition" that controlled Congress.

Fast forward to 2014, and the complaints have shifted 180 degrees. Now, the problem is excessive ideological coherence: the parties are too well defined. Their candidates offer clear options on virtually every major area of public policy. On health care, civil rights, the environment, taxes, education, immigration, and fiscal policy, the parties and their nominees have clearly defined and opposing positions. Claims that "there's not a dime's worth of difference between the parties" ring especially hollow in recent years. (Chapter 2 by Nolan McCarty and Michael Barber, which explores the causes and consequence of polarization, discusses these developments in greater detail.)

To be more precise, several rough measures for ideological coherence need to be kept in mind. The first is the increase in party-line votes in Congress. In both parties there are fewer defectors on any given vote than there have been in recent decades. Previously viewed as a sign of party "strength," now this kind of partisan team support is seen as institutional weakness. Under conditions of divided government, such strong parties pose particular obstacles (all else equal) because the president then has fewer members of the ruling party in Congress that he or she can peel off to help enact preferred legislation.

Party-line voting does not, by itself, indicate *ideological* polarization, however. It only points to the strong bonds that exist among partisans when they are called on to be counted. In theory, at least, one party could want to cut $1 in taxes and the other $2, and a divided government could be unable to pass either bill or a compromise because of the rigidity of the parties' positions and the willingness of partisans to fall in line.

Other measures of ideological coherence focus on where party members stand on certain issues: in particular, the congruence among partisans and the ideological distance between the median party members. Not only are partisans unwilling to compromise in the current environment but also their bargaining positions are so far apart that compromise on many issues is impossible. If 100% of one party's membership wants to ban oil drilling, for example, and 100% of the other wants to increase it, not much room for bargaining exists. The more that such a dynamic – ideological similarity among co-partisans but extreme differences between opposite partisans – typifies the political landscape, the more we can say the parties are ideologically polarized. To be sure, there are some issues, such as foreign and national security policy, over which the parties in Congress are not internally coherent, but such exceptions are more atypical now than in recent decades.

Related to this point is the greater intensity of political preferences among co-partisans. Saying partisans are further apart from each other on some spectrum, either one as generic as liberal to conservative or more specific such as pro-life or pro-choice, does not necessarily suggest they feel intensely about such issues. In particular, it does not speak to the willingness of opposing partisans to bargain away their positions on certain issues in exchange for others. Under current conditions of ideological polarization, issues are perceived as life or death and opponents' positions are seen as beyond the pale. In today's Congress, it would appear that not only are the parties far apart on the issues but also that the ideological distance is matched by a widespread intensity of belief on a host of issues that might not have been seen as so fundamental and defining in previous eras. Moreover, because parties increasingly view bargains as zero sum from an electoral or political perspective, even policies that both parties support may not pass if one party has more to gain (in votes or public opinion) from a successful deal.

There is considerable debate as to whether the ideological polarization just described is limited to elites (particularly members of Congress) or extends to the mass public. At a minimum the following could be described as the modest scientific consensus on the question: (1) elites (i.e., members of Congress) *and* the mass public are more polarized now than in recent decades in that they are better sorted into parties and more consistently vote for their party's nominees and (2) the mass public is less polarized than elites, highlighted in no small measure by the fact that a sizable plurality now identify as independents. Beyond those points of consensus, scholars differ over the relative shape of the distribution of opinion of the mass public as compared to the parties in Congress. To some extent this distribution depends on the issue, because public attitudes on many "moral values" questions such as guns, abortion, and gay rights appear more bell-shaped than the distribution of preferences among elites. However, on many other issues, especially when framed exactly as the legislation that Congress considers, the mass public more closely mirrors elites.

One final point concerning hyperpartisanship: when people talk about polarization, they often mean more than just the division of the population or elites into two ideologically divergent and coherent camps. They also tend to imply that the camps are of nearly equal size. The parties are polarized, on this score, because the size of each of the two camps is roughly equal. If two-thirds of Americans (let alone legislators) were Democrats, then most would not consider our politics polarized, even if a smaller faction of Republicans was unified and extreme in its opposition. This is important to keep in mind when considering policy responses, because one could easily argue that the best antidote to polarization is whatever measure might lead one party to have overwhelming dominance among the population and elites. Not only would it solve gridlock but it would also replace polarization with greater consensus.

Just to summarize, the notion of hyperpartisanship entails:

(1) **Coherence** – the relative lack of internal divisions within each party
(2) **Divergence** – the ideological distance between median party members
(3) **Intensity** – the fact that partisans are not only far apart but they also care enough about their positions that they are less willing to budge
(4) **Parity** – the political parties are of roughly equal strength

Gridlock

The U.S. Constitution is designed to disperse power and to make policy making difficult. Fear of concentrated authority was a natural consequence of our particular colonial origins, as well as a common theme for much of the political conflict throughout U.S. history. Even under conditions of political harmony, the structural features of the Constitution (such as checks and balances, bicameralism, federalism) exist as considerable obstacles to policy making not seen in most other democracies.

Under conditions of divided government in a separation-of-powers system, however, hyperpartisanship can lead to gridlock. Unlike a Westminster-style parliamentary government, in which party-line voting is key to execution of the government's agenda, party-line voting in the U.S. Congress can prevent an opposing president from executing his or her agenda. For much of the last century, this did not pose a problem. Even when we had divided government, the porousness of the parties in Congress and their decentralized power structure allowed presidents to make deals with members of the other party. When the party controlling Congress is unified and power is concentrated, the opposing president is less able to peel apart the opposing party coalition to get votes on his or her preferred policy.

A cohesive party can cause gridlock even when it does not control Congress, of course. Control of either house or of a sizable share of the Senate can enable a unified party to obstruct policies supported by a majority. Many additional veto points exist in the Senate (e.g., filibuster, holds, blue slip process) that allow for obstruction by a minority or even an individual senator. As described in the next subsection, several of these avenues for obstruction, reserved for extraordinary circumstances in the past, are now part of ordinary politics.

The willingness to use both ordinary and extraordinary tactics to prevent government from performing its most basic functions constitutes the most

troubling manifestation of polarization. Budget stalemates and resulting government shutdowns are really the least of it, because those tactics might be
seen as anticipated by the separation of powers in the Constitution. In many
respects the formal constitutional barriers to policy making seem less threatening than exploitation of extra-constitutional rules, such as the filibuster,
senatorial holds on nominees, and, most devastating on this score, the threat
of debt default.

At the same time, persistent gridlock makes alternative modes of policy
making more attractive by shifting power away from Congress and toward the
president and courts. Holds and filibusters of executive branch appointments
lead to recess appointments or delegations of power to officials not requiring
Senate confirmation. Similarly, the inability to get policy through Congress
leads presidents to engage in unilateral action through executive orders, deliberate decisions not to enforce the law, and other similar tactics. Courts in
such an environment also gain tremendous power, because their decisions
interpreting or modifying statutes will often become the final word, with a
Congress and a president unable to overturn them.

Incivility and the Erosion of Politics-Constraining Norms

Hyperpartisanship and gridlock refer to measurable political phenomena, but
incivility is the aspect of polarization that truly lies in the eye of the beholder.
The term loosely indicates "meanness," but in that sense, it would be hard to
assess the relative kindness of today's politicians to those of yesteryear. (How
does Congressman Joe Wilson's shout of "You lie" to President Obama in his
State of the Union address compare, for example, to the dueling of Hamilton
and Burr or the caning of Charles Sumner on the floor of the House of
Representatives?) In a larger sense, though, the incivility distinctive to today's
politics comes from the erosion of norms that historically constrained political
discourse and action. This incivility is not limited to policy elites, of course,
but may be more broadly shared among the mass media and public.

The ingredients to this incivility are varied. The ideological distance
between partisans is mirrored, some argue, by differences in psychology and
the tendency even to believe different politically relevant facts (e.g., the human
causes of global warming, the existence of WMDs in Iraq, the birthplace of
the president). Some of this is the result of the different media echo chambers
in which the partisans exist on cable news, talk radio, and the internet. In such
an environment both conspiracy theories and incendiary rhetoric can fester
and thrive.

The claim of declining civility extends beyond the Rush Limbaughs and
Bill Mahers of the world, however. Campaigns themselves, the argument goes,

have become nastier. Here, too, we may be suffering from a selective amnesia about the past – think of the "Daisy" or "Willie Horton" ads, for example. Yet the rise of unaccountable, sometimes unknowable outside groups (such as SuperPACs or 501(c)(4) organizations) as major forces in campaigns has removed some of the transparency and associated deterrence that previously may have chilled the most extreme campaign tactics. Candidates and parties that may have previously suffered from going "a bit too far" can now rely on outside groups to do the dirty work for them.

The dissolution of boundaries for what counts as acceptable rhetoric in politics and campaigns is just one way to measure civility, however. Indeed, uncivil language, hardly unique to contemporary politics, is more a species of the larger phenomena of the erosion of norms that previously constrained politics. Or perhaps more specifically, incivility always had its place, but now has become commonplace.

The erosion of other politics-constraining norms illustrates how actions previously considered "nuclear" have become conventional. Take recall elections, for example. Since its birth in the Progressive Era, the recall has been reserved (in theory) for the most egregious of violations of an officeholder's duties (i.e., ones that could not wait for the curing effect of a regularly scheduled election). Since the successful recall of California governor Gray Davis in 2003, however, the practice has become routine. Since then, we have seen attempts to recall Wisconsin governor Scott Walker; state legislators in Wisconsin, Colorado, Arizona, and Michigan; and Iowa's Supreme Court Justices. In fact, according to Joshua Spivak, who writes the *Recall Elections Blog*, more than 168 recall elections occurred in 2012, leading to the removal or resignation of 108 local or state officials.

The rise of the recall is but one example of the larger trend of using extraordinary electoral mechanisms for ordinary politics. The mid-decade redistricting in Texas, Georgia, and Colorado are other examples. Legislatures had always had the power to redraw lines at times other than following a census (and some exercised it to cure technical defects in existing plans or for other non-political reasons). But never before had they done so for expressly political reasons. The Texas re-redistricting also engendered its own form of extraordinary norm-breaking, now repeated elsewhere and in different contexts, of legislators leaving the state to prevent a quorum necessary for the legislature to conduct business.

The examples of innovative tinkering with electoral machinery do not end there. The recent spate of laws, passed on party-line votes, to require photo ID at the polls, shorten periods of early voting, or restrict the activities of outside groups attempting to register voters also reflect an erosion in norms as to whether and on what grounds rules of the electoral game should be changed. Indeed, all of these changes, as well as much worse and more explicit efforts at disenfranchisement or outright fraud, have been tried before, as with Dixiecrat legislatures during Jim Crow. (And, for that matter, many of these recent changes could be justified, had they been passed with bipartisan support and different motives, on good-government grounds.) However, their normalized use as a tool in partisan warfare is of relatively recent vintage and is emblematic of the polarization in American politics.

Republicans and Democrats will argue as to when this erosion of politics-constraining norms began. Republicans point to the famous 1984 "Bloody Eighth" congressional district recount controversy, in which a Democratic-controlled Congress determined the victor in a hotly contested congressional election, or perhaps to the rejection of Supreme Court nominee Robert Bork. Democrats might point to the impeachment of President Clinton or perhaps *Bush* v. *Gore*. Whatever the beginning, no one can doubt that this erosion has accelerated in the last decade. Tactics once reserved for worst case scenarios or last resorts are now considered fair game for normal politics.

In Chapter 3 in this volume, Jacob Hacker and Paul Pierson warn, however, that a tendency to blame both parties for polarization fails to describe accurately the polarization problem and, worse still, could lead to wrong-headed and counterproductive reform proposals. They argue that Republicans disproportionately engage in the "constitutional hardball" tactics described earlier and that the ideological distancing of the parties has been principally due to the rightward drift of Republicans. The "polarization problem" is, therefore, really a Republican extremism problem, they maintain, and proposals to correct it will be doomed from the start unless they recognize the asymmetry in political polarization.

ADDRESSING POLARIZATION

The chapters in this volume provide a diverse array of proposals to address, manage, or partially solve the various aspects of political polarization described earlier. Some focus on electoral reforms intended to facilitate the election of moderates, others on the need to strengthen political parties, and still others on the ways to lower the barriers to policy making. None of the chapters claims to have the magic bullet to solve America's "polarization problem." Each, however, proposes interventions that might help tame the excesses of the polarized political system or otherwise mitigate the effects of hyperpartisanship, gridlock, and incivility.

The absence of a magic bullet should not be surprising given the long-run historical forces that have given rise to our current situation. Nolan McCarty and Michael Barber describe in Chapter 2 how long-term social developments, such as rising inequality, the enfranchisement of African Americans, increased immigration, and party realignment in the South, have contributed to polarization in Congress. In so doing they reject much of the conventional wisdom, which blames polarization on redistricting, closed primaries, and the like. In line with the task force of the American Political Science Association of which they were a part, they encourage a renewed emphasis on facilitating negotiation, rather than attempting to unwind the ideological polarization long in the making.

Of course, just because gerrymandering, closed primaries, and other election rules may not have caused polarization does not necessarily mean that reforms of those processes might not help mitigate polarization once it emerged. The chapters in the next part, "Reforming the Electoral System," describe several proposals in this vein. In Chapters 5 and 6, Gary Jacobson and Elaine Kamarck run through the usual suspects: redistricting commissions, reforming primaries, and raising contribution limits to candidate campaigns. Arend Lijphart in Chapter 4 and Jonathan Rodden in Chapter 7 propose more radical reforms, such as compulsory voting, both to mitigate the polarization caused by voter mobilization and to make it more likely that the median voter in a district will have greater power in determining representatives. Lijphart goes even further, putting forth 15 different proposals, including the elimination of party primaries, instant runoff voting, and proportional representation for elections to both the House and Senate.

Instead of embracing "good-government" reforms often directed at limiting the power of polarizing parties, other authors seek to embolden party leaders and organizations against extremists. The chapters from Nolan McCarty, Richard Pildes, Bruce Cain, and me – Chapters 8–11 in the "Strengthening Parties" section – are all in that tradition. These authors argue that the increased power of outside extremist groups, such as the Tea Party, at the expense of established party organizations pulls the parties further apart and retards negotiation and compromise by preventing party leaders from speaking on behalf of the whole party. In particular, they propose either generous public funding of political parties or increasing the amount of money that individuals and groups can contribute to political parties, even to the point of returning to the old days of "soft money." Such proposals arise from a recognition that increasing the number of "moderates" in the party caucuses may prove to be too difficult a task. Rather, greater promise might be found in empowering the median party members and party leadership to rein in the most extreme forces in the parties.

Other authors are not so quick to give up on getting moderates elected to Congress. Some argue that the greater polarization of Congress, as compared to that of the mass public, could be remedied by improving the information that voters have about candidates. In Chapter 12, Adam Bonica, for example, suggests giving all voters a "data-driven voter guide" that would enable them to more accurately identify the ideological distance between themselves and the candidates running for election. Markus Prior and Natalie Stroud's proposals in Chapter 13 are in a similar spirit. They blame polarization, in part, on the fact that moderates do not turn out to vote. Therefore, they propose a series of reforms targeting the turnout of moderates, as well as public education proposals to discourage young people, in particular, from developing reflexive partisan viewpoints.

Most of the proposals discussed to this point deal with hyperpartisanship; the remaining chapters in the section, "Lowering Barriers to Policy Making," consider gridlock and how to overcome it. The first set of proposals concerning gridlock recommends removing or lowering various barriers to policymaking. The second set looks at efforts to promote and foster negotiation among opposing partisans, particularly in Congress.

Because it will be very difficult to change constitutionally specified obstacles to policy making (checks and balances, bicameralism, presidential veto, etc.), most solutions to gridlock begin with reforms of Senate and House rules, both written and unwritten. Several of the chapters urge reform of the filibuster as one way to facilitate majoritarian policy making. During the writing of this book, the Senate finally began to rein in the filibuster, eliminating it for most presidential appointments. However, Alan Abramowitz, David Karol, and Steven Smith in Chapters 14–16 suggest we should go further and eliminate or limit its use for legislation as well. Abramowitz also suggests abolishing the debt ceiling, and all three authors endorse several of the election reform proposals described earlier. With respect to the House, both Elaine Kamarck in Chapter 6 and Russ Muirhead in Chapter 17 propose changes to the way we elect a Speaker. To make the Speaker truly a Speaker of the whole House, they suggest that he or she be elected by a supermajority vote. With bipartisan support, such a Speaker would be more likely to bring to the floor bills supported by a majority of the members of Congress.

The exploitation of constitutional and subconstitutional veto points in the policy-making process is only part of the gridlock story; the other part concerns systematic breakdown in negotiation between the parties. Several authors explore what it would take to get Democrats and Republicans to the bargaining table to agree on policies that both could stomach. Secrecy in negotiations is a persistent theme throughout the chapters. Sarah Binder and Frances Lee emphasize it in Chapter 18, as does Jane Mansbridge in Chapter 19. When the TV cameras are on, the public pressures to stand firm will necessarily hobble both parties' ability to negotiate. Removing some of the well-intentioned but counterproductive laws that require transparency might help foster a safe space for negotiation. In Chapter 20 George Edwards strikes a similar chord with respect to the president, urging "staying private" instead of "going public." Edwards blames the permanent campaign for the breakdown in negotiation. With every policy dispute viewed in electoral terms, successful negotiation only happens in the rare instances when neither party fears that the other will benefit from a law's passage.

Similar arguments can be made with respect to other good-government reforms. Bans on earmarks and other side payments, argues Mansbridge, may unnecessarily constrict the means available to secure agreement from hold-outs on policy. When fewer tools exist to "buy off" legislators by providing particularistic favors, ideology and party loyalty become the primary forces shaping decisions of individual members as to whether to compromise. The same may hold with respect to measures that might make incumbents less secure, Mansbridge, Binder and Lee all maintain. On the one hand, electoral checks are necessary to ensure accountability and to replace representatives who stray too far from their constituents. On the other, high turnover and a constant fear of replacement may lead to fewer representatives with the expertise and the long-term relationships necessary to build trust. Paradoxically, the more effective the electoral check on incumbent behavior, the less willing the average legislator may be to compromise.

CONCLUSION: SOLVING OR MANAGING POLARIZATION?

Most of the reforms to address political polarization fall into two broad categories. In the first are those proposals that seek to facilitate the election of moderates or empower them once elected. The second category includes reforms that take polarization at the elite level as a given and look for ways to manage it so as to minimize the potential for government paralysis. One might think of the former as "bottom-up" strategies and the latter as "top-down" strategies.

Because the roots of our current polarization run very deep, the bottom-up strategies will be successful, if at all, only over the long term. Changes to primary rules and gerrymandering, for instance, will have an effect only to the extent that they will lead to a new crop of members of Congress who have not already staked out ideological positions far from the median voter. Indeed, as several authors in this volume argue, such reforms will only have an effect if they lead to the election of a sizable number of moderates, perhaps amounting to a majority of the caucus of the party controlling the House.

The top-down strategies could have a quicker payoff, but they come with risks as well. Betting on the party leadership – either by making them relatively "richer" through campaign finance reforms or giving them greater power to negotiate – runs the risk that moderates will be reined in just as much as extremists and that the party leadership could entrench itself. For example, in the states where the Tea Party controls the Republican Party, empowering the party leadership in the nomination process or campaigns may lead to fewer moderates getting elected or having power once they do. Similarly, the reforms of the negotiation process that would make it more secret and perhaps more particularistic (by bringing back earmarks, closing off hearings, etc.) face opposition for the same reasons that motivated "sunshine" and other open-government laws in the first place.

Neither approach is mutually exclusive of the other. Indeed, given the extent of political polarization, the challenges in getting any reform passed, and the fact that many reforms will need to be done state by state, an "all-hands-on-deck" approach is warranted. Although the history of similar political reforms cautions attention to the law of unintended consequences, it is hard to envision the political situation getting worse on this score. Of course, we have not descended into violence, and news from Egypt, Ukraine, Afghanistan, and any number of other unstable regimes should give us some perspective on our problems. That being said, the U.S. political system is more polarized than at any time in the past century. The threat such polarization poses to contemporary governance requires that all serious reform proposals be given consideration.

2

Causes and Consequences of Polarization*

Michael J. Barber and Nolan McCarty

Rarely these days does a news cycle pass without new stories of political dysfunction in Washington, D.C. Reports of stalemates, fiscal cliffs, and failed grand bargains have begun to erode the public confidence in the ability of our representative institutions to govern effectively. In May 2013, only one American in six approved of the way Congress has handled its job.[1] Sadly, that level of support was a major improvement from the previous summer, when wrangling over the usually routine matter of raising the debt ceiling drove congressional approval down to 10%.

The most common diagnoses of Washington's ailments center on the emergence of excessive partisanship and deep ideological divisions among political elites and officeholders. In short, "polarization" is to blame. Consequently, the reform-minded have taken up the mantle of reducing polarization or mitigating its effects. In recent years, proposals for electoral reform to change electoral districting, primary elections, and campaign finance have been presented as panaceas. Other reformers have focused on changing legislative procedures such as those related to the filibuster, appropriations, and confirmation process to limit the opportunities for polarization to undermine government.

Although there has been intense public discussion about the causes of polarization, its consequences, and possible cures, social science research has only recently begun to help shape those discussions. The intent of this chapter is to provide a more evidence-based foundation for these debates.

* This piece was shaped profoundly by discussions of the American Working Group of the APSA Task Force on Negotiating Agreements in Politics. This group includes Andrea Campbell, Thomas Edsall, Morris Fiorina, Geoffrey Layman, James Leach, Frances Lee, Thomas Mann, Michael Minta, Eric Schickler, and Sophia Wallace. We also thank Chase Foster for his assistance with the Working Group. An earlier version of his chapter appears in Jane Mansbridge & Cathie Jo Martin, eds., *Negotiating Agreement in Congress* (Washington, D.C.: APSA, 2013).
[1] See www.gallup.com/poll/162362/americans-down-congress-own-representative.aspx.

PRELIMINARIES

The academic study on partisanship and polarization is based on a combination of qualitative and quantitative research. Noteworthy qualitative accounts, which often combine historical research and participant observation, include Rohde (1991), Sinclair (2006), Hacker and Pierson (2006), and Mann and Ornstein (2012).

The starting point for many quantitative studies of polarization is the robust observation of rising partisan differences in roll-call voting behavior in Congress. The bipartisan coalitions of the 1950s and 1960s have given way to the party-line voting of the twenty-first century. Although these trends are apparent in simple descriptive statistics about partisan divisions on roll calls, political scientists have developed more refined measures of partisan voting differences. A variety of techniques use data on roll-call voting to estimate the positions of individual legislators on a set of scales.[2] The primary scale – the one that explains most of the variation in legislator voting – generally captures partisan conflict. At the individual-legislator level, positions on these scales reflect a mix of ideological positioning and constituency interest as well as party loyalty and discipline. Political scientists continue to debate the exact weights of these factors. Some scholars argue that the scores primarily capture ideological differences (e.g., Poole 2007), whereas others interpret them as measures of partisanship (e.g., Lee 2009). Without taking a position on this debate, we refer to the primary roll-call voting scale as the "party-conflict dimension."[3] However, consistent with common usage, we may also label positions on the scale as liberal, moderate, or conservative.

All of these techniques for estimating the party-conflict dimension produce similar findings with respect to polarization. Consequently, we focus on the DW-NOMINATE measures developed by McCarty, Poole, and Rosenthal (1997). Generally, these scores range from −1 to +1 and are scaled so that the highest scores are those of conservative Republicans and the lowest are those of liberal Democrats.

Given the estimated positions of legislators on this scale, we can measure partisan polarization by computing the difference in means (or medians) across the political parties, where a larger gap indicates a greater level of polarization. Figure 2.1 presents the difference in party means on the party-conflict scale from 1879 through 2011.

---

[2] See Poole and Rosenthal (1997); Groseclose, Levitt, and Snyder (1999); Clinton, Jackman, and Rivers (2004).

[3] It is important, however, to distinguish these scores from party loyalty. Some members who have extreme positions on these scales are not always loyal partisans (e.g., "Tea Party" Republicans).

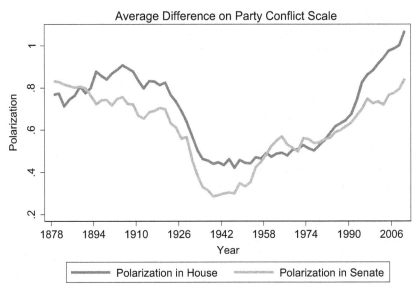

FIGURE 2.1. *Average Distance between Positions across Parties.* The *y*-axis shows the difference in mean positions between the two parties in both the House of Representatives and Senate from 1879 to 2011 using the DW-NOMINATE measures. Congress is more polarized than it has been in more than 125 years.

From the 1930s until the mid-1970s, these measures of polarization were quite low. Not only were differences between the typical Democratic and Republican legislators small but there also were significant numbers of conservative Democrats and liberal Republicans. Since the 1970s, however, there has been a steady and steep increase in the polarization of both the House and Senate. Other measures of party conflict confirm the trend of increasing polarization in the past 40 years.[4]

Although conventional wisdom often asserts that polarization resulted from the changing behavior of both parties (i.e., with Democrats moving to the left and Republicans to the right), the evidence shows that the behavioral changes are far from symmetric and are largely driven by changes in the positioning of the Republican Party.[5]

---

[4] Although Figure 2.1 shows a steady movement by the average Republican, the Republican caucus in Congress has not become more homogeneous in the same time period. The standard deviation of Republican ideal points has remained around 0.15 since the 1950s. Democrats, conversely, have become much more homogeneous in the same period with the disappearance of conservative Southern Democrats.

[5] For a discussion of methodological issues underlying this claim, see Hare, McCarty, Poole, and Rosenthal (2012).

Figure 2.2 plots the average positions of the parties by region. In the past 40 years, the most discernible trend has been the marked movement of the Republican Party to the right (for qualitative evidence, see Hacker and Pierson 2006; Mann and Ornstein 2012). It is important to note that the changes in the Republican Party have affected both its Southern and non-Southern members. The movement of the Democratic Party to the left on economic issues in the past 50 years is confined to its Southern members – reflecting the increased influence of African American voters in the South. However, it is important to note that the implied asymmetry may pertain only to the issues (primarily economic) that dominate the congressional agenda. It may well be the case that on some social issues (e.g., gay marriage), polarization is the result of Democrats moving to the left.

Another important aspect of the increase in party polarization is the pronounced reduction in the dimensionality of political conflict. Many issues that were once distinct from the party-conflict dimension have been absorbed into it. Poole and Rosenthal (1997) and McCarty, Poole, and Rosenthal (1997) both noted that congressional voting can be increasingly accounted for by a single dimension that distinguishes the parties. This situation directly contrasts with that of the mid-twentieth century, when the parties were divided internally on a variety of issues primarily related to race and region. Figure 2.3 quantifies these changes, showing the percentage of individual roll-call vote decisions in the House that can be correctly classified by one- and two-dimensional models.[6] The two-dimensional spatial model accounts for most individual voting decisions since the late nineteenth century. Its classification success was highest at the turn of the twentieth century, exceeding 90%. However, the predictive success of the two-dimensional model fell during most of the twentieth century, only to rebound to the 90% level in recent years.[7]

Increasingly, most of the work is being done by the party-conflict dimension. In the period from 1940 to 1960, adding a second dimension to account for intraparty divisions on race and civil rights led to a substantial improvement in fit. A second dimension often explained an additional 3% to 6% of the voting decisions in the House. However, in recent years, the second dimension has

---

[6] When legislators cast a vote in the way that is predicted by their estimated position on the scales, we say their vote is "correctly classified." Therefore, the figure simply plots the total number of correctly classified votes divided by the total number of votes in a given congressional session. Patterns for the Senate are similar.

[7] The high rates of classification success that we observe do not result simply because most votes in Congress are lopsided votes, where members say "Hurrah." On the contrary, Congress continues to have mostly divisive votes, with average winning majorities between 60% and 70%.

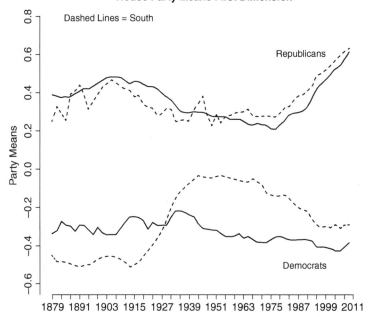

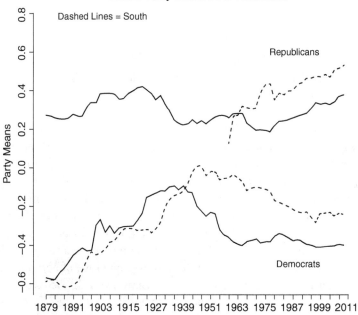

FIGURE 2.2. *Mean Party-Conflict Score by Party and Region.* The *y*-axis in this figure shows the mean position of each party by region. In this plot, the South is defined as AL, AR, FL, GA, KY, LA, MS, NC, OK, SC, TN, TX, and VA. There were no Southern Republican Senators between 1913 and 1960 and only two before that.

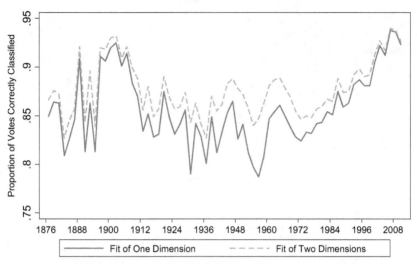

FIGURE 2.3. *The Classification Success of One- and Two-Dimensional DW-NOMI-NATE Models in the U.S. House.* The solid line plots the proportion of House roll-call voting choice correctly predicted by a single dimension. The dashed line shows the proportion predicted when a second dimension is added. During the 1950s, a second dimension that captured intraparty divisions on race improved the prediction rate from 3% to 6% per congressional term. In recent years, the improvement has been considerably less than 0.5%.

provided no additional explanatory value. In the 112th Congress, the second dimension explains only an additional 1,800 votes of the almost 600,000 cast by House members.

Although polarization and the reduction in dimensionality tend to coincide, there is no necessary logical connection between the two trends. One possibility is that partisan polarization might occur simultaneously across any number of distinct dimensions. For example, parties could polarize along distinct economic and social dimensions. However, this would imply varying intraparty disagreements on the different dimensions. To the contrary, the evidence points to similar intraparty cleavages on almost all issues. For example, the most anti-tax Republican legislators are generally the most pro-life, pro-gun, and anti-marriage equality. Similarly, the Democrats most likely to support a minimum-wage hike are those most supportive of abortion rights and gay marriage. Using the terminology of Converse (1964), *issue constraint* at the congressional level has expanded dramatically.

A second logical alternative is that polarization might coincide with the displacement of the primary dimension of partisan conflict by another issue dimension, consistent with the theory of realignments put forward by Schattschneider (1960), Burnham (1970), Sundquist (1983), and others. However, this situation also appears inconsistent with the data on roll-call voting. As McCarty, Poole, and Rosenthal (2006) documented, the partisan division on economic issues has remained the primary dimension of conflict, and other issues – such as social, cultural, and religious issues – have been absorbed into it.

Although there is a broad scholarly consensus that Congress is more polarized than any time in the recent past, there is considerably less agreement on the causes of such polarization. Numerous arguments have been offered to explain the observed increase in polarization, and these causes can be divided into two broad categories: (1) explanations based on changes in the external environment of Congress and (2) those based on changes in the internal environment. The external explanations provide arguments about how shifts in the social, economic, and electoral environments have altered the electoral incentives for elected officials to pursue moderation or bipartisanship. The internal explanations focus on how the formal and informal institutions of Congress have evolved in ways that exacerbate partisan conflict (or generate the appearance of such an increase). Although we think it is productive to divide the literature along external-internal lines, it is important to note that these explanations are not mutually exclusive. Indeed, many of the internal explanations presume a shift in the external environment that stimulates revisions of legislature rules, procedures, and strategies.

In the following sections, we review the current literature on each of these suggested causes and evaluate the evidence for and against each argument.

EXTERNAL EXPLANATIONS

A Polarized Electorate

Perhaps the simplest explanation for an increasingly polarized Congress is one grounded in the relationship between members of Congress and their constituents. If voters are polarized, reelection-motivated legislators would be induced to represent the political ideologies of their constituents, resulting in a polarized Congress. Evidence of voter-induced polarization is elusive, however.

Empirical support for the voter-polarization story requires evidence for two specific trends. First, it requires that voters be increasingly attached to political parties on an ideological basis. Liberal voters should increasingly support the

Democratic Party, and conservative voters should increasingly support the Republican Party. This process has been labeled *partisan sorting*. Second, the hypothesis requires that voters be increasingly polarized in their policy preferences or ideological identification. Extreme views must be more common so that the distribution of voter preferences becomes more bimodal.

There is considerable evidence for the first trend: voters have become better sorted ideologically into the party system. Layman and Carsey (2002) and Levendusky (2009) found that, over time, voters have increasingly held political views that consistently align with the parties' policy positions. Using data from the National Election Study, Layman and Carsey (2002) found evidence for a pattern of *conflict extension*, in which differences in the policy preferences of partisans have grown in economic as well as social and racial domains. Their results, updated through 2004, are presented in Figure 2.4.

The trends presented in Figure 2.4 are consistent with the finding that fewer voters today than in the past hold a mix of Democratic and Republican positions. As the parties become more coherent in their policy positions, voters sort themselves accordingly. This may well account for the finding of Bartels (2000) that partisan identification has become a better predictor of voting behavior over time. Also, because the terms "Republican" and "Democrat" now represent increasingly distinct clusters of policy positions, citizens who identify with one party expect the other party's identifiers to hold dramatically different political views. Consequently, party identifiers report that they dislike one another more than they did a generation ago (Shaw 2012) and state that they would be less likely to feel "comfortable" with their child marrying someone who identifies with the opposite party than was the case in the 1960s (Iyengar, Sood, and Lelkes 2012).

Fiorina (2013) argues that the patterns described herein reflect party sorting and not polarization in voters' policy positions. A lively debate has emerged about the mechanisms underlying the better sorting of voters into parties. Sorting may improve for two distinct reasons. First, voters may shift their allegiance to the party that takes their policy position. Alternatively, voters may adjust their policy views to match those of the party with which they identify. Levendusky (2009) found evidence for both mechanisms, but determined that position switching is more common than party switching. Carsey and Layman (2006) also found that party switching does occur, but that it is limited to those voters who have a salient position on one issue and are aware of the partisan differences surrounding it. However, Lenz (2012) finds little evidence favoring the party-switching mechanism. Ultimately, however, both processes are facilitated by greater polarization of partisan elites, suggesting that the

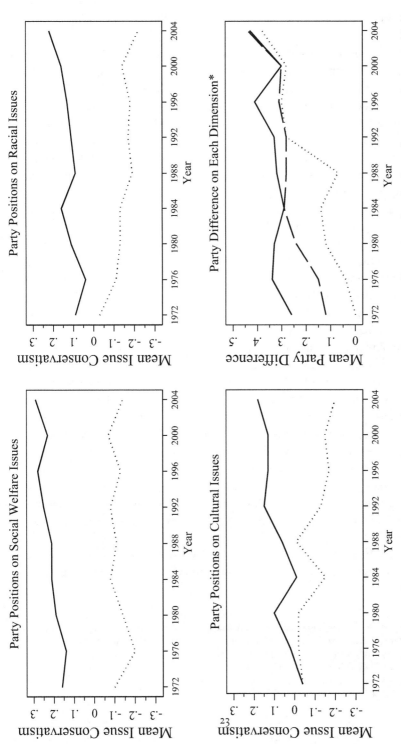

FIGURE 2.4. *Mass Party Polarization on Three Issue Dimensions, 1972–2004.* Party positions are the estimated means for each party on latent variables (ranging from −1 for the most liberal position to +1 for the most conservative position) from confirmatory factor analyses. *Party difference is the Republican mean minus the Democratic mean. *Source:* 1972–2004 National Election Studies.

trends in Figure 2.4 may be the consequence of elite polarization rather than the cause.[8]

Whereas few scholars doubt that substantial voter sorting has occurred, the evidence for voter-policy polarization is less clear. The emerging consensus is that most voters have been and remain overwhelmingly moderate in their policy positions (Fiorina, Abrams, and Pope 2005; Ansolabehere, Rodden, and Snyder 2006; Fiorina and Abrams 2008; Levendusky, Pope, and Jackman 2008; Bafumi and Herron 2010). In studies that produce estimates of voter-issue positions that are comparable to legislator positions, representatives were found to take positions that are considerably more extreme than those of their constituents (Clinton 2006; Bafumi and Herron 2010).

Figure 2.5 illustrates the main finding of Bafumi and Herron (2010). In the 109th Congress, almost every senator was more extreme than the median voter of his or her state. Although the ideological distance between representative and constituent may well have increased, some distance seems to have existed since the introduction of the earliest measurements of this issue. As early as 1960, McClosky and his colleagues found that delegates to the party conventions took positions that were more extreme than those of the voters identifying with each party.[9] Recently, Abramowitz (2010) found a more bimodal distribution of preferences among those voters most likely to participate in politics compared to the average party identifier, with further polarization still among party activists and donors.[10] The phenomenon of the more-and-more active being more-and-more extreme probably results in part from self-selection, with those having intense feelings being more willing to spend time and money on politics, and in part from the dynamic of group polarization (Sunstein 2002), in which people who talk with one another in relatively homogeneous groups end up taking more extreme positions than the party's median members. Regarding moderate voters, some have chosen middle-of-the-road positions for substantive policy reasons. Others, however, are uninformed, unengaged, or apathetic, checking off the middle position on surveys due to lack of an opinion.

Although the lack of evidence of voter polarization casts doubt on the simple link between voter and elite polarization, a dynamic version may hold

---

[8]   McCarty, Poole, and Rosenthal (2006) and Gelman (2009) also found that voters have become better sorted into parties by income over time. The question of whether partisan voters are more sorted by geography is controversial (see Klinkner 2004; Bishop 2009).

[9]   See McClosky, Hoffmann, and O'Hara (1960).

[10] Based on surveys of convention delegates, Layman et al. (2010) found evidence consistent with activists taking more extreme positions over time.

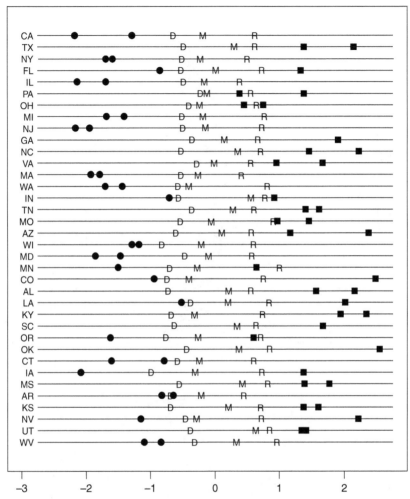

FIGURE 2.5. *Senators and Median Constituents.* The x-axis shows the median ideology of the median voter M as well as the median partisan D and R on the same policy scale as sitting senators (indicated by circles for Democrats and squares for Republicans) in each state. In almost every state, senators are more extreme than voters and partisans in their state. *Source:* Figure 2 in Bafumi and Herron (2010).

more promise. As voters sort in response to elite polarization, the incentives for parties to take positions that appeal to supporters of the other party will diminish. This leads to greater partisan polarization and greater incentives for voters to sort. Although this mechanism is not ruled out by existing evidence, it has not yet been subjected to formal tests.

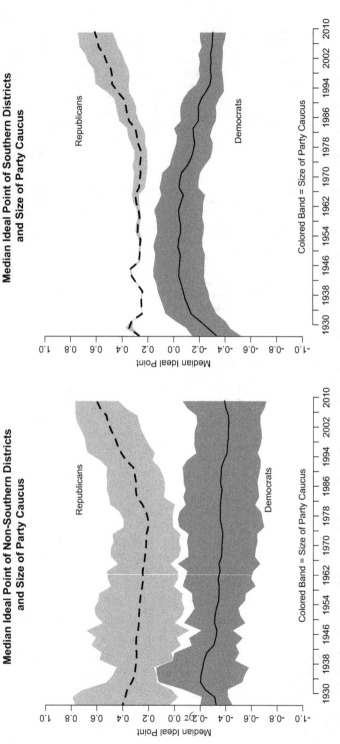

FIGURE 2.6. *Median Position of Parties and Caucus Size.* The *y*-axis shows the median position on the party-conflict scale. The colored band around each line shows the relative size of the party caucus. Republicans now hold many more seats in the South than 40 years ago, but Southern and non-Southern Republicans alike have taken increasingly conservative positions.

Southern Realignment

Although Americans still appear to remain overwhelmingly moderate, there is no denying that dramatic changes have occurred in terms of policy sorting between the parties. The realignment of the South from a solidly Democratic region to one dominated by Republicans is the starkest example of the sorting of ideology and partisanship.

Figure 2.6 places the Southern realignment in the context of the national story of polarization. The left-hand panel shows that since the 1970s there has been a dramatic increase in the number of Republicans representing Southern districts in the House of Representatives. As these Republicans replace more moderate Democrats, we see two effects. First, the median Southern Democrat becomes more liberal. By the early 2000s, most of these Democrats were representing majority-minority districts. At the same time, the new Southern Republicans were becoming increasingly conservative. However, the right-hand panel in the figure shows that the conservative path of Southern Republicans is mirrored in non-Southern districts. Thus, to blame polarization completely on the disappearance of conservative Democrats would be to ignore the conservative trajectory of non-Southern Republicans. The movement in the median ideology of Democrats, however, can be nearly accounted for by the replacement of moderate Southern Democrats with Republicans.

Whereas much attention has been focused on the effects of the Southern realignment for the emergence of a conservative Republican party in the South, the post–Voting Rights Act increase in the descriptive representation of African Americans and Latinos in the House also has had a discernible effect on polarization. Although the representatives of these groups are hardly monolithic, they are overrepresented in the liberal wing of the Democratic Party; any leftward movement of the Democrats can be accounted for by the increase in the number of African American and Latino representatives.[11]

Gerrymandering

Scholars have long suggested that allowing state legislatures to draw congressional districts may lead to overwhelmingly partisan and safe districts

---

[11] McCarty, Poole, and Rosenthal (2006) found that African American and Latino House members have more liberal DW-NOMINATE scores, even after controlling for party and the ethnic and racial composition of their districts. However, roll-call–based measures of the positions of minority legislators may understate those members' contribution to increasing the diversity of interests represented in Congress. The difference between white and minority legislators is larger on other legislative activities, such as oversight, bill co-sponsorship, and advocacy (Canon 1999; Tate 2003; Minta 2009; Minta and Sinclair-Chapman 2013; Wallace 2012).

that free candidates from the need to compete for votes at the political center (Tufte 1973; Carson et al. 2007; Theriault 2008a). However, the evidence in support of gerrymandering as a cause of polarization is not strong. First, we consider the Senate and those states in which there is only one congressional district. In these cases, gerrymandering is impossible because the district must conform to the state boundaries. Yet, in the Senate and in at-large congressional districts, we observed increasing polarization (McCarty, Poole, and Rosenthal 2006). Furthermore, McCarty, Poole, and Rosenthal (2009) generated random districts and determined the expected partisanship of representatives from these hypothetical districts given those districts' demographic characteristics. The result was that the simulated legislatures generated by randomly creating districts are almost as polarized as the current Congress. This finding holds because polarization relates more to the difference in how Republicans and Democrats represent moderate districts than the increase in the number of extreme partisan districts. Therefore, an attempt to undo partisan gerrymandering with moderate, competitive districts still leads to a polarized legislature, due to the difference between, rather than within, the parties.

Figure 2.7 illustrates this argument. The plot shows the vote-based ideologies of members of the 111th House of Representatives and the 2008 Democratic percentage of the presidential vote in that district. Scholars frequently use presidential vote shares as a proxy for a district's average ideology because the vote shares allow for a unified measure of political preferences across the country at any one point in time. Thus, a district with a larger Democratic vote share is interpreted to have more liberal constituents than a district that has a smaller Democratic vote share. Members of Congress from the same party vote quite similarly, even though they represent districts with vastly different political preferences. This difference is illustrated by the regression lines drawn in the figure for each party. Democrats who represent districts that split almost evenly in the presidential vote are not significantly more conservative than Democrats representing districts that overwhelmingly supported Obama in 2008. However, there is a dramatic difference in how representatives of the opposing parties represent districts with identical presidential vote shares. This figure does not support the argument that gerrymandering is producing districts that contain heavy partisan majorities, thereby leading to extreme representatives. Rather, more of the observed polarization can be explained by the differences between the parties in relatively moderate and competitive districts.

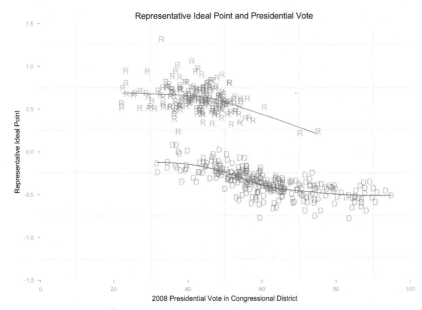

FIGURE 2.7. *Representative Position on Party Scale and Presidential Vote Share.* The *x*-axis shows the partisanship of the congressional district as measured by the Democratic percentage of the 2008 presidential vote. The *y*-axis is the representative's DW-NOMINATE score for the 111th House of Representatives. There are major differences in the way Republicans and Democrats represent similar districts. These differences account for a larger share of the aggregate party difference than the differences in the types of districts that Democrats and Republicans represent.

Primary Elections

Given the extent to which voters are now ideologically sorted into political parties, some observers suggest that only conservatives can win Republican primaries and only liberals can win Democratic primaries.[12] This suggested feature of contemporary politics has led reformers to focus on whether the rules governing participation in primaries might be altered to make it possible for more moderate candidates to win nominations. The standard recommendation is to move from closed partisan primaries to open primaries, which would allow the participation of independents. The state of California has

---

[12] Note, however, that as Figure 2.7 shows, there are many Democrats who represent districts that won less than 50% of the Democratic vote share in the 2008 presidential election and have quite moderate ideal points.

recently gone one step further with the nonpartisan "top-two" primary, in which voters of both parties cast ballots for candidates of either party and the top two vote-getters move to the general election.

Based on the historical record, it is implausible that partisan primaries are a major cause of polarization. Polarization has increased during the past 40 years despite the opening up of primaries to nonpartisans (McCarty, Poole, and Rosenthal 2006). The narrower question of whether open or nonpartisan primaries would reduce contemporary levels of polarization continues to be an active area of research, but the evidence to date provides sparse support for the argument that opening primaries to nonpartisans would reduce polarization.

A few studies have found evidence for a polarizing effect of partisan primaries. Kaufmann, Gimpel, and Hoffman (2003) found that presidential primary voters in states with open primaries hold political ideologies similar to those of the general electorate, whereas in states with closed primaries, the two electorates are more ideologically distinct. Gerber and Morton (1998) found that the positions of legislators nominated in open primaries hew more closely to district preferences, whereas Brady, Han, and Pope (2007) found that legislators who hew closely to the general-election electorate suffer an electoral penalty in primaries.

However, most of the research suggests that the effects of moving to open-primary systems are modest at best. Hirano et al. (2010) studied the history of primary elections for the U.S. Senate. Their findings cast significant doubt on the role of primary-election institutions in polarization. First, the introduction of primaries had no effect on polarization in the Senate. Second, despite the common belief that participation in primaries has been decreasing, they found that primary turnout has always been quite low. Thus, it is doubtful that changes in primary participation can explain the polarizing trends of the past three decades. Third, they find no econometric evidence that either low primary turnout or low primary competition leads to the polarization of senators. Using a panel of state legislative elections, Masket et al. (2013) investigated the effects of changing primary systems and found little evidence that such switches affect polarization. Similarly, Bullock and Clinton (2011) investigated the effects of California's short-lived move from a closed primary to a blanket primary, in which any registered voter can participate. They found that the change did lead to more moderate candidates in competitive districts but that these effects were not observed in districts that were dominated by either of the parties. This result suggests that the recent change in California to a top-two primary may affect districts that are not firmly controlled by one or the other party.

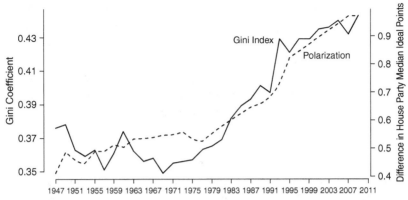

FIGURE 2.8. *Polarization and Income Inequality.* The *y*-axis shows the difference in median positions for the two parties and the Gini coefficient in the United States. The Gini coefficient is a measure of income inequality that ranges between 0 (perfect income equality) and 1 (one person controls 100% of the nation's income).

Economic Inequality

McCarty, Poole, and Rosenthal (2006) demonstrated a close correlation between economic inequality and polarization in the United States.[13] Figure 2.8 shows that economic inequality and polarization have tracked together in the past 50 years. Moreover, unlike most other hypotheses about polarization, the inequality hypothesis can explain the decline of polarization during the first half of the twentieth century, as economic inequality fell dramatically in that period (Piketty and Saez 2003). McCarty, Poole, and Rosenthal (2006) argued that inequality and polarization are linked by a dynamic relationship in which the increased inequality generated by rising top incomes produces electoral support for conservative economic policies and facilitates a movement to the right by Republicans. The resulting polarization then has a dampening effect on the policy response to increased inequality, which in turn facilitates greater inequality and polarization.

In support of the hypothesis that the distribution of income has affected polarization, McCarty, Poole, and Rosenthal (2006) demonstrated that voting behavior and partisan identification increasingly correlate with income (see also Gelman 2009) and that the ideal points of legislators are increasingly correlated with average district income. They then show (see following discussion) that polarization may have exacerbated inequality due to its negative

---

[13] See also Brewer, Mariani, and Stonecash (2002).

effects on social policy. Although the 2006 study is limited by the fact that the correlation between inequality and polarization may be spurious in the U.S. time-series data, Garand (2010) found strong evidence that state-level inequality exacerbates constituency polarization within states and predicts the extremity of Senate voting behavior. Furthermore, recent work by Bartels (2008) and Gilens (2012) showed that policy reflects the preferences of the wealthy more often than the desires of those on the bottom rungs of the economic ladder.

Money in Politics

Another common argument is that polarization is directly linked to the system of private campaign finance used in U.S. elections. Such arguments are generally premised on the idea that politicians pursue extreme policy objectives on behalf of their special-interest funders (Lessig 2011).

However, political science research suggests that any connections between campaign finance and polarization may be more subtle and complex than the conventional wisdom. Most research suggests that there is a weak connection between campaign spending and election outcomes (Jacobson 1990) or between sources of campaign funding and roll-call voting behavior (Ansolabehere, de Figueiredo, and Snyder 2003).

Conversely, the data suggest that fundraising in congressional campaigns has increased in importance, as evidenced by the steady rise in the sheer amount of money required to run for office. Since 1990, the average amount of money spent in U.S. House elections has nearly doubled in real terms. Whereas the amount of money raised in campaigns is important, the sources of funding may be more consequential for polarization. Consider the difference between the two largest sources of money for congressional candidates: contributions from individuals and contributions from political action committees (PACs). Scholars have long argued that although PACs may seek specific policy outcomes, these goals are often narrowly focused such that PACs are less concerned with the overall ideology or party of politicians and more interested in having access to members of Congress (Hall and Wayman 1990; Smith 1995; McCarty, Poole, and Rosenthal 2006; Bonica 2013).

Individual donors, however, are believed to behave quite differently. The literature on the ideology of individual donors suggests that individual contributors are more extreme than individual non-contributors and are primarily motivated by ideology when deciding who to support financially (Barber 2013; Bafumi and Herron 2010; Stone and Simas 2010; Francia et al. 2003). Furthermore, recent work estimating the ideological positions of contributors suggests that individuals are more ideologically extreme than PACs and other interest

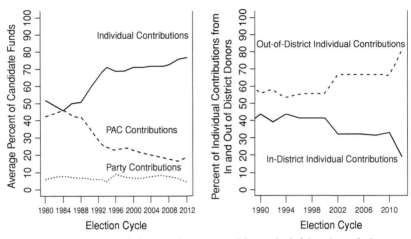

FIGURE 2.9. *Average Candidate Fundraising Portfolio.* In the left-hand panel, the *y*-axis shows the average percentage of congressional candidates' fundraising that comes from individual donors, PACs, and party contributions. In the right-hand panel, the *y*-axis shows the average percentage of individual donations that come from donors who reside inside and outside of the candidate's district.

groups (Barber 2013; Bonica 2013). Given the differences between PAC- and individual-contribution behavior, an increasing reliance of candidates on ideologically extreme individual donors might force candidates to move toward the ideological poles to raise money (Baron 1994; Moon 2004; Ensley 2009). We may also see a rise in more ideologically motivated PACs, a phenomenon that deserves further investigation.

Figure 2.9 provides evidence of an increasing reliance on individual donors. Since 1980, the average share of a candidate's fundraising portfolio comprising individual contributions has increased from less than half to nearly three quarters. At the same time, the share of individual contributions coming from out-of-district donors, who are believed to be more ideologically motivated, has increased as well (Gimpel, Lee, and Kaminsi 2006; Gimpel, Lee, and Pearson-Merowitz 2008). Together, these data suggest that there may be a direct connection between the rise in individual contributions and polarization in American politics.

However, more research is needed to convincingly link individual contributions and polarization. Although individual contributions and polarization may be increasing at the same time, this does not immediately suggest a causal relationship. Looking at individual states may provide a way to better identify the relationship. Variation in contribution limits among the states has led to differing abilities to raise money from individuals, PACs, parties, and other sources (Barber 2013). Analyzing this variation in contribution limits across time and place may provide a more conclusive view into the relationship between the increasing amount of money flowing into politics and increasing polarization.

Media Environment

Changes in the media environment of politics may also have had an important role in polarization. Many observers note that American journalism changed markedly following Watergate in a manner that may have contributed to a more confrontational style of politics. The introduction of cameras into the House chamber and the broadcasting of its proceedings on C-SPAN gave the minority Republicans, led by Newt Gingrich, a powerful new weapon against the majority party (Zelizer 2006). Others argue that the proliferation of media outlets through cable television and the internet has created an additional impetus for polarization. Recently, Prior (2007) found that partisan voters increasingly self-select into news outlets that confirm their basic partisan and ideological biases (i.e., Republicans watch Fox News and Democrats watch MSNBC). Such narrow casting was not absent in media-viewing patterns 40 years ago, but it was not nearly as extensive. One effect of this change is that elected officials have less space to deviate from their party orthodoxy for fear of being called out by party activists. Another effect is that relatively extreme activists have a platform to push forward partisan talking points to a subset of the public, contributing to societal polarization.

Equally troubling is the finding that independents increasingly prefer *Seinfeld* reruns to any news outlet. Prior (2007) called the effect of the alternative news-less media "polarization without persuasion" and suggested that the media's effect on polarization is mostly the result of nonideological Americans avoiding inadvertent news exposure through the availability of cable entertainment, whereas in the past, network television offered no alternative except the news for several hours every evening. When the only option on television was the evening news, Prior suggested, nonpolitical Americans were exposed to political information and mobilized to vote in greater numbers than they would have otherwise. He claimed that this effect is more important than partisan media by pointing to the fact that polarization and cable penetration were correlated beginning in the 1970s, long before Fox News, MSNBC, or any other partisan cable news stations existed. Others examined how the decline of newspapers, which have experienced thousands of layoffs in recent years and dramatically reduced their coverage, may also be a contributing factor.

Snyder and Stromberg (2010) found that members of Congress who represent districts that are congruent with newspaper markets compile less ideological and partisan voting records.

The reemergence of a more partisan media may also contribute to polarization. A literature attempting to measure partisan media bias and its effects on voters has developed in the past several years. Whereas debate rages as to whether the American media has an overall liberal or conservative bias, there is substantial evidence that media outlets vary in terms of their ideological and partisan orientations (e.g., see Groseclose and Milyo 2005; Gentzkow and Shapiro 2006), and the slant of coverage appears to affect voter evaluations and decisions (e.g., see DellaVigna and Kaplan 2007; Gerber, Karlan, and Bergan 2009; Hopkins and Ladd 2013). Of course, the ideological diversity of the media may be the result of polarization and not the cause. For example, Gentzkow and Shapiro (2006) found that the partisan slant of a newspaper is determined in large part by the partisanship of its local community.[14]

INTERNAL EXPLANATIONS

Rule Changes

Several scholars have suggested that the increase in measured polarization is due to changes in the rules and procedures of Congress. One argument is that the observation of rising polarization is an artifact of changes in the House regarding how votes were recorded in the Committee of the Whole (Theriault 2008b). These procedural changes made it easier for amendments to be proposed when considering legislation. These new amendments were often unrelated to the bill at hand, and they were added primarily to force the opposition party to cast unpopular votes to enable a move to considering the main piece of legislation (Roberts and Smith 2003). This simple change in the rules led to a dramatic increase in the number of party-line recorded votes and therefore led to an increase in measured polarization for indices that use roll-call voting, such as the DW-NOMINATE scores discussed previously (Roberts 2007).

Although this procedural change may have the effect of exaggerating partisan differences, it leaves many questions regarding polarization unanswered. First, the argument is centered on the House of Representatives. Polarization, as we have seen, increased in both the House and the Senate, despite no

---

[14] They also provide evidence against a reverse causal relationship between newspaper slant and local partisanship.

similar procedural change in the Senate. Second, polarization has increased gradually in the past four decades. It seems unlikely that a one-time rules change would produce such a long-term trend. Third, despite a wide variety of rules for agenda setting and recording roll-call votes operating in the American states, the level of polarization in the U.S. House is not atypical of that found in state legislatures (Shor and McCarty 2011).

Majority-Party Agenda Control

A second institutional argument focuses on the agenda-setting power of the majority party in the House (e.g., see Cox and McCubbins 2005; Aldrich 1995; Rohde 1991). Scholars have theorized that leaders of the majority party have been increasingly able to use their control over the legislative agenda to build distinctive party brands and prevent intraparty divisions. This leadership behavior, in turn, generates more party-line votes and a larger level of observed polarization. Like the rules-based explanations, these explanations struggle to explain the rising level of polarization in the Senate. Moreover, McCarty, Poole, and Rosenthal (2006) demonstrated that measures of polarization are robust to the changes in the legislative agenda that might be induced by enhanced agenda control.

Party Pressures

An additional institutional argument for increasing polarization is that party leaders in the House and the Senate have become increasingly powerful and, as such, can apply greater pressure on members to vote along party lines. Theories of party government (e.g., see Rohde 1991; Aldrich 1995) suggest that party leaders can apply strong pressures on their members to vote the way the party desires. Former and current members have indicated their impression that these pressures have increased over the years (e.g., see Edwards 2012). In developing this idea, Theriault (2008b) traced the roles of speaker and majority leader, showing that these offices have increased their institutional reach in the past 30 years. He argued that party leaders coax members to vote along party lines by offering rewards to members (e.g., committee memberships in exchange for votes with the party's agenda).

Although the plausibility of increased party pressure is strong, there are major methodological challenges in establishing the magnitude and trends of such pressures. Snyder and Groseclose (2000) attempted to distinguish the influences of parties from other factors, such as ideological preferences on roll-call voting. If we could reliably measure the effect of party pressure on members' voting behavior, we would be able to differentiate the effects of partisanship on polarization from effects of changes in ideology, constituency, and so forth. Unfortunately, the effects of party can be recovered only under strong assumptions. For example, Snyder and Groseclose assumed that members are free from party pressure on lopsided votes; therefore, a comparison between positions on lopsided and close votes can reveal the effects of party pressure. They found that, indeed, there are policy areas in which party pressure is more common, but they did not find a steady increase in partisan pressure commensurate with the increase in polarization observed during the past 40 years. McCarty, Poole, and Rosenthal (2001) criticized Snyder and Groseclose's methodology. Using an alternative methodology, they found declining party pressure in the contemporary Congress. However, methodological difficulties have prevented a consensus on this question.[15]

Teamsmanship

Lee (2009) argued that the trends in Figures 2.1 and 2.2 reflect not only an ideological divergence but also Congress members' increasing efforts to favorably differentiate their own party from the opposition as the two parties become more closely competitive in seeking control of national institutions. She argued as competitiveness increases and electoral conditions suggest a potential reversal of partisan fortunes in the next election, each party has a strategic incentive to engage in strategies of confrontation to highlight partisan differences and to deny the other party legislative victories. Tight competition gives members incentives to act together with fellow partisans, and a norm of "teamsmanship" emerges, with members' individual interests becoming increasingly linked to the fate of their parties. Teamsmanship not only deepens existing ideological divisions; it also creates conflict on issues in which legitimate ideological differences are absent. Partisan divisions on nonideological issues, Lee showed, have grown in tandem with the divisions on ideological issues. If Lee's reasoning on the strategic incentives deriving from party competition for institutional control is correct, we should see congressional polarization for as long as both political parties remain roughly equal in their electoral appeal nationwide.

---

[15] Using a different methodology, Cox and Poole (2002) provided evidence similar to McCarty, Poole, and Rosenthal (2001), but interpreted it in a way more favorable to the finding of party discipline. However, even their interpretation does not support the hypothesis that increased party pressures are associated with polarization.

Lee's teamsmanship perspective is related to the literature on strategic disagreement (Gilmour 1995; Groseclose and McCarty 2001). Strategic disagreement describes a situation in which a president, a party, or another political actor refuses compromise in an attempt to gain an electoral advantage by transferring the blame for the stalemate to the other side. Such behavior often results in the appearance of a level of polarization that exceeds the actual policy differences between the parties.

The Breakdown of Bipartisan Norms

Many personal accounts of former members of Congress link polarization to changes in the social fabric of Capitol Hill, making it more difficult to forge cross-partisan relationships (for a journalistic account, see Eilperin 2007). In the past several decades, members of Congress have increasingly chosen not to relocate their families to Washington and therefore spend far less time there and more time in their home districts. This lack of time in Washington has made it more difficult to form the personal relationships that would foster bipartisan trust and civility. Other reasons advanced for the decreasing number of interpersonal contacts across party lines include the ever-increasing workload for members of Congress and the increased amount of time devoted to fundraising. Although the social-fabric hypothesis is compelling, it has not been subjected to systematic empirical tests.[16]

CONSEQUENCES OF POLARIZATION

Although polarization generally has a negative connotation in our political discourse, it has a number of potential virtues. In the 1950s, another task force of the American Political Science Association decried the American party system for not offering meaningful policy differences to the voters. This lack of choice denied U.S. voters any meaningful influence over public policy. Centrist, undifferentiated parties are also incapable of representing the diversity of interests of contemporary American society. Undoubtedly, the polarization caused by greater representation of formerly unheard voices has benefits outweighed by any potential costs.[17] However, party polarization has negative

---

[16] A possible exception is Masket (2008), who found that randomized seating assignments in the California Assembly produced greater similarities in voting by members who shared desks.
[17] Those who feel nostalgia for the bipartisanship of the 1950s must recognize that it came at the cost of the exclusion of African Americans and other groups from the political process.

consequences to the extent that the parties primarily represent extreme policy views or impede the negotiated compromises required by democratic politics in heterogeneous societies.

As discussed previously, the evidence overwhelmingly supports the proposition that members of Congress are far more polarized than the public at large. As Bafumi and Herron (2010) showed, it is likely that legislators are taking positions that are even more extreme than those of the voters from their parties in their states and districts. Therefore, although polarization may expand the choices on the political menu, the parties are far from satisfying the palate of most voters. Thus, the effects of polarization on accountability and representation are ambiguous at best.

Theoretical Perspectives on Polarization and Policy Making

A polarized party system, however, need not have deleterious effects on policy making. Consider an idealized, purely majoritarian legislature. Imagine that we can represent policy alternatives on a single left–right spectrum and that every legislator has an ideal policy on this spectrum. In such a setting, the median-voter theorem predicts that policy would correspond to the preferences of the median legislator. The distribution of legislative preferences may become very polarized; however, if the median preference is unaffected, the outcome is the same. Although the majoritarian theory is an important benchmark, the real-world deviations from this ideal suggest that polarization should have serious consequences for policy making.

The first limitation of the majoritarian benchmark is the neglected role of legislative parties and their leaders in the policy process. Many scholars argue that legislators have strong electoral incentives to delegate substantial powers to partisan leaders in an effort to shape the legislative agenda as well as to discipline wayward members (e.g., see Cox and McCubbins 2005; Aldrich and Rohde 2010). To the extent that parties can successfully pursue such strategies, policy making becomes the domain of party leaders.

When there are strong parties and leaders, the effects of polarization are mixed. American political scientists have long suggested that more cohesive, distinct, and programmatic political parties would offer a corrective to the failures of policy making in the United States. Enamored of the party-responsibility model of Westminster-style parliaments, they argue that a system in which a cohesive majority party governs encumbered only by the need to win elections would provide more accountability and rationality in policy making.

These benefits of polarization are offset, however, when control of the executive and legislative branches is split among cohesive parties; political polarization has occurred in an era in which divided governments occur with increasing frequency. Before World War II, there was no positive association between divided government and polarization, but the two phenomena have occurred together frequently since then.

In situations of divided government with cohesive parties, party theories predict that policy making represents bilateral bargaining between the parties. The predicted consequences of polarization in this environment are not benign. Increased policy differences shrink the set of compromises that both parties are willing to entertain. They also have a second effect of increasing the incentives to engage in brinkmanship in bargaining and negotiation, thereby endangering even the feasible compromises. Low dimensionality compounds the problem of polarization by foreclosing the negotiation of solutions across distinct policy dimensions. Thus, polarization and low dimensionality lead to more gridlock and less policy innovation during periods of divided government. In contrast, polarization might lead to more policy innovation during unified governments because of increased party responsibility. We discuss later why this positive effect of polarization in unified governments might be negligible.

The second feature of the American system that generates real policy consequences from polarization is its numerous supermajoritarian institutions and veto points. Institutions such as the presidential veto and the Senate filibuster inhibit majority rule and allow polarization to hinder policy making. In the presence of these supermajoritarian institutions, policy making is driven not by the median legislator but rather by the preferences of the more extreme legislators, whose support is pivotal in overcoming vetoes and filibusters.

To illustrate how supermajoritarianism produces gridlocked policy, we suppose again that all policy alternatives and legislator ideal points can be represented as points on a spectrum from left to right, such as the liberal–conservative scale. Consider, for example, the effects of the Senate's rules for debate and cloture. Under its current rules, debate on most legislation cannot be terminated without a vote on cloture that must be supported by three-fifths of those senators elected and sworn. Thus, if all 100 senators vote according to their ideal points, the senators located at the 41st and the 60th most-leftward positions must support any new legislation because no coalition can contain three-fifths of the votes without including them. Therefore, any policy located between these pivotal senators cannot be altered or it is otherwise gridlocked. Before procedural reforms were instituted in 1975, the requirement for cloture was a two-thirds vote. Therefore, the filibuster pivots were located at the 33rd and 67th positions.

Presidential veto power also contributes to gridlock. Either the president must support new legislation, or a coalition of two-thirds of each chamber must vote to override it. Suppose that the president's position is on the left of the policy spectrum. Then the president or the legislator at the 33rd percentile must support any policy change. This legislator becomes the veto pivot. If the president is a rightist, the 67th-percentile legislator becomes the veto pivot.

Putting these institutional requirements together, a rough measure of the propensity for legislative gridlock is the ideological distance between the 33rd senator and the 60th senator when the president is on the left, and it is the distance between the 40th senator and the 67th senator when the president is on the right. When these distances are great, passing new legislation will be difficult. The level of polarization and the width of this "gridlock interval" are closely related because the filibuster and veto pivots are almost always members of different parties. Thus, as the preferences of the parties diverge, so do those of the pivots. In fact, more than 75% of the variation in the width of the gridlock interval in the postwar period is accounted for by party polarization and the 1975 cloture reforms (McCarty 2007). Therefore, this "pivotal-politics" model of supermajoritarianism suggests that polarization reduces opportunities for new legislation and increases the status quo bias of American politics (Krehbiel 1998).

It is important to note that these supermajority requirements may also lead to polarization-induced gridlock, even during periods of unified government. As long as the majority party is not large enough to satisfy all of the supermajority requirements, cross-party bargaining, negotiation, and coalition building are necessary for policy change.

This pivot perspective also underscores why the Senate's cloture rules have come under scrutiny and have produced calls for reform. Once an infrequently used tool reserved for the most important legislation, the filibuster has become – during the period of increasing polarization – one of the central features of U.S. politics. Filibusters, both threatened and realized, have been used to kill many important pieces of legislation. Perhaps even more consequentially, the ease of using the current filibuster has led the Senate to rely greatly on legislative tricks to avoid its effects. One such gimmick is using the budget-reconciliation process to pass new legislation; reconciliation bills cannot be filibustered. This was the approach taken to pass the major income and estate tax cuts in 2001, as well as major portions of the Affordable Care Act in 2009. To avoid points of order under the so-called Byrd Rule, however, such legislation can have deficit-increasing fiscal effects only for the term of the budget resolution (i.e., five to ten years). Thus, many important pieces of fiscal policy require gimmicks such as "sunset" provisions (in which the law expires after a certain predetermined time) to avoid death by filibuster.

Legislative Productivity

Despite the strong theoretical case for a relationship between polarization and policy gridlock, few scholars have addressed the issue. In his seminal work on postwar lawmaking, Mayhew (2005) considered whether divided party control of the executive and legislative branches produces legislative gridlock, but he did not consider the effects of polarization and declining bipartisanship. Indeed, he attributed his finding that divided government produced little gridlock to the fact that bipartisanship was the norm during the postwar period.

McCarty (2007) used data on landmark legislative enactments to assess polarization's effects on the legislative process. He found that the 10 least polarized congressional terms produced almost 16 significant enactments per term, whereas the 10 most polarized terms produced only slightly more than 10. This gap would be even larger except for the enormous legislative output following the September 11 terrorist attacks during the most polarized congressional term of the era. Using a multivariate model that controls for other factors that contribute to legislative productivity, McCarty found substantively large and statistically significant effects of polarization on legislative productivity. At the upper end of the range of his estimates, Congress produced 166% more legislation in the least polarized congressional term than in the most polarized term. Even at the lower range of his estimates, there was a still large – 60% – difference in legislative output. His estimates are robust to the use of other data sources, which extend the time series back to the nineteenth century.

Binder (1999) also found that as the gridlock interval increases under divided legislatures (i.e., when the distance between the House and Senate medians is largest), less legislation is passed. As these gridlock intervals grow due to polarization, her prediction was that we will observe even less legislation created and eventually passed through Congress.

The current unprecedented distance between the parties, combined with divided government between the House and the Senate, has led many media outlets to note that the 112th Congress has passed fewer laws than any other since the late 1800s (Davis 2012; Kasperowicz 2012; Sides 2012; Steinhauer 2012), when polarization was at almost the same levels as today.

Case Study: Polarization, Gridlock, and the Politics of Immigration[18]

Historically, successful immigration legislation was characterized by bipartisan coalitions between Republicans and Democrats, in addition to coalitions across chambers within Congress (Gimpel and Edwards 1998). The last significant piece of comprehensive immigration legislation that successfully navigated the legislative process passed in 1986. The Immigration Reform and Control Act (IRCA), also known as the Simpson–Mazzoli Act, was brought forward by a Democratic representative from Kentucky and a Republican senator from Wyoming, both of whom were chairs of respective subcommittees on immigration in the two chambers. The legislation was partially informed by the bipartisan Commission on Immigration Reform, which is consistent with the use of commissions on immigration throughout the legislative history of this policy area (Tichenor 2002). The legislation was considered comprehensive given the broad scope of the bill, which included criminalization of hiring undocumented immigrants, employer sanctions, and amnesty for a sizable portion of the undocumented immigrant population.

Attempts at reform since the passage of IRCA have been confronted with increased polarization on immigration both between and within the two political parties. Comprehensive immigration bills have had limited success in getting passed in one chamber, much less clearing the necessary hurdles in both chambers. Consequently, much of the legislation introduced during the 1990s and 2000s was piecemeal in nature, meaning that it addressed only one small component of immigration reform. Three major legislative initiatives stand out in the post–IRCA era as attempts at broader immigration reform. In 2006, Bill H. R. 4437, also known as the Sensenbrenner bill, was introduced. Its language was wide in scope and reach because it criminalized being an undocumented immigrant as a felony (as well as the actions of anyone assisting an undocumented immigrant), required significant construction of border fences, and imposed employer penalties and sanctions. Party polarization on the issue was intense, as demonstrated by the bill being pushed only by Republicans (with near-unanimous support within the Republican Party), whereas it was overwhelmingly opposed by Democrats. Mass mobilization of Latinos around the country occurred, leading to approximately 350 protests with millions of participants in an attempt to thwart support of the bill after it passed in the House (Wallace, Zepeda-Millán, and Jones-Correa 2014). Ultimately, the bill died, with scholars attributing the failure to the effects of the protests,

---

[18] This section was written by Task Force member Sophia Wallace.

as well as to a lack of consensus on this issue between the political parties and among the electorate (Zepeda-Millán 2011).

In 2010, the Development, Relief, and Education for Alien Minors Act (DREAM Act) was formally introduced by Dick Durbin (Democrat) and Orin Hatch (Republican), but was also announced by a number of members across both chambers, demonstrating a bipartisan effort at reform – once again in contrast to the Sensenbrenner bill. The purpose of the DREAM Act was to offer a pathway to citizenship for undocumented immigrants who had arrived in the country as minors, attended high school in the United States, and were now enrolling in college or the military. Although bipartisan in its creation, support in the House was split along party lines, with a vote of 216 to 198, with Democrats in favor. In the Senate, the bill did not achieve the necessary 60 votes to end debate, thereby leading to its failure. The DREAM Act is an important indication of the state of party polarization on immigration when one considers the context of the actual bill. In many ways, it was viewed as the least potentially polarizing immigration bill because it involved people brought to the United States as minors. Thus, the assumption was that they bore little culpability for the choices of their parents, and it targeted only those willing to pursue college or the military, which are highly valued pathways for young people. If Republicans and Democrats were going to agree on the issue of immigration reform, then this bill should have been one of the most likely cases to pass muster. However, the defeat of this bill highlights that polarization within Congress had reached nearly insurmountable levels.

More recently, in January 2013, lawmakers announced bipartisan efforts to pursue comprehensive immigration reform, with acknowledgment from both political parties that the nation's immigration system was broken. In particular, attempts to smooth polarization were made through the use of a "gang" – in this case, a bipartisan group of senators – that could work with party leaders to try to appeal to and negotiate with their own party members. The Gang of Eight, in this case, devised a bill that contained individual provisions that appealed to both parties, such as a pathway to legalization for undocumented immigrants and increased border security. The bill was able to win two-thirds of the support of the Senate but at the time of this writing has not been advanced on the House legislative agenda by Speaker Boehner. Part of the reason for his resistance is that, taken together as a package, the bill was not popular among House Republicans. Moreover, the compromised version of the bill contained provisions that House Democrats believed were too restrictionist, such as substantially expanding border security resources. This latest attempt at immigration reform demonstrates polarization on this issue not only across chambers and political parties but also within each party. For Republicans, there is divergence in opinions between moderates and Tea Party Caucus members on the issue. Boehner lacks consensus within his party in the House, which limits his power as the Speaker to move forward on this issue. For Democrats, there was enormous pressure to deliver immigration reform for the Latino electorate it so heavily relied on, to the point of excessive compromise in the view of some House Democrats. As a result, some House Democrats were so angered by the bill that they withdrew support, including one Latino representative, Filemon Vela, who resigned from the Congressional Hispanic Caucus in response to its support for the bill, despite the border security provisions.

One explanation for the breakdown of bipartisan efforts on immigration legislation may be rooted in the fact that since 1992 Congress has experienced more changes of party control than in the prior 40 years. Lee (2009) argues that these more frequent changes lead each party to believe that in the next election it may be able to win control of the chamber or increase its vote share; therefore, each party has little incentive to compromise. Rather, it has incentives to differentiate from the opposing party by taking a disparate stance on a given issue. Recent public opinion data suggest that the public is increasingly polarized along partisan lines and that Republicans' and Democrats' positions on many issues, including immigration, are quite divergent (Pew Center 2012). Despite losing traction with Latino voters and struggling to win their support (Wallace 2012) – in large part due to its position on immigration – the Republican Party continues to take a restrictionist stance that is consistent with a very active component of its electoral base. This segment of its reelection constituency comprises Tea Party supporters who played a vital role in Republican Party dominance in the 2010 elections (Skocpol and Williamson 2012; Parker and Barreto 2013). When Republicans believe party control and winning elections will be greatly influenced by the Latino electorate, their legislative strategy on immigration may change. Until then, both parties will take positions that are most appealing to the coalitions of voters they have historically relied on and thus will likely continue to be highly polarized on the issue of immigration.

POLICY OUTCOMES

Given the evidence that polarization has reduced Congress's capacity to legislate, we turn to the question of how this has affected public policy outcomes. The most direct effect of polarization-induced gridlock is that public policy does not adjust to changing economic and demographic circumstances.

There are a number of reasons to believe that these effects would be most pronounced in the arena of social policy. Given that one of the aims of social policy is to insure citizens against the economic risks inherent in a market system, it must be responsive to shifts in those economic forces. If polarization inhibits those responses, it may leave citizens open to the new risks created by economic shifts brought on by deindustrialization and globalization.

For example, consider the political response in the United States to increasing economic inequality since the 1970s. Most economists attribute increasing inequality to a number of economic factors, such as the rise in the returns to education, exposure to trade, immigration, and changes in family structure. Nevertheless, numerous Western European countries faced with the same economic forces developed policies to mitigate the consequences so that the level of inequality changed only marginally. Similarly, Hacker (2004) argued that polarization was an important factor in impeding the modernization of several of the policies designed to ameliorate social risks. A second issue concerns the ways in which social policies in the United States are designed. Many policies, especially those aimed at the poor or near poor, are not indexed with respect to their benefits. Therefore, these programs require continuous legislative adjustment to achieve a constant level of social protection. McCarty, Poole, and Rosenthal (2006) provided evidence for the effects of polarization on the minimum-wage and welfare-policy outcomes.

Delays and Brinkmanship

The recent (and upcoming) battles over raising the federal government's debt limit and dealing with the so-called fiscal cliff of January 2013 have led many observers to blame partisan polarization for Congress's proclivity to miss deadlines, "kick the can down the road" to the next legislative session or another governmental body, and govern by (artificial) crises. These same concerns have been raised about Congress's ability to deal with longer term problems such as reform to entitlements including Social Security and Medicare.

There is little doubt that partisan polarization has played a major role in creating and shaping the fiscal governance "crises" of the past few years. Clearly, the parties remain far apart on the appropriate reforms for entitlement programs. However, many of these concerns predate the contemporary rise of polarization. For example, consider the ability of Congress to pass the annual appropriation bills before the beginning of the fiscal year. Recently, Congress's track record on this score has been abysmal. From Fiscal Year 2011 to Fiscal Year 2013, Congress completed zero appropriations bills before the September 30 deadline. During the same period, Congress passed only 9 of 36 regular

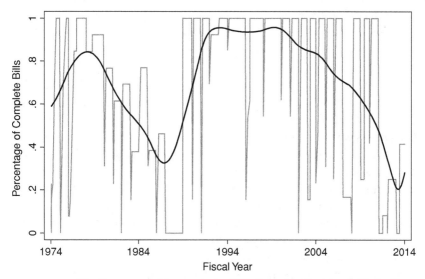

FIGURE 2.10. *The Percentage of Appropriation Bills Completed by Month.* Each observation shows the percentage of regular appropriation bills enacted prior to that month.
The dark line is a lowess smoother, which illustrates the longer term trends.

appropriations bills. (The government was funded by continuing resolution in
all of the unsuccessful cases.) It would be premature, however, to conclude that
party polarization is the prime reason for this performance. Figure 2.10 plots for
each month since 1974 the proportion of regular appropriation bills that have
been passed prior to that month (a smoothing lowess curve is also provided
to capture longer term trends). Clearly, Congress's performance has declined
significantly in the past decade, but it is important to note that it performed
almost equally poorly in the late 1980s. With the exception of the 1995–1996
government shutdown, it performed quite well in the 1990s. Thus, the trends
in congressional performance on appropriations do not closely match those of
party polarization.

Legislative Deliberation and the Quality
of Policy Outcomes

Although the quality of deliberation and policy outcomes is difficult to quantify, several studies have argued that polarization has altered Congress's deliberative and policy-making procedures and capacities (Hacker and Pierson
2006; Sinclair 2006, 2008; Mann and Ornstein 2012).

This literature identifies several changes in the norms and procedures in the U.S. House during the past two decades. First, a decentralized, committee-dominated system of policy development was replaced by a more centralized, party-dominated system. As a result, decisions about policy development and strategy are increasingly likely to be made by party leaders. Moreover, the committee system itself has become more partisan, with much less input from the minority party. Second, the role of the minority party in legislative delib-erations appears to be diminishing. The proportion of legislation considered under rules that restrict the number of amendments by the minority party has increased since the 1990s. Third, the number of violations of seniority in appointing committee leadership positions has risen. These violations gener-ally reward partisan loyalists and punish defectors. Case studies often suggest that these changes have had deleterious effects on the quality of legislation, but the question awaits more systematic study.

On the Senate side, the focus has been on the increased use of dilatory and obstructionist tactics, such as the filibuster and the hold (Wawro and Schickler 2006; Binder and Smith 1997; Koger 2010). These procedures purport to improve legislative deliberation and minority participation. Although the effects of these procedures on delay and gridlock have been established, there is little evidence of their effects on the quality of legislative output.

Although it is often difficult to quantify claims about the effects of polar-ization on the quality of legislation, recent history is replete with examples that plausibly illustrate how polarized politics undermines the quality of leg-islation. Consider the lame-duck congressional session in 2010. The session directly followed a midterm election in which the Democrats lost 63 House seats, along with their majority, and narrowly maintained control of the Senate after losing 6 seats.[19]

Even with the healthy partisan majorities it held through 2009 and 2010, the Obama administration was unable to expand on its 2009 efforts at stimulus or to provide an extension of unemployment benefits. After the election, the administration was in an even more difficult bargaining situation. The pending loss of House control and trimming of its Senate majority meant that these agenda items would have to be taken up in a lame-duck session. Thus, Democratic legislators would be called on to move on many of the same policies that the voters had appeared to repudiate in the election. There was also pressure to avoid the across-the-board tax increases that would result from the expiration of the Bush-era tax cuts on December 31, 2010. The administration had pledged to keep the tax cuts for families making less than

---

[19] This section draws heavily on McCarty (2012).

$250000 and let the rest expire. This approach, the administration argued, balanced the need to avoid tax increases in a recession with the goal of adding progressivity to the tax structure to offset growing economic inequality.

The Republicans also faced a difficult situation. The party has a long-standing commitment to making the Bush cuts permanent at all income levels. If they let the tax cuts expire, they would have little hope of restoring cuts in the upcoming congressional term. So, the lame-duck session became a "game of chicken."

Rather than push the dispute to the brink, the Obama administration reached out to Republican leaders to fashion a compromise. Yet, given the polarized environment, finding a middle ground on each of the issues – tax cuts, unemployment insurance, and other stimulus – would be impossible. Therefore, the underlying principle of the negotiation was to trade on differences in issue salience so that each side could get what it most valued and give on other issues. The Republicans procured an extension of all of the tax cuts, albeit for only two years. They also received a favorable deal on the provisions for the estate tax, with a higher exemption and lower rate than would have prevailed without the legislation.[20] The Democrats got fiscal stimulus and relief measures targeted at low-income and unemployed workers. The employee contribution to Social Security was reduced from 6.2% to 4.2% for one year, and $57 billion was appropriated for extended unemployment benefits.

Reflecting the nature of a negotiated outcome of this sort, the opposition to the plan came from the ideological extremes of both parties. Progressives were particularly upset with the extension of tax cuts for high-income families and with the estate-tax provisions. Some even expressed concern that the payroll tax deductions would undermine the Social Security system. Conservatives were similarly dismayed not to receive a more permanent extension of the tax cuts, and they worried that the extension of unemployment benefits would contribute to the deficit.[21]

---

[20] Technically, the estate tax had been repealed in 2010; therefore, establishing any estate tax was a departure from the Republican goal of extending all of the tax cuts and not raising taxes in a recession. Nevertheless, liberal Democrats were especially incensed about the high exemption and low rates. Consequently, they forced a vote on an amendment to strike the estate-tax provisions, which – had it been successful – might have unraveled the negotiated agreement (Sullivan 2010).

[21] The progressive opposition was somewhat more pronounced than that of the conservatives. Of the House members in the most liberal quartile, 71% opposed the agreement, in contrast to only 25% of the most conservative quartile. Support was highest among moderate Republicans in the third quartile, 88% of whom supported the bill.

Ultimately, polarization did not lead to gridlock, but it may have led to something far worse. Instead of a negotiated outcome that provided targeted stimulus and a transition to a more efficient, fair, and certain tax code, the bill increased the deficit by almost $900 billion and postponed important decisions to the future.

Other Policy Consequences

Perhaps one of the most important long-term consequences of the decline in legislative capacity caused by polarization is that Congress's power is declining relative to the other branches of government.[22] Recent studies by political scientists demonstrate that presidents facing strong partisan and ideological opposition from Congress are more likely to take unilateral action rather than pursue their goals through legislation.

Not only are presidents likely to become more powerful but polarization also increases the opportunities of judges and courts to pursue their policy goals because such judicial activism is unlikely to be checked by legislative statute. The courts have become the dominant arena for a wide swath of policy issues, from tobacco regulation to firearms to questions such as gay marriage.

Although most of this chapter concentrates on the effects of polarization within the legislative process, contemporary work in bureaucratic and judicial politics suggests that polarization also has detrimental effects at the policy-implementation stage. First, polarization decreases Congress's willingness to delegate authority to administrative agencies. In a systematic study, Epstein and O'Halloran (1999) showed that Congress is far less willing to delegate policy-making authority to agencies when there are significant ideological disagreements between the president and congressional majorities. Because party polarization has exacerbated these disagreements (especially during divided government), Congress relies far less on the expertise of the bureaucracy in the implementation and enforcement of statutes. The result is often excessive statutory constraints or the delegation of statutory enforcement to private actors and courts, rather than to agencies (Farhang 2010). These outcomes further weaken the executive and legislative branches vis-à-vis the judiciary. In addition, polarization has now distorted the confirmation process of executive-branch officials and judges. In studies of all major executive-branch appointments in the past century, McCarty and Razaghian (1999) found that heightened partisan polarization is the major culprit in the increasing delays in the Senate confirmation process. Consequently, long-term vacancies in the political leadership

---

[22] See Reich (2013) for a set of recent examples.

of many departments and agencies have become the norm. Because these problems are exacerbated at the beginning of new administrations, presidential transitions have become considerably less smooth. Polarization also has clearly contributed to the well-documented conflicts over judicial appointments, leading to an understaffing of the federal bench and more contentious and ideological battles over Supreme Court nominees (Binder and Maltzman 2009).

CONCLUSIONS

The negotiation failures resulting from polarization have done much to undermine governance in the United States by leading to gridlock and lower quality legislation and by harming the functioning of the executive and judicial branches. The Task Force on Negotiating Agreements in Politics was tasked not only with rekindling scholarly interest in political negotiation and bargaining but also with making concrete suggestions on how to improve the negotiation infrastructure in ways that enhance good governance.

The central idea of this chapter is not only how badly the U.S. Congress needs such medicine but also how unwilling a patient it is likely to be. Partisan and ideological divisions in Congress have grown significantly during the past three decades. Although the evidence suggests that the average voter may not have polarized significantly, engaged and attentive voters now hold issue positions that are more consistent with those of their party. Campaign funding from ideological individuals has increased, whereas the media have contributed and adapted to the increased ideological divisions.

These long-term trends have profound implications for successful negotiation. First, polarization has fundamentally altered legislators' incentives to negotiate. Expanding ideological differences and declining dimensionality have increasingly replaced win-wins with zero-sum outcomes. Increased teamsmanship has reduced the number of honest brokers who can effectively work "across the aisles" to create agreements. Moreover, polarization has exacerbated the incentives for strategic disagreement. It is difficult to negotiate when one or both sides think they are better off when bargaining fails.

Polarization has also transformed congressional institutions. The "textbook" Congress of decentralized committees has been replaced by a more partisan Congress, in which much of the negotiation occurs among party leaders. As Binder and Lee point out in Chapter 18, this change may have an ambiguous effect. On the one hand, with their near-universal jurisdiction, congressional leaders have more opportunities than committee chairs to form multi-issue

integrative solutions. On the other hand, leaders will continue to be constrained to the extent that their members do not find such negotiated settle-
ments politically advantageous.

Unfortunately, the existing political science literature suggests few opportunities for reducing polarization by electoral reforms. The evidence undermines the common arguments that reforming legislative districting or primary
elections will materially reduce polarization. Because reforming campaign
finance has been fraught with constitutional difficulties and unintended consequences, it does not seem to be a promising avenue for reducing polarization
in the short run.

Given this dreary outlook, it is entirely appropriate that we turn our intel-
lectual energies to exploring ways to negotiate and govern despite growing
partisan differences. A new political science of negotiation that can suggest
new mechanisms and protocols that help to "get the deal done," even in
polarized times, would accomplish a great deal of good.

References

Abramowitz, Alan I. 2010. *The Disappearing Center: Engaged Citizens, Polarization, and American Democracy.* New Haven: Yale University Press.

Aldrich, John. 1995. *Why Parties? The Origin and Transformation of Political Parties in America.* Chicago: University of Chicago Press.

Aldrich, John, and David W. Rohde. 2010. "Consequences of Electoral and Institutional Change: The Evolution of Conditional Party Government in the U. S. House of Representatives." In *New Directions in American Political Parties*, ed. Jeffrey M. Stonecash, pp. 234–250. New York: Routledge.

Ansolabehere, Stephen, John M. de Figueiredo, and James M. Snyder. 2003. "Why is There so Little Money in U. S. Politics?" *Journal of Economic Perspectives* 17(1): 105–130.

Ansolabehere, Stephen, Jonathan Rodden, and James M. Snyder. 2006. "Purple America." *Journal of Economic Perspectives* 20(2): 97–118.

Bafumi, Joseph, and Michael C. Herron. 2010. "Leapfrog Representation and Extrem-ism: A Study of American Voters and Their Members in Congress." *American Political Science Review* 104(3): 519–542.

Barber, Michael. 2013. "Ideological Donors, Contribution Limits, and the Polarization of State Legislatures?" Typescript. Princeton: Princeton University.

Baron, David P. 1994. "Electoral Competition with Informed and Uniformed Voters." *American Political Science Review* 88(1): 33–47.

Bartels, Larry. 2000. "Partisanship and Voting Behavior 1952–1996." *American Journal of Political Science* 44(1): 35–50.

———. 2008. *Unequal Democracy: The Political Economy of the New Gilded Age.* Princeton, NJ: Princeton University Press.

Binder, Sarah A. 1999. "The Dynamics of Legislative Gridlock, 1947–96." *American Political Science Review* 93(3): 519–533.

Binder, Sarah A., and Forrest Maltzman. 2009. *Advice and Dissent: The Struggle to Shape the Federal Judiciary.* Washington, DC: Brookings Institution Press.

Binder, Sarah A., and Steven S. Smith. 1997. *Politics or Principle? Filibustering in the United States Senate.* Washington, DC: Brookings Institution Press.

Bishop, Bill. 2009. *The Big Sort: Why the Clustering of Like-Minded Americans Is Tearing Us Apart.* New York: Mariner Books.

Bonica, Adam. 2013. "Ideology and Interests in the Political Marketplace." *American Journal of Political Science* 57(2): 294–311.

Brady, David W., Hahrie Han, and Jeremy C. Pope. 2007. "Primary Elections and Candidate Ideology: Out of Step with the Primary Electorate?" *Legislative Studies Quarterly* 32(1): 79–105.

Brewer, Mark, Mack Mariani, and Jeffrey M. Stonecash. 2002. *Diverging Parties: Social Change, Realignment, and Party Polarization.* Boulder: Westview Press.

Bullock, Will, and Joshua D. Clinton. 2011. "More a Molehill than a Mountain: The Effects of the Blanket Primary on Elected Officials' Behavior from California." *Journal of Politics* 73(3): 915–930.

Burnham, Walter Dean. 1970. *Critical Elections and the Mainsprings of American Politics.* New York: W. W. Norton.

Canon, David T. 1999. *Race, Redistricting, and Representation: The Unintended Consequences of Black Majority Districts.* Chicago: University of Chicago Press.

Carsey, T. M., & Layman, G. C. 2006. "Changing Sides or Changing Minds? Party Identification and Policy Preferences in the American Electorate." *American Journal of Political Science* 50(2): 464–477.

Carson, Jamie L., Michael H. Crespin, Charles J. Finocchiaro, and David W. Rohde. 2007. "Redistricting and Party Polarization in the US House of Representatives." *American Politics Research* 35(6): 878–904.

Clinton, Joshua D. 2006. "Representation in Congress: Constituents and Roll Calls in the 106th House." *Journal of Politics* 68(2): 397–409.

Clinton, Joshua D., Simon Jackman, and Douglas Rivers. 2004. "The Statistical Analysis of Roll Call Data." *American Political Science Review* 98(2): 355–370.

Converse, Philip. 1964. "The Nature of Belief Systems in the Mass Public." In *Ideology and Discontent*, ed. David Apter. New York: Free Press: 1–74.

Cox, Gary, and Mathew McCubbins. 2005. *Setting the Agenda: Responsible Party Government in the U.S. House of Representatives.* New York: Cambridge University Press.

Cox, Gary W., and Keith T. Poole. 2002. "On Measuring Partisanship in Roll-Call Voting: The US House of Representatives, 1877–1999." *American Journal of Political Science* 46(3): 477–489.

Davis, Susan. 2012. "This Congress Could Be Least Productive since 1947." USA Today. August 15, 2012. Retrieved from http://usatoday30.usatoday.com/news/washington/story/2012-08-14/unproductive-congress-not-passing-bills/57060096/1.

DellaVigna, Stefano, and Ethan Kaplan. 2007. "The Fox News Effect: Media Bias and Voting." *Quarterly Journal of Economics* 122(3): 1187–1234.

Edwards, Mickey. 2012. *The Parties Versus the People: How to Turn Republicans and Democrats into Americans.* New Haven: Yale University Press.

Eilperin, Juliet. 2007. *Fight Club Politics: How Partisanship Is Poisoning the House of Representatives.* Lanham: Rowman & Littlefield.

Ensley, Michael J. 2009. "Individual Campaign Contributions and Candidate Ideology." *Public Choice* 138(1): 221–238.

Epstein, David, and Sharyn O'Halloran. 1999. *Delegating Powers: A Transaction Cost Politics Approach to Policy Making under Separate Powers*. New York: Cambridge University Press.

Farhang, Sean. 2010. *The Litigation State: Public Regulation and Private Lawsuits in the United States*. Princeton: Princeton University Press.

Fiorina, Morris P. 2013. "Party Homogeneity and Contentious Politics," In *Can We Talk? The Rise of Rude, Nasty, Stubborn Politics*, eds. Daniel M. Shea and Morris P. Fiorina. New York: Pearson: 142–153.

Fiorina, Morris P., and Samuel J. Abrams. 2008. "Political Polarization in the American Public." *Annual Review of Political Science* 11: 563–588.

Fiorina, Morris P., Samuel J. Abrams, and Jeremy Pope. 2005. *Culture War? Myth of a Polarized America*. Upper Saddle River: Pearson Education.

Francia, Peter, John Green, Paul Herrnson, Lynda Powell, and Clyde Wilcox. 2003. *The Financiers of Congressional Elections*. New York: Columbia University Press.

Garand, James C. 2010. "Income Inequality, Party Polarization, and Roll-Call Voting in the US Senate." *Journal of Politics* 72(4): 1109–1128.

Gelman, Andrew. 2009. *Red State, Blue State, Rich State, Poor State: Why Americans Vote the Way They Do*. Princeton: Princeton University Press.

Gentzkow, Matthew, and Jesse M. Shapiro. 2006. "Media Bias and Reputation." *Journal of Political Economy* 114(2): 280–316.

Gerber, Alan, Dean Karlan, and Daniel Bergan. 2009. "Does the Media Matter? A Field Experiment Measuring the Effect of Newspapers on Voting Behavior and Political Opinions." *American Economic Journal: Applied Economics* 1(2): 35–52.

Gerber, Elisabeth R., and Rebecca B. Morton. 1998. "Primary Election Systems and Representation." *Journal of Law, Economics and Organization* 14(2): 304–324.

Gilens, Martin. 2012. *Affluence and Influence: Economic Inequality and Political Power in America*. Princeton, NJ: Princeton University Press.

Gilmour, John. 1995. *Strategic Disagreement: Stalemate in American Politics*. Pittsburgh: University of Pittsburgh Press.

Gimpel, James, and James R. Edwards. 1998. *The Congressional Politics of Immigration Reform*. London: Longman Publishing Group.

Gimpel, James, Frances Lee, and Joshua Kaminski. 2006. "The Political Geography of Campaign Contributions in American Politics." *Journal of Politics* 68(3): 626–639.

Gimpel, James, Frances Lee, and Shanna Pearson-Merkowitz. 2008. "The Check Is in the Mail: Interdistrict Funding Flows in Congressional Elections." *American Journal of Political Science* 52(2): 373–394.

Groseclose, Timothy, Steven D. Levitt, and James M. Snyder Jr. 1999. "Comparing Interest Group Scores across Time and Chambers: Adjusted ADA Scores for the US Congress." *American Political Science Review* 93(1): 33–50.

Groseclose, Timothy, and Nolan McCarty. 2001. "The Politics of Blame: Bargaining before an Audience." *American Journal of Political Science* 45(1): 100–119.

Groseclose, Timothy, and Jeff Milyo. 2005. "A Measure of Media Bias." *Quarterly Journal of Economics* 120(4): 1191–1237.

Hacker, Jacob S. 2004. "Privatizing Risk without Privatizing the Welfare State: The Hidden Politics of Social Policy Retrenchment in the United States." *American Political Science Review* 98(2): 243–260.

Hacker, Jacob S., and Paul Pierson. 2006. *Off Center: The Republican Revolution and the Erosion of American Democracy*. New Haven: Yale University Press.

Hall, Robert L., and Frank W. Wayman. 1990. "Buying Time: Moneyed Interests and the Mobilization of Bias in Congressional Committees." *American Political Science Review* 84(3): 797–820.

Hare, Christopher, Nolan McCarty, Keith T. Poole, and Howard Rosenthal. 2012. "Polarization is Real (and Asymmetric)." Voteview Blog. May 16, 2012. Retrieved Dec. 2013, from http://voteview.com/blog/?p=494.

Hirano, Shigeo, James M. Snyder Jr., Stephen Ansolabehere, and John Mark Hansen. 2010. "Primary Elections and Partisan Polarization in U.S. Congressional Elections." *Quarterly Journal of Political Science* 5(2): 169–191.

Hopkins, Daniel J., and Jonathan Ladd. 2014. "The Consequences of Broader Media Choice: Evidence from the Expansion of Fox News." *Quarterly Journal of Political Science* 9: 115–135.

Iyengar, Shanto, Gaurav Sood, and Yphtach Lelkes. 2012. "Affect, Not Ideology: A Social Identity Perspective on Polarization." *Public Opinion Quarterly* 763(3): 405–431.

Jacobson, Gary C. 1990. "The Effects of Campaign Spending in House Elections: New Evidence for Old Arguments." *American Journal of Political Science* 34(2): 334–362.

Kasperowicz, Pete. 2012. "Parties Trade Blame for 'Least Productive Congress' in Decades." The Hill. Sept. 14, 2012. Retrieved Dec. 2013, from http://thehill.com/video/house/249597-cantor-hoyer-trade-barbs-on-the-way-out-the-door-to-2012-elections.

Kaufmann, Karen M., James G. Gimpel, and Adam H. Hoffman. 2003. "A Promise Fulfilled? Open Primaries and Representation." *Journal of Politics* 65(2): 457–476.

Klinkner, Philip A. 2004. "Red and Blue Scare: The Continuing Diversity of the American Electoral Landscape." *The Forum* (2)2.

Koger, Gregory. 2010. *Filibustering: A Political History of Obstruction in the House and Senate*. Chicago: University of Chicago Press.

Krehbiel, Keith. 1998. *Pivotal Politics: A Theory of US Lawmaking*. Chicago: University of Chicago Press.

Layman, Geoffrey, and Thomas Carsey. 2002. "Party Polarization and 'Conflict Extension' in the American Electorate." *American Journal of Political Science* 46(4): 786–802.

Layman, Geoffrey C., Thomas M. Carsey, John C. Green, Richard Herrera, and Rosalyn Cooperman. 2010. "Activists and Conflict Extension in American Party Politics." *American Political Science Review* 104(2): 324–346.

Lee, Frances. 2009. *Beyond Ideology: Politics, Principles, and Partisanship in the U. S. Senate*. Chicago: University of Chicago Press.

Lenz, Gabriel S. 2012. *Follow the Leader: How Voters Respond to Politicians' Policies and Performance*. Chicago: University of Chicago Press.

Lessig, Lawrence. 2011. *Republic, Lost: How Money Corrupts Congress – and a Plan to Stop It*. New York: Hachette Book Group.

Levendusky, Matthew. 2009. *The Partisan Sort: How Liberals Became Democrats and Conservatives Became Republicans.* Chicago: University of Chicago Press.

Levendusky, Matthew S., Jeremy C. Pope, and Simon D. Jackman. 2008. "Measuring District-Level Partisanship with Implications for the Analysis of US Elections." *Journal of Politics* 70(3): 736–753.

Mann, Thomas E., and Norman J. Ornstein. 2012. *It's Even Worse than It Looks: How the American Constitutional System Collided with the New Politics of Extremism.* New York: Basic Books.

Masket, Seth. 2008. "Where You Sit Is Where You Stand: The Impact of Seating Proximity on Legislative Cue-Taking." *Quarterly Journal of Political Science* 3: 301–311.

Masket, Seth, Boris Shor, Steven Rogers, and Nolan McCarty. 2013. "*A Primary Cause of Partisanship? Nomination Systems and Legislator Ideology.*" Typescript. Princeton: Princeton University.

Mayhew, David R. 2005. *Divided We Govern: Party Control, Lawmaking, and Investigations, 1946–2002.* New Haven: Yale University Press.

McCarty, Nolan 2007. "The Policy Effects of Political Polarization." In *The Transformation of American Politics: Activist Government and the Rise of Conservatism,* eds. Paul Pierson and Theda Skocpol. Princeton: Princeton University Press: 223–255.

———. 2012. "The Politics of the Pop: The U. S. Response to the Financial Crisis and the Great Recession." In *Coping with Crisis: Governmental Responses to the Great Recession,* eds. Nancy Bermeo and Jonas Pontusson. New York: Cambridge University Press: 201–232.

McCarty, Nolan, Keith T. Poole, and Howard Rosenthal. 1997. *Income Redistribution and the Realignment of American Politics.* Washington, DC: AEI Press.

———. 2001. "The Hunt for Party Discipline in Congress." *American Political Science Review* 95(3): 673–688.

———. 2006. *Polarized America: The Dance of Ideology and Unequal Riches.* Cambridge, MA: MIT Press.

———. 2009. "Does Gerrymandering Cause Polarization?" *American Journal of Political Science* 53(3): 666–680.

McCarty, Nolan, and Rose Razaghian. 1999. "Advice and Consent: Senate Responses to Executive Branch Nominations 1885–1996." *American Journal of Political Science* 43(4): 1122–1143.

McClosky, Herbert, Paul J. Hoffmann, and Rosemary O'Hara. 1960. "Issue Conflict and Consensus among Party Leaders and Followers." *American Political Science Review* 54(2): 406–427.

Minta, Michael D. 2009. "Legislative Oversight and the Substantive Representation of Black and Latino Interests in Congress." *Legislative Studies Quarterly* 34(2): 193–218.

Minta, Michael D., and Valeria Sinclair-Chapman. 2013. "Diversity in Political Institutions and Congressional Responsiveness to Minority Interests." *Political Research Quarterly* 66(1): 27–140.

Moon, Woojin. 2004. "Party Activists, Campaign Resources and Candidate Position Taking: Theory, Tests and Applications." *British Journal of Political Science* 34(4): 611–633.

Parker, Chrisopher S., and Matt A. Barreto. 2013. *Change They Can't Believe In: The Tea Party and Reactionary Politics in America*. Princeton: Princeton University Press.

Pew Center. 2012. "Partisan Polarization Surges in Bush and Obama Years." Pew Research Center for the People and the Press. Retrieved from www.people-press .org/2012/06/04/partisan-polarization-surges-in-bush-obama-years.

Piketty, Thomas, and Emmanuel Saez. 2003. "Income Inequality in the United States 1913–1998." *Quarterly Journal of Economics* 118(1): 1–39.

Poole, Keith T. 2007. "Changing Minds? Not in Congress!" *Public Choice* 131: 435–451.

Poole, Keith T., and Howard Rosenthal. 1997. *Congress: A Political-Economic History of Roll Call Voting*. New York: Oxford University Press.

Prior, Markus. 2007. *Post-Broadcast Democracy: How Media Choice Increases Inequality in Political Involvement and Polarizes Elections*. New York: Cambridge University Press.

Reich, Robert. 2013. "The Real Price of Congress's Gridlock." New York Times, August 13.

Roberts, Jason M. 2007. "The Statistical Analysis of Roll-Call Data: A Cautionary Tale." *Legislative Studies Quarterly* 32(3): 341–360.

Roberts, Jason M., and Steven S. Smith. 2003. "Procedural Contexts, Party Strategy, and Conditional Party Voting in the US House of Representatives." *American Journal of Political Science* 47(2): 305–317.

Rohde, David W. 1991. *Parties and Leaders in the Postreform House*. Chicago: University of Chicago Press.

Schattschneider, E. E. 1960. *The Semisovereign People*. New York: Holt, Reinhart, and Winston.

Shaw, Daron. 2012. "If Everyone Votes Their Party, Why Do Presidential Election Outcomes Vary So Much?" *The Forum* 3(1), Article 1.

Shor, Boris, and Nolan McCarty. 2011. "The Ideological Mapping of American Legislatures." *American Political Science Review* 105(3): 530–551.

Sides, John. 2012. "Your Do-Nothing Congress (in One Graph)." Washington Monthly. Sept. 21, 2012. Retrieved Dec. 2013, from www.washingtonmonthly.com/ten-miles-square/2012/09/your_donothing_congress_in_one040039.php.

Sinclair, Barbara. 2006. *Party Wars: Polarization and the Politics of National Policy Making*. Norman: University of Oklahoma Press.

Sinclair, Barbara. 2008. "Spoiling the Sausages? How a Polarized Congress Deliberates and Legislates." In *Red and Blue Nation? Consequences and Corrections of America's Polarized Politics*, eds. Pietro S. Nivola and David W. Brady. Washington, DC: Brookings Institution Press: 55–79.

Skocpol, Theda, and Vanessa Williamson. 2012. *The Tea Party and the Remaking of Republican Conservatism*. New York: Oxford University Press.

Smith, Richard A. 1995. "Interest Group Influence in the US Congress." *Legislative Studies Quarterly* 20(1): 89–139.

Snyder Jr., James M., and Tim Groseclose. 2000. "Estimating Party Influence in Congressional Roll-Call Voting." *American Journal of Political Science* 44(2): 193–211.

Snyder Jr., James M., and David Stromberg. 2010. "Press Coverage and Political Accountability." *Journal of Political Economy* 118(2): 355–408.

Steinhauer, Jennifer. 2012. "Congress Nearing End of Session Where Partisan Input Impeded Output." New York Times, Sept. 18. 2012. Retrieved Dec. 2013, from www.nytimes.com/2012/09/19/us/politics/congress-nears-end-of-least-productive-session.html.

Stone, Walt J., and Elizabeth N. Simas. 2010. "Candidate Valence and Ideological Positions in US House Elections." *American Journal of Political Science* 54(2): 371–388.

Sullivan, Paul. 2010. "Estate Tax Will Return Next Year, but Few Will Pay It." New York Times, December 17.

Sundquist, James L. 1983. *Dynamics of the Party System: Alignment and Realignment of Political Parties in the United States*. Washington, DC: Brookings Institution Press.

Sunstein, Cass R. 2002. "The Law of Group Polarization." *Journal of Political Philosophy* 10: 175–195.

Tate, Katherine. 2003. *Black Faces in the Mirror: African Americans and Their Representatives in the US Congress*. Princeton: Princeton University Press.

Theriault, Sean M. 2008a. *Party Polarization in Congress*. New York: Cambridge University Press.

Theriault, Sean M. 2008b. "The Procedurally Polarized Congress." *Presentation at the Annual Meeting of the American Political Science Association*, Boston.

Tichenor, Daniel. 2002. *Dividing Lines*. Princeton: Princeton University Press.

Tufte, Edward R. 1973. "The Relationship between Seats and Votes in Two-Party Systems." *American Political Science Review* 67(2): 540–554.

Wallace, Sophia J. 2012. "It's Complicated: Latinos, President Obama, and the 2012 Election." *Social Science Quarterly* 93(5): 1360–1383.

Wallace, Sophia J., Chris Zepeda-Millán, and Michael Jones-Correa. 2014. "Spatial and Temporal Proximity: Examining the Effects of Protests on Political Attitudes." *American Journal of Political Science* 58(2): 433–448.

Wawro, Gregory, and Eric Schickler. 2006. *Filibuster: Obstruction and Lawmaking in the US Senate*. Princeton, NJ: Princeton University Press.

Zelizer, Julian E. 2006. *On Capitol Hill: The Struggle to Reform Congress and Its Consequences, 1948–2000*. New York: Cambridge University Press.

Zepeda-Millán, J. Chris. 2011. Dignity's Revolt: Threat, Identity, and Immigrant Mass Mobilization. PhD diss., Cornell University.

3

Confronting Asymmetric Polarization

Jacob S. Hacker and Paul Pierson

The goal of this volume is to explore possible solutions to a host of problems associated with polarization. Effective prescription, however, hinges on accurate diagnosis. Far too many discussions of polarization are based on a flawed one: that polarization is broadly similar in degree and kind at both ends of the political spectrum. This claim that political polarization is symmetrical is false: polarization is mainly driven by a sharp retreat from moderation on the right side of the spectrum. This development has occurred across multiple dimensions, from voting patterns and intensity of preferences to concrete policy demands and willingness to use once-rare hardball tactics. Prescriptions that ignore or downplay this reality are very likely to be ineffective and may even make the real problems worse.

This chapter briefly summarizes the evidence that contemporary polarization is asymmetric, before turning to a slightly longer discussion of the mechanisms that generate and sustain this outcome. This discussion in turn provides the basis for identifying initiatives that might address the central and most corrosive aspect of our "polarized politics": the ever greater extremism of the modern Republican Party.

POLARIZATION IS ASYMMETRIC

Although it is still not conventional to frame discussions of polarization as asymmetric, there is mounting evidence that the increasing distance between the two parties is primarily a consequence of the Republican Party's 35-year march to the right (Hacker and Pierson 2005; Mann and Ornstein 2012; Theriault 2013). As the creators of DW-Nominate scores, the core data that have been used to document rising elite polarization, recently put it, "We should be careful not to equate the two parties' roles in contemporary political polarization: the data are clear that this is a Republican-led phenomenon where very conservative Republicans have replaced moderate Republicans and Southern Democrats... Moreover, the rise of the 'Tea Party' will likely only move Congressional Republicans further away from the political center" (Hare, McCarty, Poole, and Rosenthal 2012).

Extensions of DW-Nominate to presidents and to vice-presidential candidates show the same pattern. So do (more weakly) data on state legislatures (Shor 2013). Similar techniques used to place Supreme Court justices on a left–right scale show that, although current Democratic appointees on the Court are moderate by modern standards, four of the current GOP appointees are among the six most conservative justices to serve on the Court in the last 75 years, whereas the fifth (Kennedy) is in the top 10 (Liptak 2010).

Other signs of asymmetry are more difficult to quantify, but increasingly hard to ignore. Most important is the striking and intensifying pattern over the past 20 years of what Tushnet (2004) has called "constitutional hardball." In the past two decades – since asymmetric polarization entered a new and more intense phase with the rise to power of Newt Gingrich – the GOP has repeatedly violated established norms (without breaking legal restrictions) to gain partisan advantage. Admittedly, categorizing such instances is a tricky exercise. Moreover, as can be expected when intense partisan conflict escalates, one can point to transgressions on both sides. When norms are broken and conflict intensifies, both sides feel strong pressure to "fight fire with fire." Nonetheless, Republicans have largely led the way and deserve exclusive or primary responsibility for the following:

- routinized use of the filibuster to block virtually all initiatives of the majority party
- the 1995 government shutdown
- the impeachment of President Clinton
- resort to mid-decade reapportionments
- systematic efforts to disenfranchise voters viewed as unlikely to support the GOP
- refusal to allow Senate votes on *any* appointments for statutorily established bodies as a means to prevent those bodies from functioning or to force legislative concessions (what Mann and Ornstein [2012] call "the new nullification")
- "hostage-taking" related to debt ceiling increases

This list is neither short nor are the items trivial. Indeed, taken together they constitute a slow-moving constitutional crisis.[1] It is this set of practices

---

[1] To avoid getting bogged down in side arguments, this discussion excludes two very significant episodes that we would personally include: the Supreme Court's decision in *Bush* v. *Gore* and

that led Mann and Ornstein (2012), two of the most respected and moderate voices in the profession, to recently conclude, "The GOP has become an insurgent outlier in American politics. It is ideologically extreme; scornful of compromise; unmoved by conventional understanding of facts, evidence and science; and dismissive of the legitimacy of its political opposition."

Why an Accurate Description Matters

Elite discourse – in journalism, academia, and foundations – is intensely resistant to the very strong evidence that polarization is primarily about steadily increasing GOP extremism. Regardless of what the evidence may show, to argue that one party is more responsible than another for political dysfunction is seen as itself evidence of bias, not to mention bad manners.[2] Political scientists have an additional reason for resistance: our dominant "Downsian" theoretical apparatus, which emphasizes the centrality to political outcomes of voter opinion and formal rules, has a hard time explaining how asymmetric polarization can persist over time.

There is a plausible argument that symmetrical polarization can be explained in Downsian terms. Politicians are not punished for moving toward the extreme if their opponents are doing the same thing to an equal degree (Fiorina 2005).[3] In this framework asymmetric polarization is much harder to understand – indeed, it should not even be possible over the medium run. Instead, we should anticipate what we call the "Downsian corrective": fear of losing elections should force the more extreme party to moderate. Yet those waiting for "the fever to break" (as President Obama memorably put it) have been waiting for Godot. The GOP has continued to move right for more than a generation. If anything, the process seems to be accelerating rather than reversing.[4] Understanding why the Downsian corrective remains so weak in practice helps clarify what is driving asymmetric polarization and, by implication, how effective various possible reforms might be.

the willingness of four GOP appointees to strike down the entirety of the Affordable Care Act – the signature statutory result of the Democrats' sweeping electoral victory in 2008 (and a bill that essentially no prominent figures regarded as raising major constitutional issues during the long and intense debate over passage).

2 Despite their long-standing status in the establishment, Mann and Ornstein were unable to get a single airing for their views on the Sunday Washington talk shows.

3 Although it is not clear to us why this constitutes an equilibrium. Shouldn't one party see an advantage in taking a small step toward the center?

4 We have short memories. John Boehner may be the GOP's "establishment" figure today, but two decades ago he was the chairman of the Conservative Opportunity Society, a major organizational vehicle for Gingrich's efforts to break the moderate faction of the GOP and push the party sharply to the right.

It is easy to see why *as individuals* GOP politicians in the House and Senate have faced strong incentives to move rightward. Most GOP extremists will not pay an electoral price at all for moving in that direction – on the contrary, they pay a price for moderation. GOP elected officials (especially in the House, but to a lesser degree in the Senate) generally represent electorates that lean strongly Republican. In the House, a combination of gerrymandering and the electorally inefficient distribution of Democratic voters (with high concentrations in urban areas) gives the GOP a sizable structural advantage. Most members of the Republican caucus quite reasonably see a loss of support in a GOP primary as their largest electoral danger (Jacobson 2013). For example, the 80 GOP representatives who signed a letter urging House Speaker John Boehner to pass the Continuing Resolution defunding Obamacare hail from districts where Mitt Romney had defeated the president by an average of 23% (Lizza 2013).

The GOP's base is not just large. It is also intense – quicker and quicker to perceive the stakes in political conflict as very high and to seek to punish those whom it sees as insufficiently loyal. That intensity is reflected and strongly reinforced by the presence of increasingly organized groups that monitor the behavior of elected officials and are ready and often eager to mount or back a credible primary challenge. Standing alongside these groups is a large and fiercely partisan media (Fox News and talk radio) for which there is simply no equivalent on the other side. Given the strength (size, intensity, and organized backing) of this base, it is far more costly to be moderate (and face a well-funded primary challenge) than to stay at or move toward the extreme. Even if extremism modestly increases the risk of general election defeat, the electoral tradeoff remains beneficial.

All that being said, asymmetric polarization may carry risks for the party as a whole. During the last two cycles, the selection of extremist candidates in winnable contests may well have cost the GOP control over the Senate (Jacobson 2013). And the GOP has now lost the popular vote in five of the last six presidential elections. Many political scientists continue to believe that these results should send strong signals to party leaders (and, indeed, to many GOP voters and affiliated interest groups) about the need to move toward the center. In short, they should foster a Downsian correction.

Yet there is absolutely no sign of anything like this happening. It did not happen after the devastating 2008 election, and it has not happened after the 2012 election (despite the fact that the GOP lost ground in the House and Senate as well as losing the White House yet again). In both cases, the party moved rightward rather than moderating.

It is not that the incentives associated with a Downsian corrective do not exist. The problem is that that they are far weaker sources of pressure on the

GOP than political scientists have assumed, for two main reasons. The first is that the "electoral price" exacted when a party moves further away from the center may (reasonably) be perceived as modest. Research in political science has recently identified a range of factors that militate against any automatic process through which voters detect and punish extremism:

- Voters are often only dimly aware of the policy positions and legislative actions of politicians, and politicians can do many things to diminish what awareness they have (Bawn et al. 2012 call this "the electoral blind spot").
- Voters often have a hard time distinguishing more moderate candidates from more extreme ones (Ahler, Citrin, and Lenz 2013). The mainstream media's "horse-race" orientation and its strong incentive to maintain an appearance of neutrality often make it unwilling to describe one party or candidate as more extreme than the other.
- Voters make decisions on the basis of factors (such as the very recent performance of the economy) that are unrelated to the policy stances of politicians (Bartels 2008; Healy and Lenz 2014).
- There are signs that voters may be (increasingly) willing to support the candidate perceived to be on "their" team rather than the one whose policy positions are closer to their own.
- Extremism may produce political effects (e.g., dysfunction, poor economic performance) that voters will attribute to the party of the president, rather than the party producing the dysfunction.
- Less easy to verify but probably quite important, the GOP may benefit if intensifying gridlock contributes to voter alienation and negative views of Washington. Unless dysfunction is clearly attributable to a particular set of politicians affiliated with the GOP, it generally hurts the party associated with an active use for government (that is, Democrats).[5]
- Given the intensity of the base, extremism may generate compensating support (in money, endorsements, or enthusiasm) that offsets any potential lost ground among moderates (Theriault 2013).

All of these factors suggest that, although GOP moves away from the center may pose some electoral risk to the party, we should not exaggerate those risks nor suggest that they operate on Republicans in exactly the same way they operate on Democrats. *As Republicans move from the center, we should picture a gradual slope of modestly declining electoral performance rather than an abrupt plunge into the political abyss.*

---

[5] This insight was Newt Gingrich's fundamental contribution to American politics.

The second reason why the penalty for extremism is limited is that the typical Downsian formulation sees the mobilization of centrist, countervailing forces as far too automatic. Instead, moderation may require the emergence of a reasonably cohesive center-of-the-road faction that can impose discipline on more extreme members. In principle, these (relative) moderates should often have the greatest incentive to push back against extremists. They are the ones most likely to be in swing districts and thus the ones most likely to pay a price for asymmetric polarization. Moreover, the status of moderates as "pivotal" voters between the two main blocs potentially gives them considerable leverage.

Historically, the leverage that moderates gain from their decisive position has often played a crucial disciplining role, ranging from the Progressive revolt against Speaker Cannon to the pivotal status of Southern Democrats during and after the New Deal (Katznelson 2013). More recently, the rise of the Democratic Leadership Council (DLC) in the 1980s and 1990s provides a textbook illustration of a Downsian corrective. Animated by widespread concerns about Democratic electability, the DLC was strongly backed by business groups that wanted a more centrist party. The moderate formula espoused by the group was a striking political success. After 1990, most of the leading figures in the Democratic Party (Clinton, Gore, Lieberman, Gephardt, Reid, Daschle, Bayh, and many more) were affiliated with the DLC.

Needless to say, this is not occurring in the GOP. The task of organizing a durable party faction raises formidable collective action problems and entails serious political risks (Rubin 2013). In contrast to the case of the DLC, the balance of organized political forces within the GOP (Christian conservatives, the Tea Party and, at least until very recently, the most politicized elements of the business community such as the Chamber of Commerce) have proved highly unfavorable to moderate organization.

Given all this, extremism may be individually rational even if it is costly for the party; that is, damaging to its brand and its prospects for winning overall majorities as well as presidential elections.[6] Even the price to the party may be limited because of the factors just mentioned.[7] In contemporary politics,

---

[6] In addition, Downsian analyses, which make reelection the sine qua non of politics, may understate the willingness of politicians to accept a level of electoral vulnerability. Professional politicians are increasingly connected to (and often recruited by) organized networks. This probably strengthens their attachment to (potentially extreme) policy agendas. And the development of strong, well-financed networks of "intense policy demanders" may create substantial private benefits for reliable politicians.

[7] Moreover, because much of the GOP policy agenda relates to constraints on government activism, the policy costs of failing to win majorities may be smaller in a context where a minority party may be able to engage in obstruction (the filibuster) and constitutional hardball (e.g., debt-ceiling hostage-taking).

how closely a party adheres to the preferences of the median voter may have a surprisingly modest impact on its political prospects.

In our view, it is the combination of a strong, intense, and well-organized base and a weak organizational base for moderate groups that distinguishes the GOP and makes it more prone to extremism. The "electoral blind spot" resulting from the limited capacity of most voters to identify the sources and nature of extremism creates *opportunities*. It is the balance of organized forces within each party (along with the asymmetric opportunity structures facing the pro- and antigovernment parties) that primarily explains why the GOP, and not the Democrats, have most aggressively exploited those opportunities.

SOLUTIONS FOR ASYMMETRIC POLARIZATION

This section begins with two basic implications of the previous analysis for the development of reform proposals. The first is a cautionary lesson. At a minimum, proposals based on the idea that polarization is largely symmetrical need to be "stress-tested" to consider the implications if that premise turns out to be false. It is not just that these reforms might turn out to be ineffective – they might also turn out to be counterproductive.

For instance, many advocate reform of the Electoral College's winner-take-all structure (e.g., by awarding electors to the candidate who carries each congressional district) as a way to make majoritarian outcomes more likely or increase incentives for party candidates to seek support in states (potentially making them more "purple") that they might be tempted to write off. But if one party is more inclined to play constitutional hardball, such a proposal might be attractive in states where that party controls the legislature and has gerrymandered congressional districts, but expects to lose the popular vote in presidential elections. If this dynamic played out, a plausible reform initiative could be hijacked to reinforce extremism.[8] In all cases, we need to consider the extent to which the effectiveness of reform proposals rests on a particular understanding of the forces generating and sustaining polarization. "Stress-testing" means asking what the consequences of the reform would be if that understanding is seriously flawed.

The second implication is that we need to complement our thinking about the reform of formal rules with greater attention to the social-structural roots of our current dysfunction. Political scientists are excellent at thinking through

---

[8] Following the 2012 election Republicans gave serious consideration to such proposals in several swing states carried by Obama but governed by Republicans (Wilson 2012).

the first-order consequences of formal rule structures; they are less good at thinking about social structures. When we think of symmetrical polarization, we tend to focus on questions such as "Does rule X create incentives for greater moderation among political candidates?" When we think about asymmetric polarization, however, we are considering contexts in which the same set of rules produces different effects in the two parties. In these contexts, we need to think systematically about the impact of *interactions between rules and the distinctive coalitional structures of the two major parties*. Given the particular set of incentives existing within the increasingly off-center and confrontational GOP, what reforms might increase the benefits of moderation or the costs of extremism?

Here, we outline three types of reforms that might be helpful. These are necessarily just brief sketches, in part because of the priority placed on delineating the mechanisms involved in asymmetric polarization, and in part because they center on influencing (often indirectly) fairly complex political and social interactions that would require much more sustained analysis.

Reestablish Norms of Moderation

The most alarming feature of asymmetric polarization has been the increasing resort to forms of "constitutional hardball." These strategies aggressively exploit permissive features of existing institutions (e.g., the appointment process, the filibuster, the debt limit). American political institutions once functioned reasonably well because of widely shared norms that certain things "weren't done." Another way to think about this is that actors renounced certain possible strategic moves because they anticipated that the likely repercussions would be too costly. Because these costs appear to have diminished dramatically, a critical reform priority should involve efforts to raise them again. Political actors need to pay a real price for engaging in constitutional hardball.[9]

There is no simple way to raise these costs, but the two critical and interconnected fronts are the media and elite discourse. The media's contribution to our challenges has been substantial, because in too many crucial venues, the desire to maintain the appearance of neutrality trumps the need for truth-telling. The inevitable complexity of the governing process further increases the temptation to offer narratives that do not help more casual

---

[9] For evidence that the current crisis over the budget and debt limit reflects strategic choices made by GOP leaders following Obama's reelection (see Chait 2013).

observers of our politics to determine accountability. This stance enables extremism. The "mainstream" media need to be encouraged to recognize the very high cost of "plague on both their houses" reporting.

An equally important audience for this effort to reestablish norms of permissible political conflict is the elite business community. The immense financial and organizational resources of business leaders make this a crucial constituency in establishing the contours of acceptable debate and behavior. The circumstances under which business elites can play a constructive role in such processes is a large and complex but vitally important subject (Mizruchi 2013). For reasons we explore briefly in a moment, we are not especially optimistic, however, that corporate leaders will emerge as a major brake on GOP extremism.

Reduce the Incentives for Obstruction

One reason asymmetric polarization persists is that obstruction has produced very substantial benefits for the GOP. It has limited the policy victories that Democrats could achieve, even following major electoral victories. Obstruction through the filibuster, as well as by extending weapons of gridlock to previously routine procedures such as appointments and debt limit increases, has given conservatives a new capacity to extract policy concessions even without gaining electoral majorities. This reflects a crucial, underappreciated political reality: gridlock and mounting frustration with government systematically favor the antigovernment party.

Reformers need to think about how to design policy initiatives and institutional reforms in such a way that the adoption of extreme policy positions and an unwillingness to compromise do not systematically benefit obstructionists. Recent reforms of the filibuster are a limited step in this direction. Additional changes, which might preserve some protections for intense minority interests while preventing the wholesale resort to obstruction, would also be helpful.

Another idea with potential is to craft agreements containing "reversion points" that put pressure on or isolate conservative extremists by increasing the costs of failure to reach a broad consensus on policy reforms. This was, of course, the intent of the sequester proposal agreed to by the Obama administration and congressional Republicans in 2011. The agreement failed in practice (revealingly, because it underestimated the intensity of GOP preferences regarding tax increases). Nonetheless, the concept is built on a political logic that holds some promise.

Strengthen the Forces of Moderation within the GOP

A telling feature of contemporary politics is the virtual absence of serious organized effort among GOP moderates, whether in or out of office, over the last two decades (Kabaservice 2012). If modern American government needs a capacity for bipartisanship to function – and it does – then we need the Republican equivalent of the DLC.

No single, direct initiative is likely to bring this about. Instead, it is likely to require a number of developments that shift the cost-benefit calculations of some subset of ambitious Republican politicians. Progress on either or both of the first two reform items described earlier would help. So, arguably, would some changes in formal rules (related to elections and campaign finance) that strengthen the electoral prospects of moderates.

As we have stressed, however, asymmetric polarization stems not simply from rules but also from the interaction of those rules with changes in social structure. Over the last generation, social transformations have created a large and intense Republican base, reinforced by well-resourced organizations and an extremist media. Some now hold out hope that the business community will emerge as a moderating force. Indeed, the development of such pressures over time would likely made a considerable difference, as they did in nurturing the Democratic Leadership Council. Yet although the emergence of such organized action in the GOP would matter, we are not optimistic about the prospects. We should not forget that large business organizations such as the Chamber of Commerce have been a principal factor encouraging the GOP's long rightward march (Hacker and Pierson 2010). The wealthy Americans who finance such organizations have benefited enormously from the GOP's increasingly aggressive stance on taxes, government spending, and deregulation, as well as from the GOP's embrace of gridlock as an essential tool for constraining government activism (Bonica, McCarty, Poole, and Rosenthal 2013).

Still, efforts to consider what might shift these underlying social coalitions in ways that disrupt asymmetric polarization at least have the merit of asking the right questions. Finding solutions to our current challenges requires recognition that the two parties are not mirror images and they are not equally responsible for rising polarization. The interaction between the electoral base and organizational environment of the GOP creates much stronger incentives for extremism than exist within the contemporary Democratic Party. To effectively tackle polarization, we must recognize this basic difference and tailor our proposals accordingly.

References

Ahler, Doug, Citrin, Jack and Lenz, Gabe. 2013. "Do Open Primaries Help Moderate Candidates? An Experimental Test of the 2012 Primary." Working Paper.

Bartels, Larry. 2008. *Unequal Democracy: The Political Economy of the New Gilded Age*. Princeton, NJ: Princeton University Press.

Bawn, Kathleen, Martin Cohen, David Karol, Seth Masket, Hans Noel, and John Zaller. 2012. "A Theory of Political Parties: Groups, Policy Demands and Nominations in American Politics." *Perspectives on Politics* 10(3): 571–597.

Bonica, Adam, Nolan McCarty, Keith Poole, and Howard Rosenthal. 2013. "Why Hasn't Democracy Slowed Rising Inequality?" *Journal of Economic Perspectives* 27(3): 103–124.

Chait, Jonathan. 2013. "The House GOP's Legislative Strike." Retrieved from http://nymag.com/daily/intelligencer/2013/09/house-gops-legislative-strike.html.

Fiorina, Morris. 2005. *Culture War? The Myth of a Polarized America*. New York: Longman.

Hacker, Jacob, and Paul Pierson. 2005. *Off-Center: The Republican Revolution and the Erosion of American Democracy*, New Haven: Yale University Press.

———. 2010. "Winner-Take-All Politics: Public Policy, Political Organization, and the Precipitous Rise of Top Incomes in the United States." *Politics and Society* 38(2): 152–204.

Hare, Christopher, Nolan McCarty, Keith Poole, and Howard Rosenthal. 2012. "Polarization is Real and Asymmetric." *Project Voteview Blog*, May 16, 2012. Retrieved from http://voteview.com/blog/?p=494.

Healy, Andrew, and Gabriel Lenz. 2014. "Substituting the End for the Whole: Why Voters Respond Primarily to the Election-Year Economy." *American Journal of Political Science* 58(1): 31–47.

Jacobson, Gary. 2013. "The Economy and Partisanship in the 2012 Presidential and Congressional Elections." *Political Science Quarterly* 128(1): 1–38.

Kabaservice, Geoffrey. 2012. *Rule and Ruin: The Downfall of Moderation and the Destruction of the Republican Party, from Eisenhower to the Tea Party*. Oxford: Oxford University Press.

Katznelson, Ira. 2013. *Fear Itself: The New Deal and the Origins of Our Time*. New York: Norton.

Liptak, Adam. 2010. "Court under Roberts Is Most Conservative in Decades." *New York Times*, July 24.

Lizza, Ryan. 2013. "Where the GOP Suicide Caucus Lives." *New Yorker*. Retrieved from http://www.newyorker.com/online/blogs/comment/2013/09/meadows-boehner-defund-obamacare-suicide-caucus-geography.html.

Mann, Thomas, and Ornstein, Norman. 2012. *It's Even Worse than It Looks: How the American Constitutional System Collided with the New Politics of Extremism*. New York: Basic Books.

Mizruchi, Mark. 2013. *The Fracturing of the American Corporate Elite*. Cambridge, MA: Harvard University Press.

Rubin, Ruth Bloch. 2013. "Organizing for Insurgency: Intra-Party Organization and the Development of the House Insurgency, 1908–1910." *Studies in American Political Development* 27(2): 86–110.

Shor, Boris. 2013. "Asymmetric Polarization in State Legislatures? Yes and No." Retrieved from http://americanlegislatures.com/2013/07/29/partisan-polarization-in-state-legislatures.

Theriault, Sean. 2013. *The Gingrich Senators*. Oxford: Oxford University Press.

Tushnet, Mark. 2004. "Constitutional Hardball." *John Marshall Law Review* 37: 523.

Wilson, Reid. 2012. "The GOP's Electoral College Scheme." *National Journal Online*. Retrieved from www.nationaljournal.com/columns/on-the-trail/the-gop-s-electoral-college-scheme-20121217.

Reforming the Electoral System

4

Polarization and Democratization

Arend Lijphart

Are there solutions to the serious problem of political polarization in the United States? The two main approaches would be efforts to change attitudes and efforts to change institutions and rules. Both are difficult, especially in the short run, but institutional changes are probably somewhat less daunting. I focus on the latter approach.

My point of departure is the fact that polarization between Democrats and Republicans is almost entirely caused by the increasing extremism of the Republican party and especially its right Tea-Party wing – as extensively documented by Thomas E. Mann and Norman J. Ornstein (2012). Democrats may have moved slightly to the left in recent decades, but Republicans have moved much further to the right. In comparison with progressive parties in other advanced industrial democracies – in Europe, Australia, and New Zealand – the Democratic Party looks like a center or slightly left-of-center party instead of a party of the far left. In a similar comparison with conservative parties elsewhere, however, the Republican Party is not just clearly on the right of the political spectrum, but considerably further to the right. A striking example of this difference is the acceptance of universal health insurance by almost all conservative parties, but not by the Republican Party in the United States, which not only opposes it but rejects it with great passion and vehemence. Paul Krugman (2013) has recently called the Republican Party the "crazy party." This is a judgment with which European conservatives are likely to agree.

We probably cannot change the minds of Republicans like Ted Cruz and Eric Cantor, but we can try to reduce their extraordinary influence – which cannot be justified in terms of basic democratic principles. The key to my recommendations for institutional reform is to try to limit the power and influence of (1) the Republican Party as a whole, which has drifted far to the extreme right, and (2) in particular the extreme right wing of the party. These recommendations are also intended to make the American political system more democratic. In fact, my diagnosis of the polarization problem is that it reveals a serious democratic deficit in the United States and the need for far-reaching democratization. Most of my proposals are radical in American, but not in comparative terms. Are they so radical that they are not practical or feasible? I am not holding my breath, but in this chapter I argue that they are certainly not impossible to implement.

ABOLISH PRIMARY ELECTIONS

There is broad agreement that the primary system fosters extremism, because primary elections tend to have low turnout and the more committed and ideologically extreme voters are much more likely to turn out to vote than more moderate voters. If primaries are the problem, one logical solution is to get rid of them and to return the function of nominating candidates for office to the formal party organizations. Because primaries were originally instituted to make the political system more democratic, the proposal to abolish them looks undemocratic. What has happened, however, is that low levels of voter participation have made primaries a means for small minorities, especially more extreme minorities, to wield undue – and undemocratic – influence. Moreover, it is hard to argue that elections without prior primary elections are undemocratic because no other democracy has anything similar to American primaries. A few may have voting procedures that are called "primaries," but they are limited to formal dues-paying party members or to elections adopted by parties on a voluntary basis. American-style primaries have four distinctive characteristics (with some variations from state to state): they are imposed on the parties by the state, they are conducted by public officials, they allow any voter who declares him- or herself to be a member of a party to vote in that party's primary, and they apply to almost all elections. The United States is unique in this respect; primaries are clearly not a necessary ingredient of democracy.

INSTITUTE FAIRVOTE'S TOP FOUR PROPOSAL

A proposal that would reform, instead of abolish, primaries, but that would also decrease the influence of extremist minorities is the top-four method advocated by FairVote of the Center for Voting and Democracy (2012). Like California's top-two system, all candidates must run against each other in a single primary election, but instead of only the two candidates with the most votes advancing to the general election, the top four candidates qualify.

FairVote further proposes that in the general election "ranked choice voting" (which I describe more fully in the next section) be used to determine the eventual winner. This proposal has two advantages. First, about 20% support in the primary is sufficient to advance to the general election, which is therefore likely to have a broader spectrum of candidates, including more moderate and independent-minded candidates. Second, moderate candidates stand a better chance of election in the higher turnout general election than in the low-turnout primary.

USE INSTANT RUNOFF VOTING WITHOUT PRIMARIES

In Australia, this method has been used since the 1920s for elections to the House of Representatives. (It is basically the same method as ranked choice voting, mentioned in the previous section, and is often also called the alternative vote or preferential voting.) The voters are asked to indicate their first preference, second preference, and so on among the candidates in a single-member district. If a candidate receives an absolute majority of the first preferences, he or she is elected. If there is no such majority, the candidate with the lowest number of first preferences is dropped, and the ballots with this candidate as the first preference are transferred to the second preferences. This procedure of excluding the weakest candidate and redistributing the ballots in question to the next highest preferences in each stage of the counting is repeated, until a majority winner emerges. It has the same advantages as FairVote's Top Four proposal – providing better chances for moderate candidates to participate in the general election and for them to get elected in this higher turnout election – and in addition it saves the money that would need to be spent on primary elections.

These first three suggestions have focused on ways to reduce the influence of the far right in the Republican Party. The next twelve deal with reforms that decrease the disproportionate influence of the Republican Party as a whole.

REMOVE THE UNFAIR REPUBLICAN ADVANTAGE
IN HOUSE ELECTIONS

Republicans won a clear majority in the House of Representatives in the 2012 election in spite of the fact that Democratic candidates won about 1.4 million more votes than Republican candidates. The 1996 House election had a similar outcome (Shugart 2012). It is entirely normal in plurality single-member district (SMD) elections that the parties' seat proportions do not correspond to their vote proportions. Usually, large parties win disproportionately many and small parties disproportionately few seats (roughly according to the so-called cube rule). But it is very rare that a party winning the most votes receives fewer seats than the runner-up. The main examples in other plurality SMD elections are the British 1951 election, won by the Conservatives even though Labour had won more votes, and the 1978 and 1981 elections in New Zealand, won by the conservative National Party although the Labour Party won more votes in both of these elections. The 1951 outcome in Britain was very controversial, and the 1978 and 1981 results in New Zealand even more so: they eventually led to the abolition of plurality SMD and the adoption of a proportional representation (PR) system. The spurious Republican majority in the 2012 House election was the result partly of gerrymandering and partly of the natural concentration of Democratic voters. In all five of these instances, the conservative parties were the spurious winners, at least partly due to the tendency of left-wing voters to be concentrated in urban areas. Congress could take action to prevent gerrymandering by mandating impartial commissions to draw election districts in each state or ideally by establishing a single national commission, and the courts could put constraints on excesses of partisan gerrymandering. To make sure that no spurious majorities could ever occur, additional seats could be awarded to the party winning the popular vote to give it a legislative majority. This is a solution that has no empirical precedents in any other plurality SMD system, but in PR systems it is often used to make the outcomes more purely proportional (Lijphart 1994, 146–148).

The importance of this spurious-winner factor can be seen in the hypothetical situation of the Democratic Party having won the 2012 House election. The Republicans would have still been the same extreme right-wing party, but it would not have mattered much: there would have been no or much less gridlock and no threats to shut down the government or to default on the country's debt. Polarization would have been manageable. The conference that produced this volume on "Solutions to Political Polarization in the U.S." might not have taken place either!

USE PROPORTIONAL REPRESENTATION FOR
HOUSE ELECTIONS

More radical than the reform of the plurality SMD system would be the adoption of proportional representation (PR) for House elections. The most likely result would be a system of about four main parties (and a few small ones); the major parties would be liberal Democrats, more centrist Democrats, moderate Republicans, and extreme right-wing Republicans. Winning voting coalitions would probably consist of mainly centrist Democrats and centrist Republicans – which would diminish the power of extreme parties, especially what is now the extreme wing of the Republican Party. Getting rid of plurality SMD would not be a radical move in comparative terms: among the advanced industrial democracies, only the United Kingdom and Canada still use this electoral system.

REDUCE THE REPUBLICAN ADVANTAGE IN SENATE ELECTIONS

The Republican advantage in House elections does not always or inevitably lead to a spurious majority. Their advantage in Senate elections is much greater. Small states tend to the Republican side, and the equal represen-tation of the states gives the Republican Party disproportionate power. This problem is harder to solve because the U.S. Constitution sets the equal rep-resentation of all states, large and small, in unamendable stone. The extreme voter inequalities that are the result plus the obstacles to change them are the main reason why Robert A. Dahl (2001) judges the United States to be democratically deficient in his *How Democratic is the American Constitution?* In principle, however, the solution would be to make the number of seats somewhat more proportional to the population of the states, as in the Senates of Canada and Australia, or much more proportional, as in the similar federal houses in Germany, India, Austria, and Belgium (Lijphart 2012, 195).

GIVE FULL VOTING RIGHTS FOR THE DISTRICT OF COLUMBIA

An additional violation of democratic principles that helps the Republican Party is the denial of representation (except in presidential elections) to the District of Columbia, which is solidly Democratic and which has a larger population than Vermont and Wyoming. A single DC voting representative in the House would not make much difference, but two more Democratic Senators would entail a significant boost to the Democratic Party in the often closely divided Senate.

USE PR FOR SENATE ELECTIONS

The Australian example suggests a possible reform of Senate elections that would not require a change in the equal state representation rule. Australian senators are elected in multimember districts (six states and two territories) by PR. If, in the United States, each state's two senators would similarly be elected simultaneously – that is, in two-member districts – by PR, it would be more likely for the minority party to win one of the seats; slightly more than a third of the vote would be sufficient. This would generally help Democrats in the smaller states and Republicans in the larger states. On balance, it would decrease the Republican advantage to some extent. This system would work even better if the number of senators per state were to be increased to three or four; with four seats at stake, the minority party would be able to win a seat with about 20% of the vote. It would obviously require an increase in the total membership of the Senate to 150 or 200 members – a major change in American but not comparative terms: second chambers in other bicameral legislatures are generally smaller in size than first chambers, but generally larger than 200 members.

ABOLISH THE FILIBUSTER RULE

Even after the elimination of the filibuster on almost all judicial and administrative appointments in November 2013, it remains a potent veto instrument on proposed legislation. Its complete abolition should be regarded as a basic and necessary democratic reform. In the current context, however, it is also worth emphasizing that the filibuster gives even more influence to the smaller states and therefore to the Republican Party.

INCREASE VOTER TURNOUT

Low voter turnout is a serious democratic problem, because it means unequal turnout that is systematically biased against less well-to-do citizens – and hence also against progressive parties and in favor of conservative parties. Compared with other democracies, voter turnout has been especially low in the United States, and the gap between more and less privileged citizens especially wide. The main culprit is the American rule of voter registration as an individual responsibility, combined with burdensome requirements for individuals to get registered. It contrasts with the many other democracies where voting is also voluntary but where voter registration is the government's responsibility. The obvious solution would be for the United States to adopt this more usual and more democratic practice – and thus, by raising the total turnout, to lower the relative share of the votes received by the increasingly extremist Republican Party.

MAKE VOTING MANDATORY

An even better method to guarantee high – indeed, almost universal – turnout is to make voting participation compulsory. It is the one solution that can effectively level the playing field between more and less privileged citizens and between progressive and conservative parties: it would completely eliminate the unfair advantage that Republicans have derived from low and unequal voter participation. I have advocated this solution for many years (Lijphart 1997), and I am pleased to see that Mann and Ornstein (2012, 140–143) also include "making attendance at the polls mandatory" among their proposals. Their phrasing also means that we agree that mandatory "voting" does not entail any obligation to cast an actual vote. The only obligation is to go to the polls; at that point, citizens can make use of their right not to vote, to refuse to accept a ballot, and to go home. Mandatory voting is relatively rare – Australia and Belgium are the main examples – and many citizens of democracies have an instinctive (although not really rational) dislike of it.

USE A LOTTERY AS AN INCENTIVE TO VOTE

A potentially useful, although so far untried, alternative to mandatory voting suggested by Mann and Ornstein (2012, 143) is "a lottery – an election PowerBall with a large prize, in which a person gets a ticket in exchange for a voting receipt. Lottery mania could enhance turnout substantially." (In addition to mandatory voting, I agree with several other Mann-Ornstein proposals, such as instant runoff voting, nonpartisan districting commissions, limits on filibustering, and proportional representation.)

HALT ATTEMPTS AT VOTER SUPPRESSION

Some political scientists have argued that low and unequal voter turnout does not make much of a difference to the relative success of left-wing and right-wing parties. However, the overall evidence does not support this position, and significantly, politicians clearly do not agree with it. Calls for abolishing compulsory voting in Australia and Belgium have come mainly from conservative parties and have been opposed by progressive parties. In the United States, Republicans have been trying to improve their electoral fortunes by suppressing the right to vote. I do not know of any other instance of such efforts at voter suppression in advanced industrial democracies. It is a unique American phenomenon – and one more deficiency of American democracy. The big problem is the decentralized system of election administration in the United States. Nationwide rules for voter registration and other election rules would be the best solution.

INSTITUTE PUBLIC FINANCING OF ELECTIONS

If unequal voter turnout is a help to conservative parties, unequal participation in terms of financial contributions is even more of a true boon. The Supreme

Court's *Citizens United* decision has already helped the Republican parties and its most extreme wing a great deal. All kinds of halfway solutions, such as rules requiring disclosures by donors and recipients, would be of some help, but the only solution that can truly level the playing field is the public financing of elections.

REFORM THE SUPREME COURT

The U.S. Supreme Court has been systematically favoring the Republican Party in recent years. The *Citizens United* case and the invalidation of a key part of the Voting Rights Act are the most recent, but not the only examples. Mann and Ornstein (2012, 73) lament the retirement of Sandra Day O'Connor, which changed "the political and ideological complexion of the Supreme Court... Had O'Connor not retired, *Citizens United* either would [have been a narrower decision] or would have been decided 5–4 the other way." But it was O'Connor who paved the way for this development by casting the crucial vote to elevate George W. Bush to the presidency in 2000. Had Al Gore been elected president, it is very unlikely that John G. Roberts and Samuel Alito would be on the Court now. The current rules governing the composition of the Supreme Court – its small membership of nine justices, their sequential appointment when a vacancy occurs, and life tenure – do not necessarily or permanently guarantee a conservative majority. However, the example of the German Constitutional Court, the closest equivalent to the U.S. Court of a powerful and assertive supreme judicial body among the advanced industrialized democracies, shows that alternative rules – its larger membership of 16 justices (8 elected by the Bundestag and 8 by the Bundesrat); the 12-year term limit; the requirement that justices retire at age 68; and the fact that usually two or more justices are elected at the same time, virtually guaranteeing that the new justices do not belong to the same side of the political and ideological spectrum – can promote broader and more balanced representation. Justices appointed by Republican presidents have been in the majority since the mid-1970s – with an average lopsided advantage of about 7 to 2 until 2009 (Blow 2013). Making the composition of the Court more balanced and less Republican-friendly would take away another advantage that the Republican Party has unfairly enjoyed.

CONCLUSION

Are these proposals too radical, politically unrealistic, and also too partisan because they are tilted in favor of the Democratic Party? I have already answered the first of these objections: they are radical only in American terms, not in comparison with the democratic rules in almost all other advanced industrial democracies. The United States is a truly "different democracy," to cite the title of a book on American government that compared and contrasted – mostly contrasted – it with the democratic systems of 30 other countries (Taylor, Shugart, Lijphart, and Grofman 2014). However, because my proposals are undoubtedly radical and far-reaching in American terms, is there any realistic chance that they can be adopted? This is a serious objection, because the proposals would require a willingness of parties and politicians to vote against their own interests. The most difficult reform would be to make the Senate less unequal in terms of voter representation, because it would require the small states to give up their overrepresentation. However, respect for democratic principles may trump such narrow self-interests. Remember that universal suffrage was adopted in most of the older democracies by parties and politicians who voted against their own self-interest, given that they had fared well under the older system of restricted suffrage.

Moreover, the premature conclusion that these basic reforms are not feasible becomes a self-fulfilling prediction: if we do not even try, we are certain to fail! What is needed is a concerted effort by both Democrats (capital D) and democrats (lowercase d) to highlight the democratic deficiencies of the current political system. It is difficult to understand why there is so little of this effort. Why has the Democratic Party not been more vocal in pointing out the undemocratic outcome of the 2012 House election, and why has it not been more insistent on calling John Boehner's Republican majority democratically illegitimate?

Finally, are my proposals too partisan? They would certainly help the Democratic Party and progressive interests, but only by making the system more democratic (lowercase d) and leveling the political playing field. They would hurt Republican interests, but only to the extent that Republicans have benefited from undemocratic features of the political system. Therefore, Democrats and democrats – and also moderate and democratically sensitive Republicans – should be able to support these reforms with a clear conscience.

References

Blow, Charles M. 2013. "Court Fight." *New York Times*, November 2, A19.
Center for Voting and Democracy. 2012. "FairVote's Fix for Top Two in California." Retrieved from http://www.fairvote.org/fairvote-s-fix-for-top-two-in-california.
Dahl, Robert A. 2001. *How Democratic Is the American Constitution?* New Haven: Yale University Press.
Krugman, Paul. 2013. "The Crazy Party." *New York Times*, September 20, A27.

Lijphart, Arend. 1994. *Electoral Systems and Party Systems: A Study of Twenty-Seven Democracies, 1945–1990*. Oxford: Oxford University Press.

————. 1997. "Unequal Participation: Democracy's Unresolved Dilemma." *American Political Science Review* 91(1): 1–14.

————. 2012. *Patterns of Democracy: Government Forms and Performance in Thirty-Six Countries*. New Haven: Yale University Press.

Mann, Thomas E., and Norman J. Ornstein. 2012. *It's Even Worse than It Looks: How the American Constitutional System Collided with the New Politics of Extremism*. New York: Basic Books.

Shugart, Matthew S. 2012. "Spurious Majorities in the US House in Comparative Perspective." Retrieved from http://fruitsandvotes.com/?p=6513.

Taylor, Steven L., Matthew S. Shugart, Arend Lijphart, and Bernard Grofman. 2014. *A Different Democracy: American Government in a 31-Country Perspective*. New Haven: Yale University Press.

5

Eroding the Electoral Foundations
of Partisan Polarization

Gary C. Jacobson

THE ELECTORAL FOUNDATIONS OF POLARIZED POLITICS

The problem with polarization is not simply that political leaders and ordinary Americans alike are divided into opposite partisan camps on a broad range of national issues, but that these divisions lead to partisan intransigence and gridlock in Washington, rendering the national government incapable of addressing national challenges in any coherent or effective fashion. Partisan divisions in the public certainly contribute to the problem, but current electoral configurations and practices, combined with the Constitution's Madisonian architecture, make it especially acute by delivering a national government divided between a Democratic president and Republican House and Senate majority who owe their election to starkly divergent electoral coalitions (Jacobson 2013a). The foundations of polarized ideological conflict and legislative gridlock thus lie in various interacting features of the electoral process. Some of these features may be amenable to deliberate adjustment; others are clearly not. The most feasible policy changes are likely to have only modest marginal effects on political polarization, but they are at least worth contemplating for want of anything more effective. The challenge as I see it is to alter electoral incentives to make participation in cross-party coalitions more attractive and partisan posturing less so, because in my view, polarized ideological conflict and legislative gridlock will not diminish much until partisan warriors in Congress are punished – or anticipate being punished – rather than rewarded at the polls. Figuring out how to make this happen is no simple matter, because it requires offsetting the trends, practices, and institutional features that generated the problem in the first place, most of which are not amenable to calculated modification.

The polarizing trends are well known. Widening partisan and ideological divisions in Washington over the past four decades have coevolved with complementary changes in electoral politics in a mutually reinforcing spiral (McCarty, Poole, and Rosenthal 2006; Sinclair 2006). National leaders were the first movers – ratcheting up partisan conflict was, for example, a central component of Newt Gingrich's successful strategy for winning Republican control of the House in 1994 – but the drift toward ideological extremes (most pronounced among Republican members) could be sustained only if greater extremity did not cost members their seats. It did not, because in response to the more sharply differentiated alternatives presented by the national parties and their candidates, voters have sorted themselves into increasingly distinct political camps (Baumer and Gold 2008; Levendusky 2009; Abramowitz 2010; Jacobson 2012). Their ideological views and policy opinions have grown more internally consistent, more divergent between parties, and more predictive of voting in national elections. The electoral units into which voters are sorted have also become more lopsidedly partisan (Stonecash, Brewer, and Mariani 2003; Bishop 2008; Levendusky 2009). Changes in the preferences, behavior, and distribution of voters have thus given the national parties more internally homogeneous, ideologically divergent electoral constituencies, providing a robust electoral foundation for polarized national politics.

In 2012, these trends culminated in the most partisan, nationalized, and president-centered federal elections in at least six decades (Jacobson 2013a). Record levels of party loyalty in the presidential contest carried over into the House and Senate elections, and the consistency in voting across offices, measured at both the individual and aggregate levels, was the highest observed in the postwar period. Figure 5.A1 in the Appendix displays two striking consequences: a very high correlation between the district-level House and presidential vote, and a very small number of districts delivering split verdicts between presidential and House candidates.

Ironically, the extraordinary coherence displayed by the electorate in 2012 delivered incoherent divided government, with a Democratic president and Senate squared off against an intransigent Republican House majority. This perverse outcome is the consequence of the current distribution of partisans across electoral units. In the presidential election, high rates of party-line voting favored Barack Obama because Democrats substantially outnumbered Republicans in the 2012 electorate and the distribution of partisans across the states favored his side in the Electoral College (Jacobson 2013b); he won reelection by nearly five million popular votes and with a 332–206 margin in the Electoral College. In House elections, however, party-line and straight-ticket voting strongly favored Republicans because of their structural advantage in the distribution of partisans across congressional districts. Although Republican gerrymanders reinforced this advantage after the 2000 and 2010 censuses

(Jacobson 2003; 2014), it has existed for decades as a product of coalition demographics. Democrats win the lion's share of ethnic minority, single, young, secular, and gay voters who are concentrated in urban districts that deliver lopsided Democratic majorities. Regular Republican voters are spread more evenly across suburbs, smaller cities, and rural areas, so fewer Republican votes are "wasted" in highly skewed districts. Thus despite Obama's substantial popular vote margin, Romney outpolled him in 226 districts, whereas Obama ran ahead in only 209. This imbalance was as great in the 1970s as it is today (see Figure 5.A2 in the Appendix), but with the rise of party-line voting and decline in ticket splitting, it has become much more consequential. Democrats actually won a majority of the major-party vote cast nationally for House candidates in 2012, 50.7%; but with party loyalty so high and split outcomes so rare, they won only 46.2% of House seats. The divided government in place today is not the result of ambivalent loyalties and preferences among voters, but of the way their votes are aggregated by the electoral system.

The high rate of party-line voting in the 2012 congressional elections gave the congressional parties in both the House and Senate their most divergent electoral bases in at least 60 years (see Figures 5.A3 and 5.A4). Back in the early 1970s, House districts won by Democrats and those won by Republicans differed in their average presidential vote by only about seven percentage points, which was a low point for the postwar period. Since then, the gap has more than tripled; in 2012, Obama's share of the vote in districts won by Democrats was on average 26 percentage points higher than in districts won by Republicans (66% compared to 40%). A similar though less pronounced trend appears in comparable Senate data. In both chambers, the congressional party coalitions now represent constituencies that are far more dissimilar, in terms of their partisan composition, than at any time in the postwar era. Very few Republicans owe their election to any significant proportion of voters who supported Obama.

Historical experience shows that divided government need not always produce stalemate, gridlock, and intense partisan conflict in Washington (Mayhew 1991). But when, as now, the president and one or both houses of Congress owe their election to starkly divergent and barely overlapping electoral coalitions, the range of mutually agreeable policy options is severely limited. There are no obvious policy prescriptions that will broaden the party coalitions, make them less homogeneous, or move their medians closer together on issues or ideology. The sorting of voters into separate ideological camps and into more homogeneously red or blue districts and states is largely the product of broad social, economic, and demographic trends that, although not immutable, defy deliberate modification. Still, some feasible actions might mitigate the effects of these trends until the political landscape evolves into a less contentious configuration.

REDISTRICTING REFORM

To the extent that redistricting practices have furthered partisan polarization, intervention here might have some effect. As is evident in Figure 5.A2, the proportion of districts with a close partisan balance – settings that encourage if not dictate moderation – has declined substantially since 1992. This was partly because of (largely pro-Republican) gerrymandering after the 2000 and 2010 censuses (Jacobson 2003; 2014), but notice that most of the decline occurred between 1992 and 2000, indicating that it had more to do with changes in voting behavior than with changes in district lines. Although gerrymandering is popularly blamed for producing uncompetitive districts that fuel polarization, the evidence indicates that its contribution to the problem has been quite modest (Jacobson 2006; Mann 2006; McCarty, Poole, and Rosenthal 2009), and of course it cannot account for the increasing partisan polarization in the Senate. Still, it is one part of the process open to manipulation.

Handing the task of redistricting to a supposedly neutral panel, exemplified by California's new process, is one proposed option. The California commission produced about a dozen competitive House districts out of the state's 53, up from essentially zero in the previous map. An initial study concluded that redistricting reform did not diminish the ideological polarization of the California delegation, but its authors also pointed out correctly that it may take a series of elections for its effects to register (Kousser, Phillips, and Shor 2013). Ideological extremity is related to a district's partisan balance, with more lopsided districts producing more extreme representatives, although the effects are asymmetrical between the parties: Democrats moderate more than Republicans as the local party balance becomes less favorable. Any change that increases the number of balanced House districts should thus encourage greater moderation, but estimates of these relationships suggest that the effects are likely to be small. It makes for considerably greater moderation if the representative serves a district that actually leans toward the other party, but such representatives have become exceedingly rare (12 members in the current House), and redistricting reform by itself cannot make them more common.

As a means of reducing polarization, redistricting also faces a special political problem. Nonpartisan line drawing that did not take the more efficient distribution of Republican voters into account would tend to harm Democrats. That is, a strictly neutral process, especially one pursuing "compactness" and protecting "communities of interest," would likely have clear partisan effects, favoring Republicans. The only way for Democrats to win a share of seats commensurate with their share of votes in many states is through deliberate gerrymanders aimed at achieving this goal. Republicans will never support any such scheme, and thus Democratic partisans have good reason to be leery about giving up any chance of controlling the process themselves.

PRIMARY ELECTIONS

California voters addressed another aspect of the electoral process by adopting an open primary system in which candidates from all parties compete in a single primary open to all registered voters; then the top two vote-getters compete in the general election, even if they are from the same party. The idea is to promote moderation by inducing candidates to broaden their appeal to attract independents and opposite-party voters in primaries and, if both general election candidates are of the same party, in general elections as well. There is some evidence that open primaries do produce more moderate winners (Gerber and Morton 1998), but California's initial experiment with the process in 2012 evidently did not (Kousser, Phillips, and Shor 2013). Like redistricting reform, primary reforms of this sort may help induce greater moderation in the long run, but so far countervailing forces seem to be considerably stronger. Nonetheless, they may be worth pursuing for want of better options.

CAMPAIGN FINANCE

Primaries have long been blamed for promoting extremism on the ground that ideological zealots are more strongly motivated to participate in these low-turnout events than are more moderate citizens. Primary electorates do indeed tend to be more extreme than general electorates (Jacobson 2012) and thus present a problem to centrist candidates in many states and districts. Broadening the electorate, as open primaries are meant to do, may thus eventually help. But a more important hindrance to moderates seeking nominations in recent elections has been the emergence of ideologically oriented groups willing and able to intervene lavishly in primaries to help ideological purists prevail. Aided by such groups on the right, more extreme candidates defeated three incumbent Republican senators in the two most recent elections, sending a strong message – backed up by explicit threats – to Republicans who might be tempted to cooperate with congressional Democrats or Obama. The consequences were on full display in the absurd game of chicken on the budget and debt limit initiated by Republicans trying to demonstrate their unwavering dedication to erasing "Obamacare" in 2013.

More generally, party and nonparty groups and individuals spending huge sums on independent campaigns have emerged in the past decade as a major new electoral force (see Figures 5.A5 and 5.A6). Most of this money is spent in a relatively small number of close House and Senate contests, and in the last couple of elections, outsiders have spent about as much as the candidates' campaigns in such races (Jacobson 2014). The Supreme Court has ruled that unlimited independent spending is protected by the First Amendment, so nothing short of amending the Constitution can curb it – and the prospects for amendment are nil. If well-funded nonparty groups with strong ideological preferences contribute to polarization by helping extremists win and by cowing incumbents who fear becoming targets, an eminently feasible (if rather unlikely) way to counteract their influence would be to fund equally lavish independent campaigns *against* extremist candidates. Fight fire with fire. Use the same tactics – including aggressively negative ads – to shift the electoral ground in favor of centrists. Threaten to punish intransigent extremists. It is not obvious who would organize such campaigns or where the money would come from, but assuming that outside campaign spending continues to be as important as in recent elections, this would be one way to increase the electoral incentive to engage in a more cooperative, less confrontational politics.

The effects on polarization of independent spending by the Hill party committees and groups allied with them are less obvious. On one hand, heavy financial assistance from party sources should promote loyalty; on the other hand, party leaders care mainly about winning majorities and thus may on pragmatic grounds support moderate party dissenters in primary and general elections in states and district where they have the better chance of winning. Such a strategy helped the Democrats take over Congress in 2006, although most of the moderates elected that year were gone after 2012. Statutory changes that channel more money through party committees might thus contribute in a small way to enlarging the number of more moderate members. Party money could also be used to protect members who support leaders willing to make the deals necessary for divided government to work – if they decide to make the deals. This is a crucial point. Strategic positioning by party leaders in pursuit of majority status has been and continues to be a major source of polarized politics in Washington. Until leaders decide that partisan intransigence does not serve their party's collective interest in winning majorities (and can convince backbenchers to go along), there is no reason to expect them to get back to negotiating the compromises necessary to govern.

Another way to improve the prospects of moderate candidates would be to raise contribution limits to candidates' campaigns. Campaigns run by outsiders nationalize and polarize electoral politics. The more resources available to candidates to shape and convey the message, the greater their capacity to adapt it to local political conditions, for example, by taking unorthodox positions that expand their appeal beyond the party base. Nothing guarantees that they will do so, but if a greater share of campaign funds were under their control, they would at least have more opportunity to pursue strategies emphasizing independence from their party and ideological moderation despite outsiders' efforts to undermine them.

THE NEWS MEDIA

The proliferation of ideologically diverse national news and opinion sources over the last couple of decades has almost certainly contributed to the widening of partisan and ideological divisions in the public (Mutz 2006; Kernell and Rice 2008; Levendusky 2009). Americans can now draw on variously slanted sources of political information – not just on television but also in newspapers and magazines and on radio and the internet – and there is plenty of evidence that they tend to select sources more likely to confirm than to challenge their political opinions (Jacobson 2013b). Whether the media landscape is more a cause or more a manifestation of polarization remains unclear, but it obviously does make it easy for rival partisans to maintain separate cognitive worlds. Its contours reflect a business model of cultivating niche audiences and delivering the purest form of the messages they want to hear, and nothing is likely to change this model as long as it continues to attract the desired audiences. Again, the only option may be to fight fire with fire, developing, for example, attractive media outlets that celebrate politicians who engage in the traditional politics of deal making and excoriate extremists who foster gridlock. Many centrist sources of news and information already exist; the challenge is to build an audience of ideologically moderate and politically independent citizens for whom politics is at best a peripheral concern, as well as to attract the selective attention of the more open-minded partisans. Again, I do not know how to bring this about, but anything that helps turn a reputation for partisan zealotry into an unfashionable electoral liability should help.

CONCLUSION

Polarized national politics in the United States is largely the product of long-term social, economic, cultural, and demographic trends, most of which are highly resistant, perhaps impervious to deliberate reversal. These trends, combined with the separate electoral bases and calendars of presidents, representatives, and senators that in current configurations deliver divided government, give partisan divisions in Washington a sturdy electoral foundation. A few aspects of the electoral process are open to modifications that might begin to erode this foundation by making it a bit easier for moderates to win and for partisan warriors to be punished on election day. More radical changes (e.g., altering the Constitution to make it easier for majorities to prevail, making voting mandatory to broaden the electorate) might be more effective, but are so unlikely as to be not worth discussing.

If there is to be a solution under present electoral institutions, it will come from voters fed up with dysfunctional government who find a way to punish its perpetrators (or to threaten credibly to do so) and from political leaders who view their individual and collective fates as better served by cooperative problem solving than by gridlock-inducing position taking. Unfortunately, it may take a national disaster of the kind threatened by present Republican efforts to defund Obamacare for that to happen, at least in the short run. In the longer run, some currently polarizing issues are likely to fade (e.g., if Obamacare takes effect and the world as we know it does not end); a stronger economy may dampen hysteria over deficits and make entitlement reform less contentious; and demographic trends may move American society toward consensus on some issues (same-sex marriage, a pathway to citizenship for undocumented immigrants) that now divide the parties. Moreover, it is difficult to imagine that Obama's successor will be as polarizing a figure as he has become. The polarized ideological conflict and legislative gridlock of today are neither inevitable nor inalterable, but they remain at present more conditions to be managed than problems to be solved.

APPENDIX: ILLUSTRATIVE FIGURES

Figure 5.A1 displays two measures of the relationship between presidential and House voting at the district level: the percentage of variance shared by the district-level House and presidential vote, and the percentage of districts that delivered split verdicts, with pluralities voting for a presidential candidate of one party and the House candidate of the other. By both measures, 2012 stands out as the extreme extension of a long-term trend toward greater electoral coherence. The district-level vote shares for president and House candidate are correlated at greater than .95, and hence 90.7% of their variance is shared. The incidence of districts delivering split verdicts, 6%, is less than half the previous low of 14% established in 2004. Moreover, only six states favored different parties in the Senate and presidential elections, the smallest

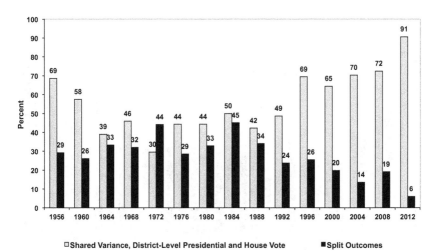

FIGURE 5.A1. Presidential Voting and District Level Results, 1956–2012

number and proportion for the entire period. For further details, see Jacobson (2013b).

Figure 5.A2 shows that over the past four decades a substantially larger proportion of House seats have leaned Republican than have leaned Democratic ("leaning" defined here as having the district vote for their party's presidential candidate at least two percentage points above the national vote for that year

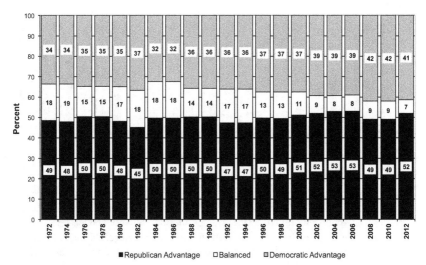

FIGURE 5.A2. District Partisan Advantage, 1972–2012

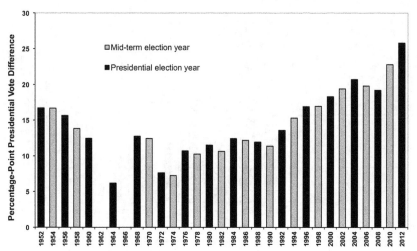

FIGURE 5.A3. Polarization of U.S. House Districts, 1952–2012. *Note*: Entries are the percentage-point differences in the average presidential vote between districts won by Democrats and districts won by Republicans; data for 1962 and 1966 are unavailable because of redistricting; entries for midterm elections are calculated from the previous presidential election. *Source*: Compiled by author.

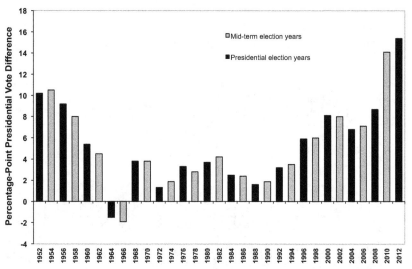

FIGURE 5.A4. The Polarization of State Constituencies, 1952–2012. *Note*: Entries are the percentage-point differences in the average presidential vote between states won by Democrats and states won by Republicans in the Senate elections; entries for midterm election years are calculated from the presidential election two years earlier. *Source*: Compiled by author.

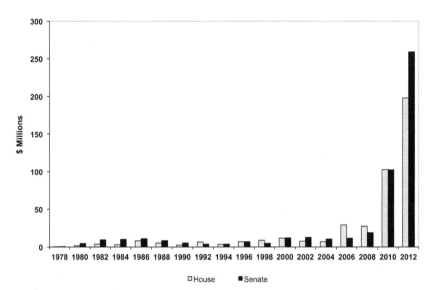

FIGURE 5.A5. Independent Spending by Nonparty Committees, 1978–2012 (Adjusted for Inflation, 2012=1.00). *Source*: Norman J. Ornstein, Thomas E. Mann, Michael J. Malbin and Andrew Rugg, *Vital Statistics on Congress*, July 2013, Table 3–14, at www.brookings.edu/research/reports/2013/07/vital-statistics-congress-mann-ornstein.

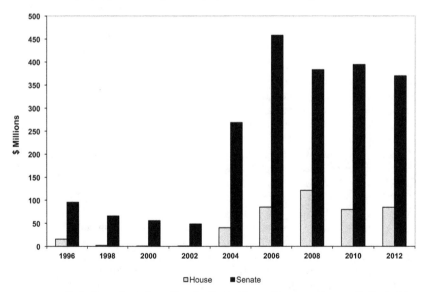

FIGURE 5.A6. Independent Spending by Party Committees, 1996–2012 (Adjusted by Inflation, 2012=1.00). *Source*: Norman J. Ornstein, Thomas E. Mann, Michael J. Malbin and Andrew Rugg, *Vital Statistics on Congress*, July 2013, Table 3–12, at www.brookings.edu/research/reports/2013/07/vital-statistics-congress-mann-ornstein.

or, for midterms, for the previous presidential election). Meanwhile, the proportion of closely balanced districts (delivering presidential results within two percentage points of the national vote) has declined and after 2012 was down to only 6.7%; very few representatives (29 to be exact) now serve districts without a clear partisan tilt. Only 12 of the other 406 districts are currently held by the disadvantaged party.

References

Abramowitz, Alan I. 2010. _The Disappearing Center: Engaged Citizens, Polarization, and American Democracy._ New Haven: Yale University Press.

Baumer, Donald C., and Howard J. Gold. 2008. _Parties, Polarization, and Democracy in the United States._ Boulder: Paradigm Publishers.

Bishop, Bill. 2008. _The Big Sort: Why the Clustering of Like-Minded America is Tearing Us Apart._ Boston: Houghton Mifflin.

Gerber, Elizabeth, and Rebecca Rebecca B. Morton. 1998. "Primary Election Systems and Representation." _Journal of Law, Economics, and Organization_ 14(3): 304–324.

Jacobson, Gary C. 2003. "Terror, Terrain, and Turnout: The 2002 Midterm Election," _Political Science Quarterly_ 118(1): 1–22.

_____. 2006. "Why Other Sources of Polarization Matter More" In _Red and Blue Nation?_, Vol. 1, eds. Pietro S. Nivola and David W. Brady. Washington, DC: Brookings Institution Press: 284–290.

_____. 2011. "The Republican Resurgence in 2010." _Political Science Quarterly_ 126(1): 27–52.

_____. 2012. "The Electoral Origins of Polarized Politics: Evidence from the 2010 Cooperative Congressional Election Study." _American Behavioral Scientist_ 56(12): 1612–1630.

_____. 2013a. "Partisan Polarization in American Politics: A Background Paper." _Presidential Studies Quarterly_ 43(12): 688–708.

_____. 2013b. "Barack Obama and the Nationalization of Electoral Politics in 2012." Presented at the Conference on the Confirming U.S. Presidential Election of 2012, Mershon Center, The Ohio State University, October 10–11.

_____. 2014. "Congress: Partisanship and Polarization." In _The Elections of 2012_, ed. Michael Nelson. Washington, DC: CQ Press: 145–171.

Kernell, Samuel, and Laurie L. Rice. 2011. "Cable and the Partisan Polarization of the President's Audience." _Presidential Studies Quarterly_ 41(12): 693–711.

Kousser, Thad, Justin H. Phillips, and Boris Shor. 2013. "Reform and Representation: Assessing California's Top-Two Primary and Redistricting Commission." Presented at the 2013 Annual Meeting of the American Political Science Association, Chicago.

Levendusky, Matthew. 2009. _The Partisan Sort: How Liberals Became Democrats and Conservatives Became Republicans._ Chicago: University of Chicago Press.

Mayhew, David R. 1991. _Divide We Govern: Party Control, Lawmaking, and Investigations, 1946–1990._ New Haven: Yale University Press.

Mann, Thomas E. 2006. "Polarizing the House of Representatives: How Much Does Gerrymandering Matter?" In _Red and Blue Nation?_, Vol. 1, eds. Pietro S. Nivola and David W. Brady. Washington, DC: Brookings Institution Press: 263–283.

McCarty, Nolan, Keith T. Poole, and Howard Rosenthal. 2006. *Polarized American: The Dance of Ideology and Unequal Riches.* Cambridge, MA: MIT Press.

————. 2009. "Does Gerrymandering Cause Polarization?" *American Journal of Political Science* 53(7): 666–680.

Mutz, Diana. 2006. "How the Mass Media Divide Us." In *Red and Blue Nation? Characteristics and Causes of America's Polarized Politics*, Vol. I, eds. Pietro Nivola and David Brady. Washington, DC: Brookings Institution Press.

Sinclair, Barbara. 2006. *Party Wars: Polarization and the Politics of the Policy Process.* Norman: University of Oklahoma Press.

Stonecash, Jeffrey M., Mark D. Brewer, and Mack C. Mariani. 2003. *Diverging Parties: Social Change, Realignment, and Party Polarization.* Boulder: Westview Press.

6

Solutions to Polarization

Elaine C. Kamarck

Polarization makes it far more difficult to conduct the essential tasks of governance, from passing a budget that would keep the government functioning, to staffing an administration. And polarization makes it almost impossible to address complex problems whose solutions require bipartisan support. Polarization does make it easier for elected officials to cross the line separating robust democratic discourse from deliberate misrepresentation and personal calumny. It contributes to diminished trust and confidence in our public institutions, and it leads to a view of politics as warfare in which contested issues are never resolved but rather are endlessly re-litigated.

Polarization has, at its roots, deeply held philosophical differences about the public sphere and what should or should not go on there. Short of one side finally winning the argument – through gradual demographic change or sudden catastrophic change – we have no easy answers for resolving deeply held differences. What we can do, however, is look at how our democracy is structured and examine the possibility that changes in the structure of government and politics might reduce some of the most severe political polarization.

Hence, what follows are three ideas for structural reforms that might mitigate some of the worst aspects of polarization and a final note on why they may not be necessary after all.

IDEA #1: REFORM CONGRESSIONAL PRIMARIES IN WAYS THAT WILL INCREASE TURNOUT

Low turnout is an enduring characteristic of all primary elections, and congressional primaries are no different. Turnout (as a percentage of voting age population [VAP]) in congressional primaries does not even break into double digits in a year like 2010 when a great deal of attention was paid to primaries. Turnout in contested primaries in 2010 was 7.5% of VAP, compared to turnout in contested primaries in 2006 of 4.6% of VAP and in 2002 of 5.4% of VAP (Galston and Karmarck 2011).

There are two ways to try and expand turnout in congressional primaries – get rid of closed primaries[1] and mandate that all primaries be held on the same day for each political party.

Given the greater interest and intensity of ideologically motivated voters in both parties, odds are that they would still dominate most primaries most of the time. But the possibility of expanding the primary electorate would cause candidates to look at primaries differently. Opening up the possibility that independents and/or voters from the other party would vote in a primary could, from time to time, dilute the impact of the ideologically driven factions within the party, thereby making it possible that moderation and compromise might be rewarded rather than punished.

Another option would be to institute California's top-two method. In the California election held on June 8, 2010, Proposition 14 – "Top Two Primaries Act" – passed with 53.8% of the vote. It overturned the closed primary process by creating, in essence, one political primary for both parties, in which voters are allowed to vote for any candidate, regardless of the voter's party affiliation. The top two candidates then face off in the general election. Prop 14 applies to all elections, with the exception of presidential primaries and elections for party office. Its proponents argued that it might cause more moderates to be elected to the California state legislature. The passage of Prop 14 is evidence of the fact that many Californians felt that their government had become dysfunctional as a result of extreme partisanship stemming, at least in part, from the closed primary process.

It remains to be seen whether Prop 14 will result in more moderate governance. Several political scientists studied the first use of this new system in California in 2012 and found little evidence that it favored more moderate candidates – mostly due to the fact that voters had a hard time discerning who was the more moderate. Nonetheless, this was an early test and the authors cautioned, "Open primaries may still moderate the behavior of elected officials even if voters fail to recognize or explicitly reward such moderation" (Ahler, Citrin, and Lenz 2013). However, the 2014 primaries also failed to offer any evidence that this system will result in the election of more moderate candidates or that it will increase voter turnout. In Washington State, which has used this form of primary since 2007, the results are also not very clear-cut.

---

[1] A "closed" primary is one in which only voters who register with a party preference can participate. Of the 50 states, 26 have closed primaries.

Even though we have little evidence so far on the impact of increased primary turnout, common sense tells us that if, over time, the primary electorate expands to look more like the general election electorate, the impact of moderates will increase and members of Congress will be somewhat liberated from the tyranny of small, ideologically dominated primary electorates, potentially enabling them to engage in more productive governance without risking their political careers.

A second way that turnout in congressional primaries could be increased would be to hold all the primaries of one party (or both) across the country on the same day. Primary election days are set by state law and have been, traditionally, set for the purpose of protecting incumbents. The Appendix lists the dates of primary elections in 2010 – the year the Tea Party surprised many incumbents. As you can see, many of these elections occurred in the middle of the summer. Press coverage was very sparse, until it became clear that the grassroots movement that had begun on cable television in February 2009 (a year earlier) with a rant by CNBC business editor Rick Santelli was resulting in something significant. Connections between the Tea Party movement and the year's little publicized primaries were made only *after* the fact. Concerned voters could easily have missed the fact that a party primary was happening.

We know from voting behavior in presidential primaries that competition and media coverage go together in stimulating high turnout – which is why early primaries like New Hampshire's have very high turnout levels and later primaries do not. If the primaries in every state were on the same day, that alone would create a story worthy of coverage. The voters would be exposed to more information about factional divisions within their parties. Debate over the direction of a party would happen *before*, not after, an important election. Of course, in some years, Republicans might still decide to nominate Tea Party sympathizers or in other years, Democrats might still decide to nominate far-left candidates, but at least the decision would not be a surprise.

In the presidential primary system a great deal of attention and bipartisan activity have been directed at rationalizing the primary calendar. Incumbents have tended to prefer obscure, low-turnout primaries, but to the extent that fear of "getting primaried" continues, they may find that they have incentives to change the primary dates in ways that will garner more attention.

IDEA #2: INSTITUTE REAL REDISTRICTING REFORM

It is easy to overestimate the impact of gerrymandering on our politics. Polarization has been increasing at all levels of government, including those – such as the state and county levels – where lines are not periodically redrawn for partisan advantage. To be sure, other factors, in addition to gerrymandering, have contributed to the creation of safe seats. For example, in *The Big Sort: Why the Clustering of Like-Minded America is Tearing Us Apart*, Bill Bishop (2008) shows how Americans have been moving, voluntarily, into geographic communities where they find others who are like them economically, culturally, and politically.

Given these trends, there is clearly a limit to the number of competitive congressional districts that could be created if redistricting were removed from the self-interested political process in state legislatures and if gerrymandering was reduced. Thomas Mann of the Brookings Institution cautions that there are little data to support a link between independent redistricting and changes in Congress. Nonetheless, scholars including Mann agree that partisan redistricting has some effect and are involved in projects to increase the transparency of the redistricting process.

In the broader public, the same dissatisfaction with partisan gridlock that led California voters to do away with party primaries has also been felt in states that have decided to put the redistricting process in the hands of nonpartisan bodies. The number of independent redistricting commissions has grown over time, albeit slowly. The first four were established in Hawaii, Iowa, Washington, and Montana in the 1980s. They were followed by Idaho, New Jersey, and Arizona in the 1990s, and then by California's passage of Proposition 11 in June 2008, establishing the California Redistricting Commission that began work on redistricting following the 2010 census.

Although scholars tend to study either congressional primaries *or* congressional redistricting in isolation, it is the *combination* of the two that heightens the impact of ideology and thus contributes to polarization. Over time we can see the effects of polarization in legislative behavior. Scholars who have studied congressional voting behavior find that in the middle of the twentieth century there was substantial overlap among the two political parties: there were Southern conservative Democrats and Northern liberal Republicans. Each political party in this era was indeed a big tent, home to some House members and senators whose ideological predispositions were closer to members of the opposite party than to their own. Reinforcing these broad coalitions was the fact that in this era all members of Congress shared a common understanding of the threats to the United States as primarily involving the Cold War.

With all these caveats, reforming the process of drawing legislative districts by taking redistricting out of the hands of state legislatures and placing it in the hands of non-partisan commissions is an obvious place to start to reduce polarization.

IDEA #3: INSTITUTE SUPERMAJORITY SELECTION OF
CONGRESSIONAL LEADERSHIP

In the very first vote of every new Congress, those seeking leadership positions are required only to win votes from their caucus. They are *not* required to reach across the aisle. The result is that House and Senate leaders reflect a majority of the majority, which is almost always a *minority* of the entire legislative body. Rather than promoting compromise and comity, the method of selecting congressional leaders reinforces the influence of dominant factions within each party. In a system of equal powers among branches of government, the result of this leadership mechanism is that it leaves only the president to speaking for the majority of the country.

How would things change if it took 60% of each body to elect the Speaker of the House and the Majority Leader of the Senate? Unless one party commands a supermajority as the result of the previous election, the very first vote of each new Congress would test the ability of aspiring leaders to construct the bipartisan coalitions that are so integral to effective governance. In most years a 60% rule would require the leadership of the majority party to establish a relationship with at least some faction of the minority party.

The consequences for the ability to pass legislation are obvious. In the Senate, the magic number needed to break a filibuster would be achieved first in the leadership elections. Although the Senate amended its filibuster rule last fall, it did so only for some points in the legislative process and for appointees to the executive and judicial branches. The need for 60 votes on legislation is far from dead. If, under this reform, the leadership coalition held throughout the legislative life cycle, it would be easier to obtain 60 votes for the passage of legislation.

In the House, the leadership election would establish a majority large enough to overcome the inevitable lapses in party discipline – assuming, that is, that the legislative agenda the Speaker supports is consistent with the thinking of the supermajority needed to attain that position of leadership.

This proposal goes somewhat against the grain of current thinking. Some have called for eliminating the filibuster rule in the Senate altogether so that legislation could be passed with simple majorities. However, there are good reasons why we should want major legislation in the United States to be passed by large majorities. First, supermajorities guarantee ownership by both political parties. In such circumstances, it is more likely that the legislative process can address difficult problems – for instance, our long-term structural budget deficit – without proposed solutions being manipulated by either party for political gain. Second, significant pieces of legislation require years of careful implementation. During this period, party control of government is likely to shift. Leaders of a political party that has no stake in a program are not likely to work hard to make sure that the program is well implemented. In fact, just the reverse might occur – with failure leading the former opposition party to say, in effect, "We told you so."

This idea, like the others cited earlier, has its downsides. As my colleague Sarah Binder (see Chapter 18) reminds me, in the nineteenth century there were some very fractious leadership elections. Under this proposal, gridlock or dysfunction could indeed manifest itself in the leadership election and not wait for the budget or debt ceiling vote.

IDEA #4 – JUST WAIT

A final thought: it might just make sense to wait this out. A few final bits of data suggest this option.

It is possible that the strength of the Tea Party faction within the Republican Party is waning. According to Gallup, Tea Party supporters in the electorate now account for 22% of voters compared to a high of 32% at the end of 2010 (Saad 2013). Other polls have shown similar trends, and the effects of their "take no prisoners" style in Congress could further weaken the Tea Party's influence within the GOP (Edwards-Levy 2013). And the mobilization of the business community in the 2014 midterm elections was successful in denying the Tea Party the kind of high-profile wins they had in the 2010 mid-term elections. With the exception of Congressman Eric Cantor, the Tea Party did not manage any attention-getting wins.

Second, there is some polling indicating that Tea Party supporters are older, with an average age of 66+, than some baby boomers and Gen Xers and Millenials.[2] If that is indeed the case and if the Republican Party more broadly continues to have trouble attracting younger voters, this pull of the far right could diminish with time.

A third indicator is an interesting piece of data about the Fox News channel, one of the most important actors in a heavily polarized society. Its viewership consists of the oldest people in the country. According to Nielson data, half of its viewers are 68 years old and older, and it is having trouble attracting younger viewers (Thompson 2014).

Finally, political parties change. The Democrats pulled themselves out of a long losing streak when they reformed in ways that would allow Bill Clinton

---

[2] "Tea Party Support Declines Somewhat: Support strongest among older, white men who did not graduate from college," Harris Interactive, March 8, 2011.

to win the presidency not once but twice. It is possible that the Republicans will do this as well, especially if the political consequences of their internal polarization get even worse than they have been.

But while we are waiting for the sources of our current hyperpolarization to decrease we can, perhaps, change some pieces of our system so that philosophical political differences do not lead to destructive governmental gridlock.

APPENDIX

Dates for 2010 Primaries

Date	Primary for Federal Office
February 2, 2010	Illinois
March 2, 2010	Texas
May 4, 2010	Indiana, Ohio,
May 11, 2010	West Virginia
May 18, 2010	Arkansas, Kentucky, Oregon, Pennsylvania
May 25, 2010	Idaho
June 1, 2010	Mississippi
June 8, 2010	California, Iowa, Maine, Montana, South Carolina, South Dakota, Virginia
June 22, 2010	Utah
July 20, 2010	Georgia
July 27, 2010	Oklahoma
August 3, 2010	Kansas, Michigan, Missouri
August 5, 2010	Tennessee
August 10, 2010	Colorado, Connecticut, Minnesota
August 17, 2010	Washington, Wyoming
August 24, 2010	Alaska, Arizona, Florida, Vermont
August 28, 2010	Louisiana
September 14, 2010	Delaware, Washington, DC, Maryland, Massachusetts, Rhode Island, Wisconsin
September 18, 2010	Hawaii

References

Ahler, Doug, Jack Citrin, and Gabriel Lenz. 2013. "Can California's New Primary Reduce Polarization? Maybe Not." *The Monkey Cage*, March 27. Retrieved from themonkeycage.org/2013/03/27/can-californias-new-primary-reduce-polarization-maybe-not.

Bishop, Bill. 2008. *The Big Sort: Why the Clustering of Like-Minded America Is Tearing Us Apart*. New York: Houghton Mifflin.

Edwards-Levy, Ariel. 2013. "Tea Party Hits Record Level of Unpopularity in Public Opinion Poll." *The Huffington Post*, January 7. Retrieved from www.huffingtonpost .com/2013/01/07/tea-party-poll_n_2425833.html.

Galston, William A., and Elaine C. Karmarck. 2011. *The Still-Vital Center: Moderates, Democrats, and the Renewal of American Politics.* Washington, DC: Third Way.

Rucker, Phillip. 2013. "Some Tea Party Congressmen Find Signs of Political Backlash at Home." *Washington Post*, October 7. Retrieved from http://www.washingtonpost .com/politics/some-tea-party-congressmen-find-signs-of-political-backlash-at-home/ 2013/10/06/d13d698a-2d27-11e3-b139-029811dbb57f_story.html.

Saad, Lydia. 2013. "Tea Party Support Dwindles to Near-Record Low." *Gallup Politics*, September 26. Retrieved from www.gallup.com/poll/164648/tea-party-suppor-dwindles-near-record-low.aspx.

Thompson, Derek. January 27, 2014. "Half of all Fox News' Viewers are 68 and older," *The Atlantic*. Retrieved from http://www.theatlantic.com/business/archive/2014/01/ half-of-fox-news-viewers-are-68-and-older/283385/.

7

Geography and Gridlock in the United States

Jonathan Rodden

Political polarization in the United States causes inefficiency and policy uncertainty. This occurs not because of unusually high levels of ideological polarization among voters or legislators that generate large policy swings. Rather, it is a problem of extreme gridlock under a unique form of two-party presidential democracy in which changes from the status quo frequently require defections from opposition legislators.

This chapter explores the argument that these defections are increasingly difficult to achieve because of a profound transformation of American political geography associated with deindustrialization and suburbanization. Our understanding of this transformation is still limited, as should be the hubris with which we dispense reform advice. This chapter advocates a cautious and experimental approach to reform at the state level, focusing on the potential advantages of some form of compulsory voting.

WHAT IS THE PROBLEM?

The United States has a unique constitution. It is one of the only countries in the world that combines a strict two-party system with a presidential form of government. Its only peers are Venezuela, Ghana, and Sierra Leone. As demonstrated in Figure 7.1, all other former British colonies with single-member districts and strict two-party systems have a parliamentary form of government. These countries have no need for bipartisanship. Members of the government party almost always vote for the legislative proposals of the executive, and members of the opposition vote against. A bimodal distribution of roll-call voting scores without centrists is neither remarkable nor troubling in a parliamentary system.

	Parliamentary	Semi-presidential	Presidential
Two-party	12	2	4
Multiparty	32	19	30

FIGURE 7.1. Regime Types and Party Systems

The problem in the United States is that for two-thirds of the years since 1950, the president has not presided over a partisan legislative majority. To achieve any change from the status quo, the president must assemble the votes not only of co-partisans but also of some members of the opposition party. In most other presidential systems, the chief executive is able to assemble multiparty coalitions rather than relying on defections from a single opposition party that controls the legislative agenda.

In what reformers now view as a golden era of bipartisanship, U.S. presidents were able to forge relatively stable relationships with moderate representatives known as blue dogs, boll weevils, and Rockefeller Republicans. We have come to appreciate these "moderate" representatives as the lifeblood of American presidentialism now that they are gone.

Investors are justifiably concerned with polarization in the United States, but not because Americans are divided into two radically opposed camps of Marxists and Randian conservatives, such that every election is a lottery that might end up with either nationalization of the means of production or a dismantling of the regulatory state. Rather, the current fear is that internecine battles between self-interested groups within parties that lack clear platforms will be resolved in unpredictable ways as part of high-stakes bargaining between the executive and the legislature. Divided government in the presence of partisan control over the legislative agenda produces drama and uncertainty even over votes that are clearly in the public interest, such as funding the government or avoiding default.

In short, the United States faces a problem of dysfunctional two-party presidentialism. U.S. parties are typical of what political scientists have learned about parties in presidential systems, especially those in the opposition: they are fractious, undisciplined, and have few incentives to develop realistic alternative government programs outside of presidential campaigns. They have no unifying ideological statement around which members have agreed to compete and govern if they are victorious. Rather, there are two loose groups of factions that cannot make promises about what they might do if elected, because it will inevitably involve complex negotiations with other factions in the party and then, in the likely event of divided government, negotiations with the other party.

Voters must try to cobble together some understanding of a party's platform by making sense of a cacophony of voices that claim to speak for the party. This cacophony is especially diverse for the party that does not control the presidency. This is nothing new. However, for reasons that are discussed later in the chapter, those voices have become increasingly polarized, and voters have come to perceive the parties' platforms as increasingly polarized. Even though the parties are as fractious and incoherent as ever, voters perceive them to be highly distinctive and use the party labels as heuristics that are increasingly difficult for candidates in moderate districts to avoid.

Party leaders have gained greater control over the congressional agenda, preventing bills that might achieve bipartisan support from reaching the floor of the legislature (Cox and McCubbins 2007; Harbridge 2011), which only reinforces the public perception of the parties as taking polarized positions.

The dominant rhetoric in the reform literature is that Americans are centrists, but elected politicians, in collaboration with interest groups, have pushed the candidates' platforms and legislative behavior to the extremes through some specific institutional features, including primary elections, redistricting, and agenda control in the legislature. The solution, we are told, is to reform those institutions.

Before accepting these conclusions, however, we must be sure that we have the correct story about the decline in the number and influence of moderate members of Congress. The bulk of this chapter suggests that changes in Congress's institutional features might be of minor importance compared to deeper shifts in the demographic and geographic support bases of the parties.

Even if the ideological positions of Democrats and Republicans in the electorate as a whole have not moved substantially apart over time, and there are still a number of "centrist" congressional districts or states, a form of partisan polarization can nevertheless emerge *within* precisely the districts or states that once gave us "moderate" or ideologically complex representatives such as Charlie Wilson or Arlen Specter.

Since World War II, the parties have undergone an astounding process of geographic segmentation, whereby the Democrats have become the party of the inner city, the low-income suburb, and the postindustrial town (in addition to rural pockets of blacks, Latinos, and Native Americans), while the Republicans have become the party of white suburbs, exurbs, and the rural periphery. At the same time, the most rapidly growing suburban areas are becoming more racially diverse and politically competitive.

As a result of this transformation, a seemingly "moderate" district is often either (1) a small, very Democratic city and its very Republican periphery or (2) a sprawling, racially heterogeneous suburb of a major metropolis that contains pockets of Democrats and Republicans. Armed with the modern toolkit of micro-targeting and get-out-the-vote, incumbents face incentives to build their electoral strategies around the mobilization of their party's electoral base rather than appealing to unreliable and unpredictable moderates.

If this depiction is correct, investment in the reform of primaries, campaign finance, or redistricting practices might lead to disappointing results. Responding to incentives, candidates in many districts have invested heavily in a strategy of turnout mobilization in which ideological appeals to moderates are an afterthought. As desirable as they may be, I ignore more radical reforms to the electoral system or the structure of the legislature, and take a real-ist/incremental approach that advocates state-level experiments with a reform that could undo the entire logic of within-district polarization: compulsory voting.

HOW DID THE PROBLEM EMERGE?

A central puzzle in the literature on U.S. politics is that most voters appear to be centrists, in spite of the growing polarization in congressional voting. Relative to voters in other advanced democracies, Democrats and Republicans are not especially far apart in their answers to batteries of policy questions. To the extent that the Democrats and Republicans have meaningful written platforms, they are no further apart on average than platforms of parties in other democracies. Yet American voters (and political scientists) *perceive* the parties to be further apart than their counterparts in any other advanced democracies. I provide data in support of these assertions in Appendix 1.

What accounts for this polarization in perceptions of party platforms? And why are legislators so unwilling to vote across party lines? These questions must be answered together.

The most obvious possibility is that liberals and conservatives have sorted themselves not only into the ideologically proximate party (Levendusky 2009) but also geographically into increasingly homogeneous districts, such that there are simply too few moderate districts left (Bishop 2008). Though it is certainly not a perfect proxy for mean district ideology, it is useful to look at the evolution of presidential votes aggregated to the level of congressional districts. To contrast the era of bipartisan cooperation with the present, Figure 7.2 displays kernel densities of (standardized) Republican vote shares as well as first dimension DW-Nominate scores for the 90th and 110th Congresses. The

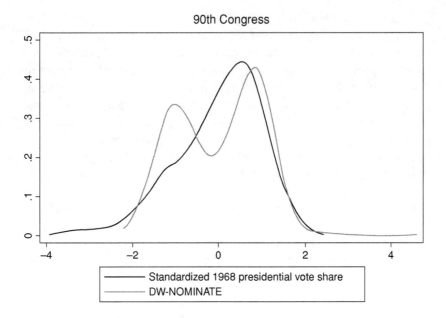

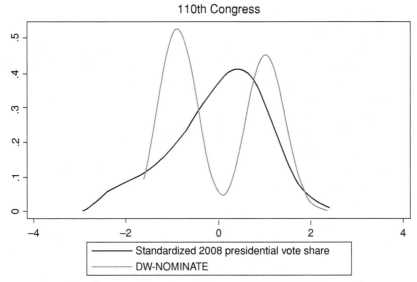

FIGURE 7.2. Distribution of Presidential Votes and NOMINATE Scores: Contrasting the Era of Bipartisanship with Today

distribution of presidential votes across districts has changed somewhat: the tails of the distribution have been pulled out slightly, especially on the left, and the density of districts in the middle is now a bit smaller.

However, there is nothing in the distribution of the district presidential vote that would explain the increasingly bimodal distribution of congressional voting. There is still a large density of districts that are evenly divided between Democrats and Republicans. The early postwar period demonstrated that the U.S. presidential system can function with only a small rump of moderate legislators in the opposition party who negotiate with the president, and there are still more than enough "moderate" districts to fulfil that function. The crucial question is why the legislators from these districts will no longer vote across party lines.

The answer may lie in the same demographic trends that are pulling the tails of the district-level distribution outward as they play out *within* the districts in the middle of the distribution. In short, districts where the presidential vote share is near 50% do not necessarily contain a large density of moderates.

Figure 7.3 displays the county-level two-party presidential vote (outside the South) on the horizontal axis, and the logged population density of the county on the horizontal axis. The size of the marker corresponds to the population of the country. Figure 7.3 displays a fascinating transformation. In the early postwar period, there was a very weak correlation between population density and Democratic voting. The relationship has become steadily stronger in each election, and by 2000 it is stunning. Democratic presidential candidates no longer compete in very rural counties, and Republicans no longer compete in cities.

Perhaps the more interesting and unheralded parallel relationship, however, is below the county level. Figure 7.4 displays the precinct-level relationship between population density and the 2008 Obama vote share within Pennsylvania counties. In the nonmetropolitan counties, there is a stark geographic segmentation between the sparse rural precincts and locally dense enclaves – for example, smaller postindustrial towns, college towns, or even county seats of very rural counties containing clusters of rental housing and public employees. The relationship is even stronger in the suburban and exurban counties surrounding Philadelphia and Pittsburgh and their postindustrial satellite cities. Democrats dominate the relatively dense communities containing apartment buildings and small, tightly spaced, older single-family homes, whereas Republicans dominate the communities with larger single-family houses built in newer developments with lower density.

This relationship holds up virtually everywhere in the United States. Urban America is overwhelmingly Democratic, and very rural places are overwhelmingly Republican. Much of supposedly red "rural" America is a patchwork

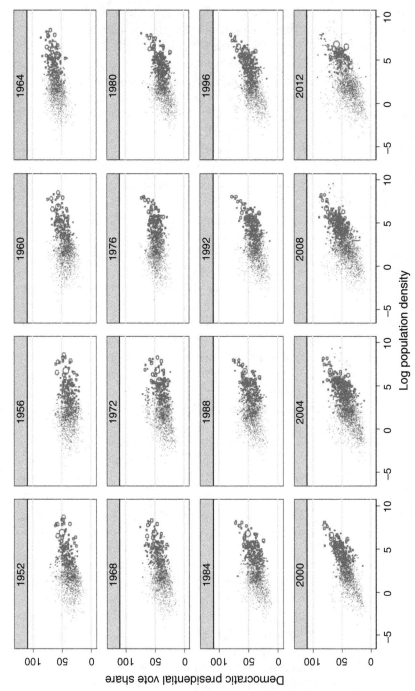

FIGURE 7.3. County-Level Population Density and Democratic Presidential Vote

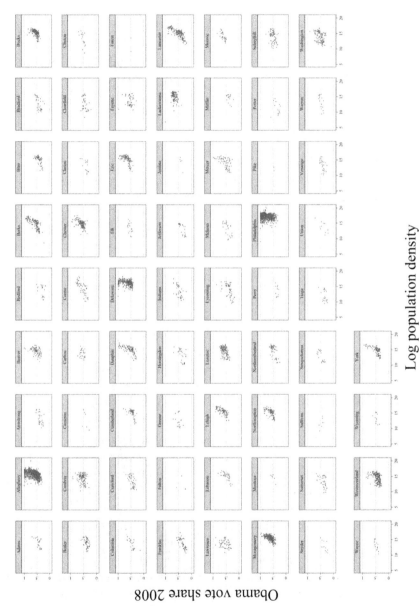

Log population density

FIGURE 7.4. Population Density and Democratic Presidential Vote, Pennsylvania Precincts

of very Democratic towns, many of which are losing population as they lose manufacturing jobs, and a largely Republican periphery. Perhaps more importantly, the image of suburbia as homogeneously white and Republican is inaccurate. The suburban and exurban counties that are most rapidly gaining population are becoming far more racially diverse and, contra Bishop (2008), more heterogeneous in their voting behavior. Minorities, especially Latinos, are moving to the locally dense suburban areas where employment opportunities are expanding (Orfield and Luce 2012).

Elsewhere I have pointed out that this pattern creates substantial partisan bias in favor of Republicans (Rodden 2013). The relevant implication here is that the anatomy of a "moderate" district has changed since the golden era of bipartisanship. Before globalization and the collapse of manufacturing, the political differences between nonmetropolitan industrial towns and their surrounding rural peripheries were less pronounced. Even in the 1960s, white flight from large cities was incomplete, and the sharp political differences between major cities and their surrounding suburbs had not yet fully emerged (Nall 2012).

Over time, the Democrats became the party of urban and postindustrial America and the Republicans the party of rural America and the outer suburbs. As part of this transformation, national party labels have become increasingly meaningful heuristics for voters in House and Senate elections. The number of House districts that split their votes between presidential and congressional candidates has been steadily declining. Moreover, when Democrats manage to win in Republican districts (and vice versa), they face few incentives to emphasize policy, focusing instead on advertising their role in appropriations (Grimmer 2013). Furthermore, party leaders suppress a potentially large number of votes that would obtain bipartisan support. Thus, policy debates are dominated by extremists from urban Democratic districts or rural Republican districts, generating the polarized platform perceptions described earlier.

Increasingly, today's "moderate" districts are those with relatively even mixtures of highly Democratic communities (such as smaller postindustrial or college towns or growing Latino suburbs) and highly Republican exurbs and rural areas. Thus a presidential vote share near 50% in a district or state does not imply that it contains a large density of moderates.

Tausanovich and Warshaw (2013) have linked several surveys together so as to obtain large sample sizes on several policy questions in order to characterize the distribution of preferences within districts. McCarty et al. (2013) use these data to show that the most "moderate" districts have the most internally polarized electorates. They go on to show that differences in roll-call votes between Democrats and Republicans in otherwise identical districts are much larger when the districts are internally polarized.

Incumbents in such districts face weak incentives to cultivate moderate voting records. McCarty et al. (2013) argue that a heterogeneous internal distribution of political preferences, combined with uncertainty about turnout, creates uncertainty among candidates about the spatial location of the median voter, weakening their incentives to converge to the district median. Moreover, incumbents must cater not only to the district median but also to the median of their party primary electorate. As primary electorates are pulled further apart, incumbents with moderate voting records are in increased danger of losing primaries.

As the geographic segmentation of the electorate within districts has increased, so has the technology of geographic and household-level targeting of messages and mobilization activities. When the district electorate is internally polarized, candidates find it increasingly advantageous to invest in activities related to turnout among their supporters rather than attempting to attract unreliable moderates.

WHAT CAN BE DONE?

A number of factors have changed during the period from the 1960s to the present. Party leaders have gained agenda control, credible primary challengers have become more common, majority-minority districts have emerged, *Roe v. Wade* introduced the rising salience of issues related to moral values, and campaign funding and strategies have changed. As I argued earlier, this period has also seen a thorough geographic and demographic transformation that interacts with each of these changes.

We only have one run of history from which to draw inferences, leaving us in a very weak position to attribute causal primacy to one of these factors and recommend institutional change. Given this morass, it is tempting to recommend wholesale constitutional revisions that would change the basic nature of the game, thereby exiting the constitutional trap of dysfunctional two-party presidentialism. Woodrow Wilson's proposed solution was to adopt a parliamentary form of government. A related proposal might be to change House and Senate terms to four years and coordinate with presidential elections so as to reduce the prevalence of divided government. Alternatively, the United States might retain its presidential system, but double the size of both the Senate and House, adding an upper tier with list proportional representation (a German-style two-tiered system) – hoping to achieve a multiparty system that would allow presidents to assemble flexible multiparty coalitions, as happens in virtually all of the world's presidential systems.

Such radical constitutional changes are extremely unlikely to come to fruition, however, and some of their effects are very difficult to predict.

Rather than focus on first-best solutions, I turn attention to a more realistic reform agenda that would focus on smaller changes, ideally ones that do not require constitutional amendment. Even better, it is useful to focus on reforms that can be rolled out at the state level in the spirit of experimentation.

We simply do not know how much of the growth of congressional polarization has been caused by increasing agenda control by party leaders because we cannot observe the bipartisan votes that never took place. Some suggest that rules changes, such as the anonymous discharge petition, could help a band of centrist legislators occasionally buck the party leadership and negotiate with the president. Yet it is not clear how often this would help, if ever, because moderates in the party controlling the House consistently underuse the institutional tools currently at their disposal.[1]

Other medium-scale reforms, such as the reform of primaries or redistricting institutions, are worthy of consideration and further research, but there are reasons for skepticism. If crucial districts are internally polarized and incumbents can rely on mobilizing their base as described earlier, it is not clear how institutions such as "Top Two" primaries or even the alternative vote would provide incumbents with incentives to cast moderate roll-call votes. Moreover, an increasingly large empirical literature produces mixed or null results when attempting to link primaries to polarization (Hirano et al. 2010; McGhee et al. 2013).

The demographic trends described earlier are easily conflated with gerrymandering. Although gerrymandering takes place, of course, its impact on polarization is unclear, and those who advocate redistricting reform as a fix for polarization simply cannot explain Senate polarization (McCarty, Poole, and Rosenthal 2009).

The basic problem described in this chapter is that many of the best candidates for bipartisan compromise in Congress have made a calculation that it is in their best interest to ignore or demobilize moderates and to attempt to maximize turnout among the clusters of voters who are most likely to support them. Even if Democrats and Republicans in these districts are not especially ideologically polarized, they have come to perceive the parties as such, and

---

[1] Further research on state legislatures would be useful. Anzia and Jackman (2013) have collected data on roll-rates and various indicators of majority party agenda power in state legislatures. They find that indeed, the majority party is more likely to be "rolled" when it does not have strong agenda control. It would be useful to explore whether these higher roll rates are associated with different experiences under periods of divided government. Leaving aside executive-legislative relations, Jackman (2012) finds that strong party agenda control in state lower chambers is associated with greater policy volatility.

given the strength of partisan agenda control in Congress, candidates cannot make credible promises to behave as moderates.

An appealing experiment has already been proposed by Norman Ornstein, Peter Orszag, William Galston, and others: simply take turnout mobilization off the table as an electoral strategy by instituting something like compulsory voting in both primary and general elections. Presumably this would have little impact in safe urban and rural districts, but in the heterogeneous districts described earlier, it is likely that candidates would discover a new fondness for the median voter in the district. We would not expect absolute convergence to the district median, because candidates would still be pulled outward by their primary constituencies. However, the primary constituency would likely become more moderate, and in the general election – even in highly polarized districts – the strategy of ignoring or demobilizing the moderates and mobilizing the base would be counterproductive. I cannot think of a quasi-realistic reform that would do more to incentivize representatives in centrist districts to behave as centrists.

One might argue that this reform is just as unrealistic as parliamentary democracy or proportional representation and would likely run into constitutional hurdles. However, many of these hurdles can be circumvented by implementation at the state level. The states are free to regulate their own elections, and it is not obvious that compulsory voting in state legislative elections would run afoul of the U.S. Constitution. The turnout increase would very likely spill over to all offices on the ballot, including federal offices. As Ornstein suggests, concerns about coercion and mandates can be alleviated by experimenting with lottery-style payments for voting rather than fines, and it would be necessary to provide alternatives, especially in the primary, for independents. As a practical matter, compulsory voting would probably require a widespread vote-by-mail option.

Perhaps the most obvious objection is that such a reform would be unpalatable to Republicans. But unlike voter identification laws, which asymmetrically lower turnout among minorities and renters (Dropp 2013), the partisan effects of mandatory voting are less predictable (see, e.g., Sides, Schickler, and Citrin 2008). The Democrats have developed a very sophisticated get-out-the-vote operation in recent years, and Republicans in some states might be keen to neutralize it and call a truce.

Moreover, the long-term success of the Republicans, especially in competing for the presidency and some winnable Senate seats, may be undermined by the rhetoric and maneuvers of its overwhelmingly rural legislative incumbents. For the larger aspirations of their leadership, the efficient geography and strategic redistricting that allow the Republicans a legislative majority without a popular vote majority have a downside for the national party brand. More directly, low-turnout primaries have occasionally produced extremist candidates with poor prospects in the general election. If it generates a crop of moderate candidates in competitive districts and states, compulsory voting could be of long-term benefit to Republicans. Republicans and Democrats alike have rationally adapted to the low-turnout environment of the United States, and it is folly to believe they would not adapt their strategies and platforms to a high-turnout environment.

In the short term, compulsory voting is most likely to be taken seriously in blue or purple states during moments when Democrats control the policy agenda. Even so, all such states contain some heterogeneous districts, and a single opportunity to track changes in the behavior of representatives in such districts after the introduction of compulsory voting would provide an excellent learning opportunity, as well as a possible platform for policy diffusion.

Finally, short of compulsory voting, academics and foundations might explore ways of experimenting with alternative efforts to increase turnout among moderates, especially in primaries. For instance, they might mimic the micro-targeting efforts of the parties, but use household-level data to target nonpartisan "get out the vote" campaigns at moderate voters with low-turnout probabilities. Perhaps even a modest increase in turnout among moderates would change the incentives of incumbents who have grown accustomed to an internally polarized electorate in the district. The only way to find out is to conduct well-crafted experiments.

APPENDIX: AMERICAN POLARIZATION IN COMPARATIVE PERSPECTIVE

How does the ideological polarization of the U.S. Congress, and among U.S. voters, compare with other countries?

First, Hix and Noury (2013) have examined roll-call votes from 16 legislatures. In their data, the only thing remarkable about the United States is the extent of party indiscipline. Relative to the other countries in their study, even other presidential systems, Republicans and Democrats are *more* likely to vote across party lines than legislators in other countries.

What about the voters? The World Values Survey includes a rich set of policy questions that De la O and Rodden (2008) use to create two issue scales for all respondents: one related to economic policy and another related to social policies such as abortion, gay rights, and traditional moral values. To create Figure 7.A1, I generated these scales separately for each country

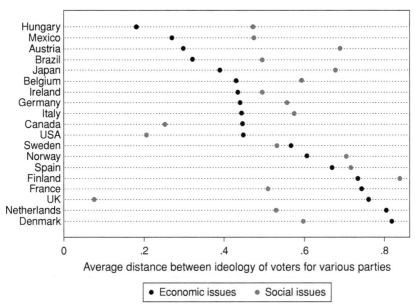

FIGURE 7.A1. Average Ideological Distance between Voters for Various Parties, World Values Survey

using exactly the same questions. For each political party in each country, I calculated the mean policy preference of respondents who reported voting for it. In each country, I calculated the absolute value of the distance between the means for all possible pairs of parties in the country. I then calculated the weighted mean of those distances across all party pairs, where the weight is the joint vote share of the parties in the most recent legislative election.

On the economic dimension, the distance between Democrats and Republicans is not especially large relative to other countries. On the social dimension, the distance is quite small in comparative perspective.[2]

Perhaps the parties' platforms are far apart even if their voters are not. A strategy for assessing this possibility is to use the text analysis of party platforms conducted by the Comparative Manifestos Project (CMP). Using the composite left–right scale created by CMP researchers, I again computed the weighted average of the distance between all party pairs as just described. Figure 7.A2 displays the mean distances for the countries covered by the CMP

---

[2] It is also useful to compare the overall standard deviation of the scales within countries. On both scales, Americans are less ideologically divided than the average country in the WVS. Note that this WVS analysis has been conducted only on Wave 2 (early-mid 1990s). Future work should examine more recent cross-country surveys.

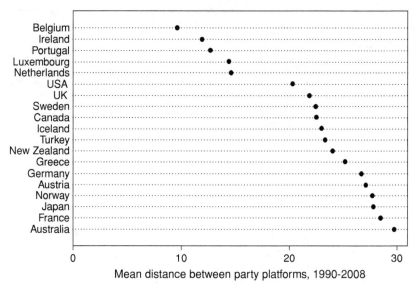

FIGURE 7.A2. Mean Distance between Ideological Platforms of Various Parties, Comparative Manifestos Project

since 1990, showing that the platforms of the Democrats and Republicans are not especially far apart.

Leaving aside party manifestos that very few people read, how do voters perceive the parties' platforms? The Comparative Study of Electoral Systems asks respondents in a variety of countries to place each of the country's parties on a left–right scale from zero to 10. For each respondent, I calculated the difference in perceived ideology between each pair of parties and again calculated the vote-share-weighted average across all pairs. Figure 7.A3 summarizes the distribution of this quantity for each country in the survey.

On this indicator the United States is quite distinctive. On average, Americans view their parties as much further apart than voters in other countries. Figure 7.A3 also suggests that Americans are unusual in the extent to which they disagree in their assessments of the difference between parties. Perhaps this is a function of geographic diversity in party labels across states, such that state-level Democrats and Republicans are relatively similar in Louisiana and Massachusetts, but very different in Colorado and California.

Finally, it is worth noting that when experts rather than voters are asked to make similar placements of parties, something very similar happens: American experts view their parties as further apart than experts in any other country.

Part of this finding might be explained by a psychological bias such that American respondents would place the Democrats and Republicans closer to

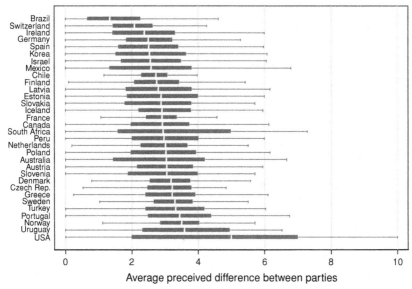

FIGURE 7.A3. Mean Perceived Difference between Platforms of Various Parties, Comparative Study of Electoral Systems

the middle if asked to also place the Tea Party, Greens, and Libertarians. It is nevertheless noteworthy that, in spite of the heterogeneity of voices within American political parties, voters and political scientists alike seem to attribute to them the platforms of their most extreme members.

References

Anzia, Sarah F., and Molly C. Jackman. 2013. "Legislative Organization and the Second Face of Power: Evidence from U.S. State Legislatures." *Journal of Politics* 75(1): 210–224.

Benoit, Kenneth, and Michael Laver. 2006. *Party Policy in Modern Democracies.* New York: Routledge.

Bishop, Bill. 2008. *The Big Sort: Why the Clustering of Like-Minded America Is Tearing Us Apart.* New York: Houghton Miffflin.

Cox, Gary W., and Mathew D. McCubbins. 2007. *Legislative Leviathan: Party Government in the House.* New York: Cambridge University Press.

Dropp, Kyle. 2013. "Voter Identification Laws and Voter Turnout." Unpublished paper, Stanford University.

Grimmer, Justin. 2013. "Appropriators not Position Takers: The Distorting Effects of Electoral Incentives on Congressional Representation." *American Journal of Political Science* 57(3): 624–642.

Harbridge, Laurel. 2011. "Congressional Agenda Control and the Decline of Bipartisan Cooperation." Unpublished paper, Northwestern University.

Hirano, Shigeo, James M. Snyder, Stephen Ansolabehere, and John Mark Hansen. 2010. "Primary Elections and Partisan Polarization in the U.S. Congress." *Quarterly Journal of Political Science* 5(2).

Hix, Simon, and Abdul Noury. 2013. "Government-Opposition or Left-Right? The Institutional Determinants of Voting in Legislatures." Unpublished paper, London School of Economics.

Jackman, Molly C. 2012. "Majority Party Rights and Majority Party Power: The Link between Procedural Rules and Policy Outcomes." Unpublished paper, Brookings Institution.

Levendusky, Matthew. 2009. *The Partisan Sort: How Liberals Became Democrats and Conservatives Became Republicans.* Chicago: University of Chicago Press.

McCarty, Nolan, and Keith T. Poole. 2009. "Does Gerrymandering Cause Polarization?" *American Journal of Political Science* 53(3): 666–680.

McCarty, Nolan, Jonathan Rodden, Boris Shor, Chris Tausanovitch, and Christopher Warshaw. 2013. "Geography and Polarization." Presented at the Annual Meeting of the American Political Science Association, Chicago.

McGhee, Eric, Seth Masket, Boris Shor, Roger Stevens, and Nolan McCarty. "A Primary Cause of Partisanship: Nomination Systems and Legislator Ideology." Unpublished paper, Public Policy Institute of California.

Nall, Clayton. 2012. "The Road to Division: How Interstate Highways Caused Geographic Polarization." Unpublished paper, Stanford University.

Orfield, Myron, and Thomas Luce. 2012. "America's Racially Diverse Suburbs: Opportunities and Challenges." Working paper, Institute on Metropolitan Opportunity, University of Minnesota Law School.

Rodden, Jonathan. 2013. "The Long Shadow of the Industrial Revolution: Political Geography and the Representation of the Left." Unpublished manuscript, Stanford University.

Rodden, Jonathan, and De La O, Ana. 2008. "Does Religion Distract the Poor? Income and Issue Voting around the World." *Comparative Politics* 41(4): 437–476.

Sides, John, Eric Schickler, and Jack Citrin. 2008. "If Everyone Had Voted, Would Bubba or Dubya have Won?" *Presidential Studies Quarterly* 38(3): 521–539.

Tausanovitch, Chris, and Christopher Warshaw. 2013. "Testing Theories of Representation in Congress, State Legislatures and Cities Using a 'Super Survey." Unpublished paper, UCLA.

Strengthening Parties

8

Stronger Parties as a Solution to Polarization

Nathaniel Persily

Conventional wisdom regards political parties as the engine of polarization. That perspective is understandable enough: if the polarization problem arises from excessive partisanship, then the parties are probably at fault. Disable the parties, the argument goes, and then the representational distortion (and concomitant gridlock) caused by the parties will be mitigated.

This chapter argues the exact opposite position. Parties, rather than being the cause of our polarization, may be the solution. This argument only makes sense if one believes, as I do, that polarization is caused (or at least exacerbated) by the relative weakness of party organizations and leaders vis-à-vis outside groups. In other words, polarization is caused (in part) by party weakness, not strength, and any solution to polarization must begin by strengthening parties; specifically, the party organizations and their leadership.

This chapter compares the most frequently proposed "good-government" anti-party reforms of the campaign finance, primary election, and redistricting processes with their pro-party analogs. The basic differences between the two approaches concern the threats targeted by the reforms and the assessments as to whether greater promise comes from reining in extremes or promoting moderation. The anti-party approach hopes to promote the election of moderates by fostering electoral competition or liberating candidates from the constraints of party loyalty and discipline. The pro-party approach aims to empower the median party member and the party leadership against the extremes.

The chapter ends with an epilogue presenting lessons drawn from my experience as senior research director for the Presidential Commission on Election Administration. Consistent with the approach outlined here, the success of that body arose from an attempt to have partisans lead the work of the Commission. It took polarization as a given and then worked successfully not to avoid it, but to manage it.

THE CONVENTIONAL "GOOD-GOVERNMENT"
"ANTI-PARTY" APPROACH

When Americans seek to reform the political system, their prescriptions usually fall into two categories: more democracy or less democracy. Such a distinction was emblematic of the differences in approach one hundred years ago between Western Populists and the Eastern Progressives in their attempt to rein in party machines, for instance. The Populists pushed for more democracy through various means, such as the initiative, referendum, recall, judicial elections, U.S. Senate elections, women's suffrage, and party primaries. The Progressives pushed for less democracy, advocating a professional civil service, nonpartisan commissions, increased reliance on experts, and restrictions on campaign finance.

The same spirit motivated reformers of the post-Watergate era. In the 1970s the parties moved toward a greater use of primaries, especially in presidential contests, in an effort to expand participation; they also adopted measures to diversify and open up participation in the party nominating conventions. At the same time, the Office of the Independent Counsel was created as a way to constrain the most significant political abuses seen during Watergate, and new campaign finance reforms were adopted through amendments to the Federal Election Campaign Act.

The newest wave of reform – this time with polarization, rather than corruption as its target – also moves to expand democracy or to cabin it. Expansion can be seen in efforts to open up primaries, lower barriers to voting, or, more radically, move to compulsory voting, as some chapters in this volume suggest. Proponents of this view see polarization as a product of a skewed electorate. If only more people participated, the argument goes, the median voter would be empowered and representatives would gravitate toward the center. In particular, the unrepresentativeness of primary electorates, which some argue are dominated by the most extreme partisans, is seen as a problem, given that for most districts the primary election is the dispositive election. Proponents of open, blanket, top-two, or nonpartisan primaries therefore hope that expanding the primary electorate will make it more diverse and representative and lead candidates to cater to the median voter of the district (or state), rather than the median voter of the low-turnout party primary electorate.

In contrast, those who view democracy as the problem deliberately seek to remove certain issues or institutions from electoral pressures. The proposal for redistricting commissions is a case in point. Because redistricting by self-interested legislators is seen as distorting the electoral filter of representation (by introducing either partisan or pro-incumbent bias), transferring the line-drawing process to an unelected and unaccountable body seems like a viable solution to the distortion. Taking politics out of the redistricting process, reformers hope, will make districts more competitive and legislators more representative. Redistricting commissions are emblematic of a larger set of nonpartisan commissions that reformers hope might "take the politics" out of politics. If electoral pressures are causing polarization and gridlock, then transferring policy making to unaccountable, unelected, and politically insulated groups may offer progress in areas where the parties' electoral ambitions prevent resolution.

Campaign finance regulation, too, is held out as a solution to the polarizing tendencies of a democracy gone off the rails. Focused both on corruption and on polarization, reformers view money as the source of multiple evils. Good-government solutions often target both the amount of money in the system and its sources. Reforms, such as the Bipartisan Campaign Reform Act (BCRA) of 2002, attacked corporate and union expenditures on TV advertisements, as well as their contributions to political parties. Because contributors are often more committed partisans or hold more intense views than the general public, limiting the amount of money they can contribute, the argument goes, would free elected officials and parties from the polarizing influences of rich donors. Forcing parties and candidates to raise a large number of small contributions would rectify the ideological discrepancy between the donor class and the median voter. In other words, by diminishing the relative influence of a small number of wealthy ideologues on the party, the voice of the average voter would be magnified, and the parties would be more responsive to it.

As other chapters to this volume explain in greater detail, little evidence to date suggests much hope for the conventional approach. Where and when these reforms have been tried, levels of polarization appear to remain unaffected. Redistricting commissions or constraints on redistricting processes may lead to differently shaped or even more competitive districts, but the types of representatives who emerge look like the ones immediately prior to the reforms. Similarly, states have experimented with all kinds of primary systems (open, closed, semi-open, semi-closed, blanket, nonpartisan, top-two), and the openness of a primary is weakly related (if at all) to the ideology of the representatives elected. The effect of campaign finance may be a bit more complicated (as suggested later in this chapter), but it appears that the good-government reforms that have been tried have, if anything, made things worse. The fault may lay with how the Supreme Court has carved holes in such reforms, but regardless, those constitutional rules constrain reform efforts going forward and shape the legal terrain that determines how such proposals will operate in practice.

Perhaps the right combination of good-government reforms has not been tried, or perhaps they have not been in effect for long enough. Or perhaps, as argued here, the reform energies have been misdirected at the wrong targets. Parties might be the solution, rather than the cause of the problem.

THE "PRO-PARTY" "BAD-GOVERNMENT" APPROACH

So, what does a "pro-party," in contrast to a "good-government," approach look like? First, such an approach starts from the proposition that the causes of polarization are long term and structural. Quick institutional fixes will not reverse demographic trends that are a half-century in the making. Second, as a result, the pro-party approach gives up on electing moderates and focuses more on reining in extremists. This is perhaps the greatest difference between the two approaches: while not disparaging the motivation of electing moderate, compromising, problem solvers, the pro-party approach cuts its losses and resigns itself to curbing the worst abuses of the current system, rather than trying to recreate the preexisting party system or attempting to cultivate the election of centrists. Therefore the approach seeks to embolden party leaders and to increase their strength relative to extremist outside groups. Party organizations need to be richer and more powerful to counteract the polarizing tendencies of outside groups, and party leaders need to have a greater array of tools to whip recalcitrant members into line.

Campaign Finance Reform to Strengthen Parties

Whereas good-government reforms of the campaign finance system try to limit the influence of money on the party and its candidates, the pro-party approach seeks to increase the influence of party money, in particular, over candidates. Such an approach takes as a given the huge demand for campaign funds and the inevitable influence of large independent expenditures in the post–*Citizens United* world. However, instead of trying to clamp down on the influence of all participants in the campaign finance system, the pro-party approach seeks to rectify the imbalance between insiders and outsiders by amplifying the voice of the parties so they can compete with outside groups.

There are basically two sets of options to enrich the political parties and magnify their financial role in elections: public funding or increasing the limits on private contributions. Public funding would, of course, provide the best of both the good-government and pro-party worlds. It would address the corruption concerns held by good-government reformers, while also enriching the parties. Increasing the role of private money in funding the parties is a second-best solution, but perhaps the only one that might be politically feasible.

There are any number of ways by which public money could be used to fund parties. Most developed democracies give free television time and direct checks from the public treasury to the parties. Since the demise of the presidential public funding system, however, most proposals for the United States have gone in a different direction. Generous matching of individual contributions to candidates, for example, is often held out as a success story in places such as New York City. In general, such methods are not proposed for contributions to political parties, but they should be. By whatever means necessary, public money should be used to drown out the influence of private money on elections and the political process.

Conceding that public funding might be a political nonstarter, increasing the limits for contributions to parties may be the only way to increase their relative influence in elections. We rightfully lament the salad days of soft money, when nights in the Lincoln Bedroom were all but auctioned off and corporations, unions, and wealthy individuals gave large checks often to both political parties. However, one would be hard pressed to demonstrate that the anticorruption interests that underlay the ban on soft money have been well served. Instead, analogous (perhaps even more dominant) influences from the push of such money outside of the parties have both stubbornly maintained the level of corporate and wealthy influence on politics (a.k.a. corruption) while at the same time removing money from the institutions (parties) best situated to counteract their independent influence. It may be a devil's bargain to bring such money back into the party tent, but without public funding, rich contributors or organizations are the only source for funds that the party can then redirect to help loyal candidates. Whether one blames the reformers for the Bipartisan Campaign Reform Act (otherwise known as McCain-Feingold) or the courts that contorted the law from what was intended, the end result is the same: outside groups are in a better position than the parties to raise unlimited funds.

To be sure, objections to facilitating private funding of political parties are not limited merely to fears of corruption. Some worry that it would increase polarization as well. Enabling rich individuals and entities to give more money to political parties does not mean they will stop spending independently – they might do both and their influence could expand considerably. Not only could they threaten candidates with outside spending but they could also effectively bribe the parties into doing their bidding, or so the argument goes.

This powerful critique assumes that outside independent spending is, with respect to polarization, no different from spending laundered through and redirected by political parties. There are several reasons to doubt this assumption. First, although earmarking (informally or formally) of donations might be common, once parties control the money they can redirect it toward races and candidates where they think it will be most useful. This will include protecting establishment candidates against insurgents. Because party leaders' top priority, as distinct from that of ideological outside groups, is to help run candidates who win general elections, whatever money they have will be directed primarily toward that end. Second, although several outsiders may want to influence the party as well, some will prefer to remain independent of the party, and still other entities that have not played the independent expenditure game will then come back in to support the party once they can. To put it bluntly, the same entities that have been funding Tea Party challengers of late are not the same entities that contributed soft money to the Republican Party before the BCRA. To some extent, this may be because corporations in the soft money days were "shaken down" and gave, reluctantly, to both political parties. But it also might be that the universe of contributors, even wealthy ones, willing to give to political parties is more diverse and not coterminous with the group of individuals and organizations willing to spend independently. Finally, it is hard to imagine certain outsiders, such as the Koch brothers and Sheldon Adelson, having greater influence than they already possess. Even if contributions from them and their ilk flow to the political parties, the larger pot of cash at the disposal of party leaders will enable them to cultivate loyalty among incumbents once elected by helping them ward off extremist challengers in primaries.

The Pro-Party Approach to Primary Reform

The same general approach regarding campaign finance reform applies to primary reform as well. In both settings, the strategy is to embolden the party organization so it is in a better position to ward off extremist challengers to more loyal (even if not exactly "centrist") candidates. In the context of campaign finance this strategy has meant enabling the party to spend more money on its favored candidates. For primary reform, it means reforming the nomination process to make it more likely that the party organization's preferred candidate will advance to the general election.

As others in this volume have indicated, the United States is an outlier when it comes to voter involvement in party nomination processes. Since the Progressive Era, and especially since the early 1970s reforms to the presidential nomination process, we have taken for granted that "democracy" requires the extensive involvement of average voters in the nominations of political parties. The experience of most democracies is precisely the opposite: "democracy" takes place in the general election, whereas nomination processes are often closely regulated by party insiders.

Of course, there are good reasons why Progressives fought to move from smoke-filled rooms to primary elections open to all party members. The corrupt party machines' stranglehold on candidates ensured that no outsiders had a chance at getting elected. It should be conceded that returning to such a system, or taking power away from primary voters, could have the same effects: mavericks from the political extremes or the political center will have a hard time getting on the general election ballot as party nominees if party leaders play a strong gatekeeping function.

How might party organizations play a stronger role in nomination processes? The most extreme and infeasible version of reform would be to eliminate primaries altogether and leave nomination to the state and local party organizations. Primaries have become too entrenched in our conception of American democracy, though, for that option even to be considered. Less radical alternatives would be to allow the party greater power to determine who can call themselves Republicans or Democrats on the primary ballot. In other words, the party organization could own the brand and decide which candidates get to use it. Less radical still would be the greater use of ballot notations in which candidates could still run with the party label, but the party organization would be able to endorse candidates officially on the ballot. In other words, the party could put its thumb on the scales by signaling to voters in the primary which candidate it prefers. Of course, in some instances, the party or the candidate may not see it as in his or her interest to have the endorsement. But if it might help add a few points of vote share for the more moderate alternative in a low-turnout election, merely having the power to endorse could pay dividends whenever a candidate must decide whether to toe the party line or not.

These types of proposals are quite different from the good-government reforms. The strategies of those reforms have a decidedly different goal: namely, expanding participation (through open or nonpartisan primaries) so that the primary electorate looks more like the general election electorate. Doing so, reformers hope, will lead to more moderate candidates emerging onto the general election ballot and to an eventual winner who will be more responsive to the median voters in the relevant jurisdiction. If the data suggested such reforms held promise, there would be good reason to endorse them. But the states have experimented with many different primary forms, and all the data suggest no effect on the ideology of candidates who eventually emerge as representatives.

Once again, because the approach taken here gives up on electing moderates and is laser-focused on reining in extremes, the pro-party proposals are ones that will necessarily be biased against both centrists and extremists alike.

That is, a party machine could withhold its endorsement or the party label
from either a candidate seen as too close to the other party or one seen as on
the fringes of the party mainstream. Because promoting the election of moderates is an (albeit admirable) fool's errand and one unlikely to deal with the
more serious problem of counteracting the polarizing forces on the political
extremes, giving the party greater power to skew primary elections is the best
of all bad alternatives.

Increasing Party Power in the Redistricting Process

Redistricting might be one of those areas in which party power appears to be at
its apex. After all, in most states, either the parties collude to draw safe districts
for each other, or one party uses its line-drawing power to bias the lines in its
favor. These practices lead good-government reformers to seek to remove the
redistricting authority from self-interested actors and place it in commissions
or to impose criteria that might constrain partisan or incumbent-related greed
in the line-drawing process. As with campaign finance and primary reform,
most good-government redistricting reform is aimed at promoting the drawing
of competitive districts (or avoiding the intentional creation of uncompetitive
districts) based on the theory that evenly balanced districts are more likely
to produce moderate representatives. However, as with primaries, the role of
redistricting in fostering polarization does not find support in the data. Indeed,
the parallel rise in polarization in unredistricted bodies such as the U.S.
Senate belies the notion that line drawing is a major contributing factor to the
growing ideological distance between elected representatives of the two major
parties.

Pro-party redistricting reform is the most radical of the proposals considered
here and, as such, is likely not to be adopted in the near term. However, even
as a thought experiment the proposal illustrates another way that we might rein
in abuses of the redistricting process and simultaneously strengthen the role of
party leaders. Of course, the most radical, pro-party reform of the redistricting
process would be to move to proportional representation. Under such systems,
which, let us not forget, are the democratic norm, voters would vote only for
parties, not candidates, and the share of the vote received by each party would
translate into a proportional share of seats. Although the Constitution says
nothing about districting (only a federal law requires it), Americans are very
well tied to the notion of electing an individual who represents a particular,
geographically defined space.

An intermediate option is available, however, that would marry the districting that Americans have come to know and love with aspects of proportionality
that can mitigate partisan bias and strengthen party institutions. The German

system, for example, uses districts, but adds bonus representatives who are elected by a statewide party vote. In this system, voters vote for a party in addition to their local representative. The final partisan composition of the legislature depends on the party vote, because a number of seats are added to the seats won through districts, so that the end result is a legislature with a partisan breakdown mirroring that of the voters. For example, if the statewide vote were evenly split between Democrats and Republicans, but the district-based results were lopsided in favor of Democrats, then Republicans would be given additional seats in the legislature – unconnected to any district constituencies – to offset the biased results from the districts and bring them to parity with the Democrats. The basic idea behind such a system is to maintain a representative that you can still call your own but to reserve a certain number of seats in the legislature chosen by party leaders to mitigate any distortion caused by the carving up of a state into biased districts.

Such a system has a double payoff from the standpoint of polarization. First, once proportionality is added to a district-based system, the incentives to gerrymander disappear. The line-drawing party has nothing to gain by drawing an additional district in its favor, when that biased district will be counteracted by the party vote at the state level. As a result, one might hope that the most polarizing enterprise in which legislators engage might become less vitriolic. Second, by adding a few seats to be determined by a party list and chosen by party leaders, the party gains additional power over its elected representatives, which it can wield along the same lines discussed earlier with respect to campaign finance and party primaries. In fact, when the party chooses the candidates who appear on the statewide list for the party-allocated seats, it can sometimes rescue an establishment candidate who gets defeated in his or her district. Whether the parties use that power often is irrelevant. The fact that they have it is sufficient to assist them in rewarding or threatening those who would stray from the party line.

CONCLUSION

The principle (or perhaps assumption) that guides the pro-party proposals described here is that extremists within the parties and nonparty groups on the outside are driving polarization. Even if they are not driving it, strengthening the parties against the extremes may be one of the only ways to mitigate polarization. In previous eras, the lack of intraparty coherence could facilitate deal-making by allowing presidents to peel off moderate defectors from their congressional parties. Most popular reforms seek to recreate that age. Because I view that age as irretrievable, I place greater faith in the ability of party organizations to curb the extremism of individual legislators and fortify the position of party leadership by giving leaders additional tools to clamp down on candidates and incumbents outside the mainstream.

This strategy comes with risks, of course. Placing one's bet on the party organization represents a gamble that the party itself will not be captured by extremists. If it is so captured, then the same tools of discipline described earlier could be used against moderates (or even mainstream party members) instead of fringe candidates. I view that gamble as worth taking because, all else equal, the party organization's leaders tend to prioritize winning elections over fighting for a cause. Because they have the greatest incentive to win elections and increase their seat share so as to capture control of Congress or state legislatures, they are less likely (all things equal) to pursue a strategy of political suicide that systematically alienates the median voter in the name of ideological purity.

The air of resignation in this approach should be self-evident. By accepting our polarization largely as given, it focuses on mitigating the worst excesses of our politics rather than fundamentally trying to break apart the party coalitions as some reforms hope to do. This strategy places faith in the electoral ambitions of the party organizations as a force that can temper the most extreme impulses evident in our current politics. Because I view the "fight" undergirding reform debates as one pitting the party mainstream against extremists, rather than the party mainstream against moderates, anything that might strengthen the party against its most fringe elements would represent a step in the right direction.

EPILOGUE

As this book on solutions to polarization was being written, I had the good fortune of serving in a position specifically mandated to overcome polarization and arrive at common-sense solutions to a heavily politicized problem. Because the lessons from my experience as senior research director of the Presidential Commission on Election Administration might be generalizable to other areas of policy making, I add this short epilogue to describe the institutional features that helped the commission succeed in achieving bipartisan consensus in an area fraught with political difficulty.

Those five features can be summarized succinctly:

1. The commission had a well-defined mission that deliberately excluded from the outset certain politically contentious, deal-breaking issues.
2. The leaders of the commission were partisans, not moderates.
3. No elected officials sat on the commission.

4. The commission worked "from the ground up" by focusing its work on state and local officials rather than the federal government.
5. The specific contents of the commission report were not made public until its final release.

In his acceptance speech on the evening of the 2012 election, President Obama noted the long lines of voters waiting in polling places in Florida and elsewhere, and he ad-libbed, "We have to fix that." In his State of the Union address three months later he announced the formation of a commission to be co-chaired by his campaign lawyer, Robert Bauer, and Mitt Romney's campaign lawyer, Ben Ginsberg, which would issue recommendations to address the problem of long lines as well as other issues concerning the administration of American elections. It would be made up of senior election administrators and representatives from private industry and have six months to write its report.

The keys to the success of the commission can be found in the executive order that created it and the personnel appointed to it. Although the issue of long lines at the polling place gave birth to the commission, the executive order assigned to it an array of issues including voter registration, absentee voting, provisional ballots, ballot design and technology, and problems concerning specific communities, such as military and overseas voters, voters with limited English proficiency, and voters with disabilities. Notably and intentionally absent from the charge were the most controversial voting issues, such as voter identification and reforms to the Voting Rights Act, over which the political parties have clearly irreconcilable differences. However, the absence of these topics from the executive order did not mean that the remaining issues were unimportant or easily solved. Indeed, from the standpoint of the numbers of voters affected, the topics covered by the executive order are much more consequential than the ones that receive the most attention from advocates and the press.

In that spirit of election management rather than advocacy, the commissioners were chosen on the basis of their expertise rather than as representatives of interest groups or as elder statespeople. The commissioners included Larry Lomax and Tammy Patrick, who had run elections for Clark County (Las Vegas), Nevada, and Maricopa County (Phoenix), Arizona, respectively. They included state election officials, such as Trey Grayson (former secretary of state of Kentucky and director of the Institute of Politics at Harvard), Chris Thomas (state election director for Michigan), and Ann McGheean (former director of elections for Texas). In addition, three representatives from private business were on the commission: Joe Echevarria (CEO of Deloitte and Touche), Brian Britton (vice president and director of theme parks for Walt Disney World), and Michelle Coleman Mayes (formerly of Allstate, now counsel to the New York Public Library).

Most important from the standpoint of producing a credible bipartisan report, however, were the two co-chairs of the commission, Robert Bauer and Ben Ginsberg. Given their client base and litigation history over the previous three decades, no one could accuse them of being shrinking nonpartisan violets. They were veterans of partisan trench warfare in recounts, voting rights lawsuits, campaign finance battles, and a host of other election-related litigation. Although credible representatives of their parties' membership, they trusted each other and shared a commitment to producing a meaningful set of proposals. As such, they were uniquely positioned to focus the commission on politically feasible proposals and to provide a critical vouch or stamp of approval from their respective camps for the eventual recommendations.

This is not to say that consensus was foreordained or that the parties will now go along with each of the commission's recommendations. Implementation of each proposal will likely depend on the idiosyncrasies of political cultures of the various states. In some cases, narrow political interests will trump reforms that both parties might admit are in the public interest. And as with all public policy proposals, turf wars, bureaucratic inertia, and funding problems could derail one or another good idea.

Yet one of the chief advantages of the commission's approach (and membership) was to derive recommendations "from the ground up;" that is, to try to unearth consensus from the testimony and experience of local and state election administrators. Throughout the course of the hearings and meetings with various officials, it became abundantly clear that the polarization expressed by national politicians on election administration issues was not representative of the views held by local and state officials. As is often true with professional bureaucrats, these officials shared a common set of concerns and, more than anything, usually wanted to get the job done and stay out of the headlines. The recommendations in the commission's report are made in that spirit: they aim to improve the voting experience through common-sense reforms to the election administration system.

Finally, although I regard the commission's work as a success story (and am admittedly biased in my assessment), some constraints made achieving that success unnecessarily difficult. In particular, the procedural constraints imposed by the Federal Advisory Committee Act (FACA) impeded deliberations and could have led the commission to fall victim to the same polarizing tendencies that most often prevent substantive reform in this domain. FACA requires that all substantive deliberations occurring in the presence of a quorum of the commission be on the record, publicly noticed, and open to the public in some fashion. No report on such a high-profile and sensitive topic, such as elections, could possibly be written in real time with play-by-play media coverage. The process of coming to a consensus requires honest debate in a safe space where ideas can be floated, false starts taken, and mistakes made. There are legal ways around FACA's draconian, if well-intentioned, requirement of transparency: the use of subcommittees is one example. However, commissions such as this one should not need to jump through hoops in order to discuss their mission and potential proposals away from the polarizing (and thereby paralyzing) echo chambers of the mass media.

There is a larger lesson to be learned here concerning the unintended consequences of good-government efforts to rid political institutions of improper influences. Transparency and open-government laws can stifle the kind of private negotiations most necessary to achieve policy agreement under conditions of partisan polarization, as Jane Mansbridge explains in Chapter 19 in this volume. As attractive as the notion may be that "sunshine is the best disinfectant" when it comes to politics, conducting negotiations in the open often leads to a hardening of partisan positions and a refusal to talk honestly about the political constraints affecting any deal. When done in the open and in view of a media likely to characterize negotiations as zero-sum, partisans feel compelled not to show any weakness. As a result, the entire give-and-take of a negotiation is likely to disintegrate into a game of chicken, as opponents view the process more as a way to win political points than to solve problems.

This argument is consistent with the ones proposed in the body of this chapter, which is primarily focused on strengthening the position of party organizations. In both settings, the critical question concerns how to empower elites so that they can make credible promises and bargains to address widely recognized problems. Our democratic impulses lead us to want an egalitarian free-for-all in which widespread participation in open public jousting will somehow lead to effective majoritarian policy making. But, as the present state of our politics demonstrates, there is no invisible hand that necessarily guides the political market toward a desirable equilibrium. On the contrary, the rules that shape the pathways of power and influence can help promote the paralysis we have now come to expect – or they can be redesigned with the goal of achieving, at least, the bare minimum of performance that a functioning democracy can provide and that our polarized polity still deserves.

9

Reducing Polarization by Making Parties Stronger

Nolan McCarty

As we meet amid yet another manufactured fiscal crisis, one hardly needs to exert much effort to argue that the polarization of our political leadership is the central challenge to good governance in the contemporary United States. So discussions about how to reduce polarization and mitigate its effects are both timely and worthwhile.

Of course, we are not nearly the first researchers to take up these questions. The polarization of America's officeholders has been at or near the top of the academic research agenda in American politics for more than 15 years. The issue has also drawn close attention from policy practitioners, journalists, and the philanthropic community. Polarization in Washington has now surpassed the desire to spend more time with one's children as the leading rationale for the retirement of legislators. Yet despite the mountain of research and discussion, we are still far short of an evidence-based agenda for reform (see Chapter 2 in this volume for a recent review of the evidence about the causes of polarization).

In this chapter, I suggest one reason why we do not know much more about how to reduce polarization than we did 15 years ago. It is because we still have a poor understanding of the role played by political party organizations in producing more or less polarization.

A central confusion in both the academic literature and public discussions of legislative polarization in the United States is the conflation of polarization and partisanship. This confusion arises naturally because the two phenomena are hard to distinguish empirically. For example, using roll-call votes and derived indices, political scientists have noted the increasingly divergent positions of the parties (see McCarty [2011] for a discussion of the measurement of legislative ideal points and polarization). But it is very difficult to discern whether those increased differences reflect true ideological changes or simply increased intraparty cooperation and interparty conflict. In light of our inability to distinguish between these explanations, scholars often use the terms "polarization" and "partisanship" almost interchangeably.

This conflation of polarization and partisanship is relevant for discussions of political reform. Many popular prescriptions for reducing polarization call for decreasing the role of political parties. But if polarization in the United States is the consequence of relatively weak parties rather than strong parties, as I argue may be the case, then such reforms may be ineffectual if not counterproductive.

In the next section, I sketch out a theoretical argument as to how weak parties might counterintuitively lead to legislative polarization. Then I review a few key pieces of evidence in favor of the proposition.

SOME THEORY

To illustrate my key point, let me consider two scenarios. The first is one with strong legislative parties. Here I assume that parties are so strong that they behave as unitary actors. The second scenario is one in which parties are very weak. The organizations and leaders impose no discipline on candidates, and therefore party labels convey no information to voters.

The strong party scenario perfectly conforms to the model of Anthony Downs (1957). In his model, as we well know, the unified political parties have very strong incentives to converge to the political center. A party that fails to position itself in the center will be defeated by one that does. This convergence prediction continues to hold even if the parties have policy preferences. So with strong parties, there is very little polarization. Two homogeneous parties promote the preferences of the median voter.

Consider the weak party scenario. Now the autonomous candidates of each party have incentives to converge on the median voter in each district. Voters would be indifferent between the candidates and would metaphorically flip coins. So half the districts would be represented by Ds and half represented by Rs. Moreover, the D districts would be statistically identical to the R districts. So there is no polarization on average. Ds and Rs represent districts ranging across the spectrum. Both parties are very heterogeneous, but the distributions of legislator positions are the same.

So neither the extreme weak or strong party system would be very polarized. What about the intermediate case? Jim Snyder and Michael Ting (2002) offer a model that closely approximates this middle ground. In their model, voters wish to use party labels to make more informed choices about legislative candidates. If Republican candidates are more conservative on average than

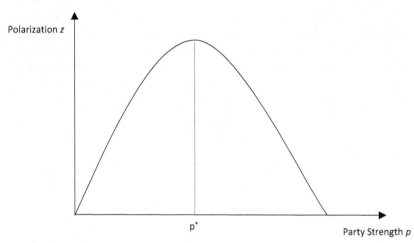

FIGURE 9.1. Hypothetical Relationship between Polarization and Party Strength

Democratic candidates, a voter might use this information in casting her vote in a legislative election even if she did not know the exact locations of the specific candidates. Snyder and Ting also assume that voters are risk averse. So, *ceterus paribus*, a voter prefers the candidate whose party label provides more precise information about that candidate's position. In other words, voters prefer candidates from homogeneous parties to those from heterogeneous parties.

This aspect of voter preferences gives each party a strong incentive to screen candidates who deviate too far, left or right, from the party's prevailing position. Strong parties are assumed to be better at screening candidates and thus better able to reduce the variance in the positions of their candidates. A party that can perfectly screen is equivalent to the Downsian party. If both parties are perfect screeners, each will position itself on the median voter and screen out any candidates with different positions.

But when parties are weaker, they screen candidates imperfectly. For such parties, Snyder and Ting (2002) obtain a distinct prediction. That such parties cannot screen out relatively more extreme candidates forces them to position themselves away from the median voter. Thus, weak parties will take divergent positions. Consequently, Republican candidates will tend to win conservative districts, Democratic candidates will win the liberal districts, and Consequently, there will be considerable polarization in equilibrium.

So in theory, the relationship between party strength and polarization is not monotonic. For the sake of illustration, suppose we could separately measure party strength p and polarization z. Then the figure would look something like Figure 9.1, which hypothesizes that there is a level of party strength that generates a unique maximum, call it p^*.

Most discussions about polarization implicitly assume that $p < p^*$. There-fore, if we were to weaken parties we could reduce polarization. But given the current state of empirical knowledge, there is no reason *a priori* to assume that the current level of party strength in the United States is below p^*. To the contrary, as I argue in the next section, there is considerable evidence consis-tent with the idea that $p > p^*$. If such is the case, a reform agenda designed to reduce polarization should strive to strengthen the role of party organizations both by enhancing their role in the selection and discipline of candidates and by giving them an enhanced capacity to withstand the pressure of extreme interest groups and voters.

WHY IT MIGHT BE THE CASE THAT $p < p^*$

"Null" Findings on Primary Electoral Systems

Despite the widespread belief that a move to less partisan primary electoral systems should lead to less polarization, there is very little evidence to support the proposition. In a recent paper, my coauthors and I used data on the positions of newly elected state legislators to test for the effect of primary election law (McGhee et al. 2014). Because we were able to incorporate state-level fixed effects, we were able to estimate the effects of changing from a partisan primary to a more open primary system on the extremity of newly elected legislators. Although most of our estimated effects were small relative to the standard errors, our one consistent finding was that polarization is higher in states with semi-closed primary systems than in states with more partisan closed primaries or with less partisan open primaries.[1] This is consistent with the argument that polarization is highest when party strength is at an intermediate level.

New Results on Campaign Finance

Barber (2013) finds that there is significantly more legislative polarization in states that allow unlimited individual contributions to candidates than in those that place tight constraints on individuals. He also finds that the candidates who are most reliant on individual contributions tend to have more extreme voting records. Importantly, he finds that the opposite is true with respect to corporate and labor union PAC contributions. Barber's results raise the possibility that,

---

[1] A semi-closed primary is one where co-partisans and independents may participate, in contrast to closed primaries in which only co-partisans participate and to open primaries where all voters may participate.

by enhancing the role of political parties in the campaign finance system, legislators might become less reliant on the contributions from ideologically extreme individuals, although he does not directly test this hypothesis.[2]

Preliminary Results on Party Organization and Polarization in the States

In a recent dissertation, Katherine Krimmel (2013) argues that the national parties polarized at least in part because they were forced to turn increasingly to organized interests for resources as traditional partisan resources such as patronage declined. She makes a very strong historical and archival case for this change in partisan strategy. Krimmel also provides some quantitative evidence that there is lower legislative polarization in states that have historically strong party organizations. Specifically, Krimmel finds a strong negative correlation between state legislative polarization as measured by Shor and McCarty (2011) and David Mayhew's (1986) measure of traditional party organizations (TPO).[3]

In this section I update Krimmel's analysis. First, I show the bivariate relationship between the differences in party medians for state lower and upper chambers and Mayhew's TPO scores. Each dot represents an annual level of polarization for each state legislature. The data cover the period of 1996 to 2008. Both Figures 9.2 and 9.3 show that on average there is a negative relationship between polarization and the historical strength of party organizations in the state. Interestingly, however, both also demonstrate very considerable heterogeneity of the states that score in the lowest of Mayhew's categories. This would be consistent with the inverted u-shape of Figure 9.1 if it were the case that p^* fell in this category.

To further explore the relationship between polarization and party strength, I estimate some simple regression models. The dependent variable of each model is either a polarization measure or a measure of the position of a party's

---

[2] McCarty and Rothenberg (2013) develop a formal model in which parties serve as brokers between interest groups and candidates. Although the paper does not directly explore the implications for polarization, the model does suggest that a moderate candidate would receive more resources in the presence of a partisan broker than would be obtained in unmediated relationships with interest groups.

[3] Mayhew (1986) classifies traditional state party organizations in the 1960s as those with local political organizations that meet five criteria. Such organizations (1) are largely autonomous from candidates and outside interests, (2) have longevity, (3) use hierarchical structures, (4) try to influence nominations for office, and (5) rely substantially more on "material" incentives than on "purposive" incentives. That Mayhew's ratings pertain to the situation in the states during the late 1960s has the advantage of making them plausibly exogenous to contemporary levels of polarization.

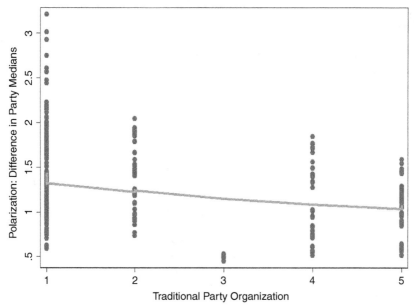

FIGURE 9.2. *Polarization and Traditional Party Organization in State Lower Houses.* Polarization is measured as the difference in the median position of Republican and Democratic legislators drawn from Shor (2013) and Shor and McCarty (2011). The measure of traditional party organization is from Mayhew (1986).

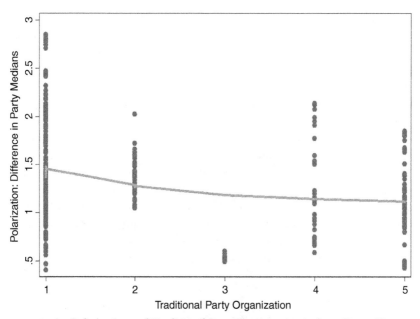

FIGURE 9.3. *Polarization and Traditional Party Organization in State Upper Houses.* Polarization is measured as the difference in the median position of Republican and Democratic legislators drawn from Shor (2013) and Shor and McCarty (2011). The measure of traditional party organization is from Mayhew (1986).

TABLE 9.1. *Total party organization (TPO) and polarization*

	House polar	Senate polar	Dem medians	Rep medians
Traditional Party Org	−0.108	−0.0945	0.0165	−0.0918
	(0.0399)	(0.0434)	(0.0295)	(0.0283)
Year	0.0126	0.0126	0.00576	0.00681
	(0.00385)	(0.00454)	(0.00290)	(0.00255)
South	−0.434	−0.255	0.716	0.281
	(0.189)	(0.180)	(0.134)	(0.141)
Income Inequality	6.009	7.436	−9.606	−3.597
	(4.451)	(3.670)	(2.010)	(3.339)
Percent African American	0.00701	0.00236	−0.0124	−0.00535
	(0.00896)	(0.00910)	(0.00848)	(0.00509)
N	617	627	617	617
R-Squared	0.240	0.180	0.464	0.290

Note: Standard errors in parentheses.
Source: Total party organization as measured by Mayhew (1986). Polarization and party median data from Shor and McCarty (2011).

legislative delegation. All of these data are drawn from Shor and McCarty (2011). The main independent variable is again Mayhew's TPO measure. I include a small set of control variables: *Year* to capture the trend toward greater polarization,[4] *South* to capture regional variation in both polarization and the prevalence of traditional party organizations, *Percent African American,* and *Income Inequality*, the Gini coefficient of family income (see McCarty, Poole, and Rosenthal [2006] for arguments linking polarization to income inequality).

Table 9.1 presents the results. The first two columns report the estimates for the lower and upper chamber, respectively. In both of these models, states with a recent history of traditional party organization have less legislative polarization than those that do not. Because Mayhew's measure is scored from 1 to 5, states with traditional party organizations have differences in party medians that are about 0.4 lower than states with weaker party organizations. The magnitude of this effect is equivalent to a one standard deviation reduction in polarization and two-thirds of the interquartile range. Therefore the correlation

[4] Shor (2013) and Shor and McCarty (2011) report that there is considerable heterogeneity across states as to whether polarization is increasing or decreasing. I ignore that heterogeneity here and estimate a single time trend.

of party organization and polarization is both large and statistically significant. Importantly, the results are robust to the inclusion of controls for region, economic inequality, and racial composition. As expected, the coefficient for year and income inequality are positive, and the coefficient for South is negative. The size of the African American population has a very small and statistically imprecise effect.

I also estimate models for each party separately. Note that Shor-McCarty scores are coded such that Democratic legislators have lower scores than Republican lawmakers. Therefore a variable with a positive coefficient for Democrats and a negative coefficient for Republicans is one that reduces polarization. The results suggest that party organization has an asymmetric effect across parties. The effect on Democratic legislators, although positive, is small and imprecise. The effect on Republican legislators, however, is quite large. This result is consistent with several findings that associate the recent increases in polarization to the rightward movement of the Republican party (Hacker and Pierson 2005; Hare et al. 2012; Barber and McCarty 2013; Shor 2013). My results suggest that these conservative shifts were concentrated in states with weaker party organizations.

CONCLUSIONS

Academic observers and journalists generally have a too simplistic view of the relationship between party organizations and polarization. This view tends to blame polarization on a strengthening of political parties. Instead, the opposite is just as plausible. Perhaps instead of sidelining parties in the nomination process and campaign finance system, we should be enhancing the role of parties.

My view is essentially that of E. E. Schattschneider (1960). Strong political parties have autonomy from and bargaining advantages over special interest groups. Weak parties are those whose elected officials are free agents who can build electoral coalitions around narrow and extreme interests.

I have no specific reform proposal to offer, and I fully recognize that prescriptions to strengthen parties run against a strong tide of American political culture. But let me conclude with a couple of reasonable approaches to reducing polarization by strengthening parties.

First, the role of formal party organizations in the nomination of candidates should be enhanced, not diminished as in reforms such as California's "top-two" primary system. The official neutrality of political parties in primary elections facilitates the entry of more extreme candidates who can receive funding and organization by extreme groups. Formal party groups ought to be able to deploy the resources necessary to counter such insurgent candidates.

Second, the role of the political parties in the campaign finance system ought to be enhanced. For all of its faults, the "soft money" loophole that once allowed political parties to receive unlimited campaign contributions was far superior to the current system that shifts more of the action to outside groups. An ideal reform would shift the balance back toward parties so that they could play a much bigger role as a conduit of money to specific candidates. Such a role for parties might provide better assurances that moderate legislators need worry less about being "primaried" by candidates backed by outside groups.

References

Barber, Michael. 2013. "Ideological Donors, Contribution Limits, and the Polarization of State Legislatures." Typescript, Princeton University.

Downs, Anthony. 1957. *An Economic Theory of Democracy*. New York: Harper & Row.

Hacker, Jacob, and Paul Pierson. 2005. *Off Center: The Republican Revolution and the Erosion of American Democracy*. New Haven: Yale University Press.

Hare, Christopher, Nolan McCarty, Keith T. Poole, and Howard Rosenthal. 2012. "Polarization is Real (and Asymmetric)." Retrieved from http://voteview.com/blog/?p=494.

Krimmel, Katherine. 2013. "Special Interest Partisanship: The Transformation of American Political Parties in Government." PhD diss., Columbia University.

Mayhew, David. 1986. *Placing Parties in American Politics*. Princeton, NJ: Princeton University Press.

McCarty, Nolan. 2011. "Measuring Legislative Preferences." In *Oxford Handbook of the American Congress*, eds. Frances Lee and Eric Schickler. New York: Oxford University Press: 66–94.

McCarty, Nolan, Keith Poole, and Howard Rosenthal. 2006. *Polarized American: The Dance of Ideology and Unequal Riches*. Cambridge, MA: MIT Press.

McCarty, Nolan, and Lawrence Rothenberg. 2013. "A Positive Theory of Group-Politician Alliances." Presented at the Pubic Choice Society meeting.

McGhee, Eric, Seth Masket, Steven Rogers, Boris Shor, and Nolan McCarty. 2014. "A Primary Cause of Partisanship? Nomination Systems and Legislator Ideology." *American Journal of Political Science* 58(2): 337–351.

Schattschneider, E. E. 1960. *The Semisovereign People*. New York: Holt, Rinehart and Winston.

Shor, Boris. 2013. "Asymmetric Polarization in the State Legislatures? Yes and No." Retrieved from http://americanlegislatures.com/2013/07/29/partisan-polarization-in-state-legislatures/.

Shor, Boris, and Nolan McCarty. 2011. "The Ideological Mapping of American Legislatures." *American Political Science Review* 105(3): 530–551.

Snyder Jr., James M., and Michael M. Ting. 2002. "An Informational Rationale for Political Parties." *American Journal of Political Science* 46: 90–110.

10

Focus on Political Fragmentation, Not Polarization

Re-Empower Party Leadership

Richard H. Pildes

Political polarization, from my point of view, is a concern primarily inso-far as it affects the capacity for governance – others might be troubled with a political culture characterized by divisiveness, lack of civil disagreement, and the like, but my concern is effective governance. Indeed, polarization might well involve tragic conflicts between the domains of voting and gover-nance; as responsible party government advocates have long argued, coherent and sharply differentiated political parties appear to increase turnout, make the most salient cue in voting – the political party label – that much more meaningful, and through that cue enable voters to hold officeholders more meaningfully accountable. Thus, party polarization has electoral benefits; it is not a matter of all cost and no advantage. As a result, we should view partisan polarization as a significant problem only if and when its costs are substan-tial enough to outweigh these other benefits. To the extent partisan polar-ization contributes significantly to political paralysis and governmental dys-function, then polarization shifts to becoming a major problem for American democracy.

But if the concern about polarization is best understood as one about effec-tive governance, the angle into this problem that is worth focusing on now and in coming years needs to be redefined. My argument is that we should identify the issue not as *political polarization* but as one of *political fragmentation*. By fragmentation, I mean the external diffusion of political power away from the political parties as a whole and the internal diffusion of power away from the party leadership to individual party members and officeholders.

Until recently, much of the commentary on polarization has focused on the difficulty of fitting America's increasingly parliamentary-like political parties into the Constitution's institutional architecture of a separated-powers system (Levinson and Pildes 2006). In times of divided government (but not only then, given the Senate filibuster rule, which remains in place on policy matters), will the absence of a "majority government" make it too difficult to generate the kind of concerted political action required for legislation? But beneath the surface fact of party polarization lies a more specific set of questions essential to getting at the capacity for effective governance. The issue is not polarization per se: it is where the sources of compromise and negotiation, deal making, pragmatism, and the like are going to come from. Polarization and divided government make those capacities and attitudes more necessary and, of course, more difficult. But polarized parties and their leaders can still forge compromises in crucial areas, at least those in which the need for action is generally viewed as compelling even if the specifics are contested (budgets, debt ceiling increases). That is, party polarization does not by itself necessarily make impossible the kind of compromises that enable government to function effectively, particularly in areas in which there is broad consensus that government must actually take action (again, passing budgets and meeting existing financial obligations are the paradigmatic examples).

My claim is that political fragmentation of the parties (most obviously visible, at the moment, on the Republican side, but latent on the Democratic side as well) is more important than polarization in accounting for why the dynamics of partisan competition increasingly paralyze American government. Were the recent government shutdown and the dancing on the knife's edge of a government default simply a product of the extreme polarization of the political parties – or of the inability of party leaders to bring recalcitrant minority factions of their parties and individual members along to make the deals that party leaders believed necessary? Ironically, stronger parties – or parties stronger in certain dimensions – might be the most effective vehicle for enabling the compromises and deals necessary to overcoming the partisan divide. The problem is not that we have parliamentary-like parties – it might well be that our political parties are not parliamentary-like *enough*. In particular, structural changes in the practices and rules of democracy have caused the party leadership to lose the capacity to control and discipline factions within the party and individual members.

Political scientists have long distinguished three domains in which political parties function: the party as an ongoing organizational entity, the party in the electorate (the party's voters), and the party of elected officials in their capacity as part of the government. To put my point most extremely, the "party-in-government" has been severely undermined in recent decades (Brinkley 2008). As in any setting, organizations require a certain unity – embodied in effective leadership – to negotiate, make credible commitments, and forge deals with other organizations. It is this capacity that "the parties in government" have lost. We tend too often to focus on individual political personalities as the explanation for the failure (or success) of government. Yet in government today, the problem is not that individual leaders are much "weaker" personalities than in the past. It is that the overall structural system, particularly communications and election financing, have disarmed party leaders of the tools they had in the past to ensure and enforce party discipline and unity. These structural changes make party leaders less able to exert the kind of control and force that they were able to in certain earlier eras.

In this chapter I offer one policy proposal designed to re-empower party leadership over other party members within the government: elections that are publicly financed through money that flows primarily to the political parties, rather than to individual candidates or officeholders. I offer this as one point of entry into the larger issue of how to reinvigorate party leaders' capacity to exert leadership on behalf of the parties and to ensure and enforce party cohesion in the midst of contentious and difficult legislative choices. This proposal is less important in itself than as an illustration of the kind of directions we should be focusing on to enable more effective governance in the midst of highly polarized political parties.

I

I am on record as arguing that the hyperpolarization of today's parties is principally a product of long-term historical and structural forces that flowered with the civil rights era of the 1960s, particularly the Voting Rights Act, as African Americans (and many poor whites) begin the process of becoming full political participants (Pildes 2011). If that claim is correct, extreme polarization might best be understood as the "new normal" for an unforeseeable but extended period of time; absent a major shock to the political order, either from external sources or internal ones (for example, if Hispanic citizens, when they fully enter the electoral process, destabilize existing partisan/ideological alignments), specific efforts to diminish polarization by one or several discrete changes in matters such as institutional design or other arenas are likely to be quixotic. As a result, polarization cannot be wished or easily reformed away. Instead, it should be accepted as a fact likely to endure for some time, with attention focused on how best to manage its consequences in ways that will nonetheless promote more effective governance. Nonetheless, those searching for means to diminish polarization itself, in the service of governance, have offered at least three potential points of leverage. Explaining why those levers are not likely to move our polarized party-governmental system much helps justify my different focus on addressing political fragmentation.

The first direction pursued by some reformers seeks to diminish polarization in government by empowering "the people" more effectively. The idea driving these proposed reforms is that greater citizen participation will be a solvent for political dysfunction and polarization. The assumption is that partisan polarization is not in us, but in our political parties: polarization in our formal politics is a corruption or distortion of the more moderate, centrist politics we would have if we could only find ways to give "the people" more direct control or influence over elections and governance. This is part of a recurring wish or vision throughout American political history. But there are good reasons to distrust this idea and even to think that institutional efforts to reflect it would make polarization worse, not better.

For one, Alan Abramowitz has shown that the "politically engaged public" is just as polarized as the parties in government (Abramowitz 2010). Being "engaged" in this sense means little more than taking part in the most basic forms of democratic participation – voting, trying to persuade a friend or neighbor to vote, displaying a bumper sticker or yard sign, giving money, or attending a campaign rally or meeting. These findings thus pose a serious challenge to the idea that more participation equals less polarization. If political engagement correlates with increased polarization, as Abramowitz documents, we should be skeptical about whether finding ways to increase popular participation will temper polarization. In addition, participation does not sprout up spontaneously and atomistically, like mushrooms after a rain. Participation has to be energized, organized, mobilized, and channeled in effective directions; all of that requires the very organizations, and the partisans, that "citizen" participation is meant to bypass.

Moreover, political engagement might not just self-select for partisanship but itself might also be an experience that generates polarization. Indeed, keep in mind that we have been living since the 1960s with an ever increasing, and largely unquestioned, cultural drive for greater popular participation – and more and more transparency to facilitate that participation – at the same time that the political culture has shown increasing disdain for government and that polarization and political paralysis have increased. We should be wary of romanticizing a more engaged public as a vehicle that will save us from hyperpolarized partisan government. As for those who talk about diminishing polarization through changing "the political culture," I have no idea how that might be done. We are not going to uninvent the internet, or cable television, or other forms of media fragmentation that shape our era's political culture.

The second approach to trying to transcend polarization itself focuses more narrowly on changing the mix of candidates and officeholders in an attempt to elect a critical mass of more centrist officeholders who can bridge partisan divides. The institutional-design proposals here include familiar ones (open primaries; independent commissions to redistrict, perhaps with instructions to maximize competition; changes to internal legislative rules) and less familiar ones (getting rid of laws banning "sore-loser candidacies, diminishing the Voting Rights Act's strict requirement of "safe" minority election districts, moving to instant-runoff voting, or, even more radically, abolishing primaries altogether and returning to a system of candidate selection by party leaders). But the empirical evidence thus far raises serious doubts that the specific institutional-design changes that can be tested (open primaries, neutral districting) would, in practice, diminish polarization. I remain concerned that the social-scientific work, by studying each specific institutional modification in isolation, might miss the cumulative effect that several of these changes together might have. Although I retain some hope that changing the structure of primary elections – particularly instituting more dramatic changes, such as instant run-off voting – would facilitate election of more centrist figures (Big Think; Pildes 2010), the evidence is not promising that institutional reform can enable election of a larger, critical mass of centrists.

Hence the third approach.

II

Democracy in America has always rested on a delicate balance between the ideology of "popular sovereignty" and the reality of how effective political and governing power is actually organized. In American political culture, appeals to the idea of popular sovereignty have always played a more central role than in other, more recent democracies: the idea that the large body of the people is, or could be with the right reforms, a decision maker on policy issues beyond the citizenry's Schumpeterian role of accepting and rejecting candidates. The reality has necessarily been, however, that effective governance requires that effective decision-making power be in the hands of those whom some would disparage as "political elites" (elected officials, party leaders, and others), with elections serving primarily as a means for holding that elite accountable for the results. The key to effective democracy might be cast as sustaining the ideas and appropriate practices of popular participation while maintaining a coherent and decisive enough structure of political leadership to enable effective governance.

Seen in this harshly realist light, political paralysis and dysfunction result from the collapse in recent decades of this accommodation. Political fragmentation reflects the way that the claims of popular participation and transparency, along with structural changes, have shifted the traditional balance between leadership and popular participation so far in the latter's direction as to make effective leadership far more difficult. The issue is not a matter of defective capacities for leadership in particular officeholders, such as those at the top of the parties-in-government. It is that these larger cultural and structural forces, which have tried, with greater and greater success, to transform the idea of popular participation into more of a reality, have created a set of conditions in which it is less possible to have the kind of political leadership necessary for effective governance. Democracies and parties frequently are riven with internal factions and latent conflicts, but political leadership, through the parties, has in many eras managed to contain and discipline those conflicts in times when democracy has functioned well (and when parties were less coherent and polarized, bipartisan ideological coalitions were possible).

This is all fairly abstract thus far. But if we reconceptualize the problem as effective governance, this perspective opens up the third approach not yet as fully explored in the polarization debate and literature: focusing on structural changes that might restore effective leadership at the elite level within the parties-in-government and the parties-as-organizations. If we cannot reduce polarization among the politically engaged, through some kind of hard-to-imagine cultural transformation, and we are unlikely to elect less polarized officeholders through institutional-design reforms, changing structural incentives to enable party leaders to exert more effective, unifying control might be the most practical approach to rebuilding the capacity for effective governance. Partly this is a numbers problem: negotiations between three to five leadership figures are easier than hydra-headed negotiations, in which new factions or individuals pop up to expand the issue dimensions at stake in negotiations. Partly it is the capacity for credible organizational commitment in negotiations that is essential to collective governance. And partly it is an empirical belief that, on average, party leaders in Congress are more likely and incentivized to be able to forge compromises, both because their election requires appeal to broad constituencies within their legislative party and because they bear more personal responsibility and blame for the failure of "their" institution to function effectively (outliers do exist, of course).

The problem, in other words, is not best defined as parliamentary parties within a separated-powers system. It is excessive political fragmentation that makes American parties today incapable of functioning as truly parliamentary ones, even as they become more polarized. The primary reason is that the party elite – leaders in the House, the Senate, and the presidency – have lost the capacity they had in some earlier eras for disciplining members of their own party. Party leaders no longer have as much leverage to force party members to accept and toe the party line. The capacity for members of the House and Senate to function as independent freelancers has increased significantly in recent years. This reality is part of the broader breakdown of traditional organizational "power" that Moises Naim (2013) so well documents across a wide array of public and private institutions.

III

The two major recent forces that bring about the political fragmentation of the political sphere are the communications revolution and the way elections are financed (replacing party leaders' power to pick candidates and imposing primary elections also contribute, but those developments date far back at the nonpresidential level). On the former factor, does recently elected Senator Ted Cruz spend more time on Twitter and television, including cable television, as well as giving televised speeches on the floor in the post–C-SPAN era, than he does meeting with Republican Party leaders? Whatever the answer might be, that question itself illustrates a central point: officeholders have the capacity now to reach large, intensely motivated audiences of potential voters and donors, in ways that simply were not possible before. They can establish a personal brand that stands for a different version of the political party than that of party leaders (think Senator Elizabeth Warren vs. President Barack Obama on the Democratic side). Party leaders do not control and cannot shut down these social media and other channels of access to direct communication with voters and donors. At the same time that these channels enable individual officeholders to reach out, they also enable more widespread populist influence to reach in – factional interests within parties can be mobilized more easily. Moreover, this capacity for massive, effective, and direct mobilization of potential supporters might have diminished somewhat the importance of committee assignments, at least for politicians who see themselves as upwardly mobile (i.e., most). Yet imagining some way to roll back or modify this communications revolution is fantasy.

Thus, the more productive direction for reducing fragmentation and empowering party leadership is attacking the other major structural change that enables officeholders today to act as independent entrepreneurs: the way elections have come to be financed. To push back against these changes, we could consider an option that admittedly would have little current political support: financing elections publicly, but not through a candidate-centered public-financing system. Instead, the key feature would be that the public money would be channeled through the appropriate political party organizations, such as the House, Senate, and national campaign committees of the parties. If such a system (which resembles the way elections are financed in many other mature democracies) were to be considered, we would also have to restructure the way the leadership of these organizations was designed and selected. Without offering one specific path, the general idea is that the leadership should be headed by a small group of the elected leaders of the parties – to empower the actors with the greatest incentives to care about the party's appeal to the broadest electorate.

If public financing is considered too unlikely as a political matter, it might be easier to envision modifying McCain-Feingold's ban on soft-money donations to the parties in appropriate ways that encourage the flow of more money to them without raising genuine concerns about corruption. Or we might modify policy so that parties can do more to coordinate their spending with candidates. Such measures might be the most effective way of making individual members more dependent, once again, on party leaders and thereby recapture some of the leverage those leaders have lost.

In the 1980s and 1990s, the party campaign committees were more important to individual candidates than they have been since political actors absorbed the changes that McCain-Feingold wrought. Even if the parties then were more "service" organizations, in John Aldrich's phrase, and no longer rested on the older "party principle" that the party was more important than its members (Aldrich 1995), the parties were extremely valuable to candidates and potential candidates because of the economies of scale and institutional expertise they could bring to bear, particularly for members who were not long-serving incumbents. These relationships of dependency made candidates and officeholders more beholden to the party leaders who ran these committees. Moreover, many of these campaign committee leaders transformed their success in that role into legislative leadership positions (consider the career paths of George Mitchell or Tony Coelho). Successful leadership of the party-as-organization was cashed in for leadership of the party-in-government. Because of the dependency of members on the party organization, these legislative leaders therefore could be far more "persuasive" in bending party colleagues to the leadership's will. When McCain-Feingold entirely cut off soft money to the parties, it drained them of a significant source of funding at the same time that powerful new incentives were created for donors to send their money to nonparty entities (La Raja 2008; Kelner 2012; on the effects on state parties, see Reiff 2012 and for a different, earlier view, see Jacobson 2010). Of course, public financing through the party organizations would have to be set at a high enough level and be adjusted rapidly over time for this public money to be meaningful enough to give candidates and officeholders strong incentives to become more dependent, once again, on the party organization and leadership. Public funding would also have to be sustained at a high enough level to diminish the marginal contribution of private funding, for otherwise the centralizing aims of public funding through the parties would be compromised.

To be sure, several other changes contribute to the loss of leadership leverage. One of the most important is "earmark reform," which eliminated the most direct quid pro quo leaders could offer wavering members in return for supporting the leadership's position. As noted earlier, the significance of committee assignments has also diminished, thus diluting the power that

Richard H. Pildes

leadership can exercise through that mechanism. That decline might partly reflect the developments in independent communication and fundraising noted earlier. Specific committee assignments have also become less valuable as it has become somewhat more difficult to turn those assignments themselves directly into major financial contributions, given the much greater transparency and scrutiny that now exist regarding these relationships. The decline of leadership leverage and power is thus a product of a number of forces, and it would be a mistake to think we could recreate in full the powers that leadership could exert in earlier eras; the question is not where are the Lyndon Johnsons of today, but could Lyndon Johnson exist today. But having campaign money flow through the parties as much as possible seems to me the most direct and immediate means to recapturing some of that lost leadership leverage.

IV

Publicly financing elections is merely one suggested means to the larger goal of re-empowering party elites and leaders and giving them the tools to more effectively enforce party discipline in the service of effective governance in a highly polarized political era that is likely to remain so for years. But the particular means is less important than the definition of the goal. My aim is to define re-empowering elected party leaders as the goal and to provoke discussion about the most effective means of realizing it.

More broadly, I believe it important to confront head-on two powerful cultural trends that will generate resistance to publicly financed elections through the parties or other means that aim at re-empowering political leaders. The first is the ideology of "popular participation." Any change in the democratic system that aims to empower political leaders will be cast in terms of Manichean conflict between "the people" and "the elites." America's cultural self-understanding of democracy has always invoked a rhetoric of "popular sovereignty" far more populist in meaning than in other Western democracies. This self-understanding is embedded in many of our political institutions and practices, such as the fact that we alone elect (state) judges and prosecutors, that we have vastly more elections for more offices than any other democracy, and that our administrative state is generally more subject to direct political control than in other democracies. But it is increasingly becoming clear, in our era at least, that the much greater participation enabled by the communications revolution also breeds polarization, as well as fragmentation. Instead of seeing a relentless expansion of participatory reforms as the cure for what ails democracy, we should start recognizing a perhaps tragic tradeoff between certain modes of participation and the capacity for effective governance. In the past, I have supported matching private-public election financing systems, such as that used in New York City and now being adopted elsewhere. But I have become leery that these systems will only exacerbate polarization and fragmentation, because the private money will tend to come from the most politically engaged citizens – and thus, the most polarized ones. Simple public financing, from that perspective, might thus be the better option.

Second, efforts to empower party leadership will also run into America's characteristic and unique distrust of political parties (Epstein 1986). Part of the culturally distinctive understanding of "popular sovereignty" here has been a romantically individualist vision of democracy – a vision that sees organizational intermediaries between citizens and government, such as political parties, as always something of a corruption from true democracy (Pildes 2004; Rosenblum 2008). And if parties must be tolerated, they must be put under the control of "the people" as much as possible; hence, the Progressive Era antiparty creation of the mandatory primary election in the early twentieth century. Thus, a robust defense of political parties – as well as of party and political leadership – will have to be willingly and forthrightly undertaken to mobilize support for any set of changes that seek to re-empower party leadership.

The obstacles to such changes, in other words, are not merely entrenched interests and entrenched ways of doing things. These obstacles are also cultural ideas whose virtues might seem unarguable, might be taken for granted, and might be widely shared; they might be ideas, such as "popular participation," that reformers have no desire to tackle head-on. But if I am right that the problem is effective governance, that political fragmentation might be the most effective focal point for effective reform efforts rather than polarization per se, and that the right direction for fresh thought is how to re-empower political and party leaders, it is also necessary to understand the deep sources of resistance that must be engaged as a prelude to any movement along this path.

References

Abramowitz, Alan I. 2010. *The Disappearing Center: Engaged Citizens, Polarization, and American Democracy*. New Haven: Yale University Press.

Aldrich, John H. 1995. *Why Parties? The Origin and Transformation of Party Politics in America*. Chicago: University of Chicago Press.

Brinkley, Alan. 2008. "The Party's Over." *Wall Street Journal*, September 6. Retrieved January 21, 2014, from http://online.wsj.com/news/articles/SB122065969178405759.

Epstein, Leon D. 1986. *Political Parties in the American Mold*. Madison: University of Wisconsin Press.

Jacobson, Gary C. 2010. "A Collective Dilemma Solved: The Distribution of Party Campaign Resources in the 2006 and 2008 Congressional Elections." *Election Law Journal* 9(4): 381–397.

Kelner, Robert. 2012. "The Truth about National Political Party Fundraising." *Inside Political Law*, July 31. Retrieved January 21, 2014, from www.insidepoliticallaw.com/2012/07/31/the-truth-about-national-political-party-fundraising.

La Raja, Raymond J. 2008. *Small Change: Money, Political Parties, and Campaign Finance Reform*. Ann Arbor: University of Michigan Press.

Levinson, Daryl and Richard Pildes. 2006. "Separation of Parties, Not Powers." *Harvard Law Review* 119(8): 2311–2386.

Naím, Moisés. 2013. *The End of Power: From Boardrooms to Battlefields and Churches to States, Why Being in Charge Isn't What It Used To Be*. New York: Basic Books.

Pildes, Richard H. 2004. "The Supreme Court, 2003 Term – Foreword: The Constitutionalization of Democratic Politics." *Harvard Law Review* 118(1): 29–154.

————. 2010. "Abolish Primary Elections." *BigThink*. August 26. Retrieved January 21, 2014, from http://bigthink.com/videos/abolish-primary-elections.

————. 2011. "Why the Center Does Not Hold: The Causes of Hyperpolarized Democracy in America." *California Law Review* 99(2): 273–333.

Reiff, Neil. 2012. "The Weakening of State and Local Parties." *Campaigns & Elections*, July 16. Retrieved January 21, 2014, from www.campaignsandelections.com/magazine/us-edition/324462/the-weakening-of-state-and-local-parties.thtml.

Rosenblum, Nancy L. 2008. *On the Side of the Angels: An Appreciation of Parties and Partisanship*. Princeton: Princeton University Press.

11

Two Approaches to Lessening the Effects of Partisanship

Bruce Cain

In recent years, scholars, journalists, and others have identified various possible causes for rising partisan polarization in U.S. government. They include underlying factors such as rising economic inequality, geographic sorting, new media, immigration, post–civil rights era party realignment and the Supreme Court's rulings on independent expenditures. In addition, there are contemporary political conditions, such as the white backlash against America's first African American president and the paralyzing consequences of divided government in Washington. Realistically, this means that any serious effort to dial down partisanship requires a comprehensive, multilevel strategy and a coherent, realistic vision of modern citizenship.

The dominant problem in U.S. politics in recent years can be characterized as democratic distortion – a skewing of process and policy in which the political system is too responsive to those with intense preferences, especially when they are ideologically extreme or oriented toward private gain at public expense. Ideally, the political process in a diverse, pluralist society should aggregate preferences fairly with a robust capacity for compromise. But the excessive influence of ideological extremists and the ability of concentrated economic interests to use the state for private gain suggest that we are drifting away from that goal.

The nub of the problem is that those with intense ideological preferences and/or concentrated material interests are better able and more willing to exert influence over elections and policy making in government. Preference intensity tends to increase with ideological extremity and the degree to which material interests are directly affected by government policies. Sometimes, ideology and material interests coincide (e.g., the Koch brothers) and sometimes they do not (e.g., Moveon.org). Party activists tend to have more polarized views than non-activists. Businesses, trade unions, and other regulated groups normally advocate for their narrow economic self-interests. Because those with intense preferences are also more willing to pay the opportunity and collective action costs associated with political participation (i.e., mobilizing the vote, contributing and spending money in campaigns, lobbying agencies, monitoring government actions, and the like), their influence is more constant and effective over time than that of less engaged citizens.

Many citizens are unaware of the issues that interest groups and party activists care about. Moreover, they only participate sporadically and in inverse proportion to opportunity and collective action costs. This creates a political participation and policy skew in elections (especially primaries), campaign finance activity, and lobbying (Fiorina 1999). Ironically, many modern political reforms have amplified the influence of intense preferences by facilitating the proliferation party primaries, open meeting laws, direct democracy opportunities, and the like (Cain 2014). The Supreme Court has also contributed to this systemic hypersensitivity to intense preferences through its expansive definition of First Amendment political rights.

The focus of this book is partisanship. Despite several years of lively political science debate over this topic (Abramowitz and Saunders 2008; see Chapter 14 in this volume), the original observation by Fiorina, Abrams, and Pope (2005) still stands: partisanship in the Congress and state legislatures mostly exceeds partisanship in the electorate as a whole. This is evident in Figure 7.2 (in Chapter 7 by Rodden), which reveals the discontinuity between the mapping of the still largely unimodal presidential vote and the now starkly bimodal congressional roll-call voting scores. Indeed, according to Bonica's data presented in Chapter 12, the congressional roll-call voting scores more closely track the sources of campaign contributions. Moreover, there are now more voters who self-identify as political independents, refusing to affiliate with either major political party.

This "disconnect" between elite behavior and public opinion frustrates many centrist and less politically engaged voters. The rising polarization in Congress contributed to government gridlock under conditions of divided government after 2010 as exemplified by the frequent threats to shut down the government and ignore debt obligations, increasing obstruction to court and political appointments, and ongoing attempts to overturn the Affordable Care Act (ACA). The Obama administration was only able to pass the ACA under budget reconciliation rules during the brief period of united government between 2008 and 2010.

The most direct way to dampen partisanship would be to ban parties and limit their involvement in raising money and supporting candidates. This approach is both constitutionally suspect and politically infeasible. Moreover, we know from experience with nonpartisan local elections that limiting the involvement of parties would increase the incumbency advantage and would not prevent ideological groups from fielding and supporting their candidates of choice.

In this short chapter, I demonstrate two constitutionally permissible approaches to dialing down the effects of partisanship: the use of public finance vouchers to enhance the general public's influence and a storage votes scheme that puts limits on the ability of extreme legislators to obstruct legislation in the U.S. Senate. These approaches do not address the underlying causes of ideological and partisan extremity. Rather, they take as a given that some individuals and groups will use the political system to further their highly partisan and ideological positions. The question is whether the effects of partisanship can be toned down without violating constitutional constraints.

In the electoral arena, capping speech even in the interests of fairness and deliberation is not an option. Hence, the first strategy enhances the voices of the electorate generally through a voucher public finance scheme. In the legislative arena, it is constitutionally possible to put a budget constraint on obstruction, allowing some degree of minority veto without violating the majority rule principle. Hence, we consider the idea proposed by Casella, Turban, and Wawro (2013) to substitute the Senate filibuster on judicial nominees with storable votes.

SOFTENING ELECTORAL PARTISANSHIP EFFECTS THROUGH VOUCHERS

Efforts to limit protected speech in the interests of equality have generally run afoul of the Supreme Court, especially recently. Although the Court might someday revisit the notion of a fair public forum, it leaves us for the foreseeable future with only a "floors, not ceilings" approach. As applied to partisanship and ideological extremity, this means empowering the less engaged, less extreme segments of the electorate. In addition to being a force for more moderation, this voting bloc could potentially serve a role analogous to that of slack in organization theory by giving representatives more room to negotiate, deliberate, and compromise.

To explore what it would mean to empower the less engaged, I focus on one increasingly salient problem: campaign finance. American politics are increasingly professionalized and expensive at all levels, which has put a premium on money as opposed to other political resources (e.g., organizing volunteers). Big and small donors are often an unrepresentative sample of the general public in terms of ideology and partisan skew. Elected officials spend significant amounts of their time raising funds for themselves and their partisan allies.

Public finance schemes in theory should have blunted the influence of this kind of private money, but they have largely failed to date. The federal presidential public funding system has collapsed, because candidates can raise more money from private donations and avoid spending limits at the same time. Moreover, some voters do not like spending more for speech that they disagree with. As a consequence, average voters are not really part of the campaign finance game even when there are public financing options. Typically, public campaign funds are either linked to small private donations in matching schemes or bureaucratically allocated as a lump sum to candidates who qualify and agree not to raise money privately. In either case, individual voters have little or no direct say in how public money is allocated to specific candidates.

Over the years, various scholars such as Rick Hasen (1996) and Bruce Ackerman and Ian Ayres (2002) have suggested a voucher system that would allow voters to allocate public money to candidates of their choosing. Although many regard vouchers as either fanciful or intriguing, a voucher system has never been given a serious try. In theory, a well-funded voucher system would allow moderate and less engaged voters to add their voice to the so-called invisible primary and to counteract the dominant influence of materially and ideologically interested donors. But there are also lots of possible ways vouchers could be foiled. Would moderate and less engaged voters even bother to allocate their money? Would vouchers be sold on a black market for profit? Can individual allocations be aggregated in a way to offset ideological money? These are design questions that must be addressed if vouchers are going to be part of a solution to hyperpartisanship.

The aim of this proposal is to get the general public into the fundraising game by reformulating public campaign financing into a voucher system that favors party and multicandidate committees with the broadest donor bases by allowing them to contribute more to candidates than those with smaller numbers of donors. This would compensate for several flaws in the current public finance systems. First, voters as donors would get to finance "speech" that they like as opposed to underwriting campaigns generally or speech with which they do not agree. Second, the candidate's receipt of money would not be tied to expenditure limits, which have all too often put the candidate who accepts the public finds at a disadvantage as against the one who does not. Finally, this scheme would tie the amount that an entity could donate to the breadth of its donor base. The elements of the voucher would be as follows:

1. Each citizen gets to allocate a specified amount of money that can be distributed to candidates or multicandidate PACs in any sum up to the total allocation.
2. Voters can either make a one-cycle, renewable allocation to a multi-candidate PAC or party or can make direct allocations to candidates.
3. Multicandidate PACs would be allowed to contribute to candidates directly, with varying contribution limits according to the number of voucher and hard money/limited contributors in their donor base.
4. Voucher allocations could be made online or be mailed.
5. The system should be first tested experimentally and then in the field with a local government to prove its value.

The purpose of allowing voters to allocate to either candidates directly or to multicandidate PACs is to compensate for the likelihood that some citizens will not bother to take the time to learn about the different candidates, but might be capable of responding to a group appeal in broad general terms. In particular, this would allow for a clearer separation between ideology and party, enabling moderates from either party to support a centrist independent PAC. PACs would be allowed to solicit these public funds, but would have strict reporting requirements about their operations and expenditures. The one-cycle allocation to PACs as well as candidates allows the less engaged to empower others to watch out for their interests.

The current federal system limits multicandidate PACs and the political parties to $5,000 dollars per candidate, ostensibly to prevent them serving as conduits to corruption. This rationale makes little sense because the inputs to both are disclosed and capped. Moreover, it forces both into independent spending (i.e., spending that is not controlled or coordinated with a candidate). Allowing the parties and multicandidate PACs to develop a sufficiently broad base of donors so they could give more to candidates directly would heighten the advantage of hard over soft/independent money, given the way the most favorable rate system operates with TV stations. If the PAC/party can give unlimited amounts of money to the candidates and the candidates would still get the more favorable candidate advertising rates, it would undercut the appeal of independent spending to some degree. The current system of media buy pricing is in effect a congestion pricing system: it allows higher charges for independent expenditures than for official candidates. The candidate price advantage could be extended to broad-based party and multicandidate organizations as well. Congestion pricing does not cap speech, but does indirectly encourage the fair use of public forum opportunities.

In the long run, democracy in the future will no doubt be increasingly conducted online. But in the short run, putting the voucher system exclusively online might cut out some disadvantaged individuals; hence the need to allow multiple ways for citizens to be able to designate their voucher allocations. Allowing broad-based party and multicandidate PACs to have higher expenditure limits will better equip them to match the efforts of the SuperPACS and other independent expenditures. Allowing multicandidate PACs as well as parties to receive vouchers opens up the field to broad-based movements, including bipartisan efforts. Given the complexities of voucher design, its viability should be tested on a small scale before rolling it out. This could mean a simulation experimentally and/or in the field with a small jurisdiction.

SOFTENING THE EFFECTS OF THE FILIBUSTER

A second approach to dampening the effects of political partisanship is to lessen the minority's capacity to obstruct legislative action through the use of supermajority rules, which seem to exacerbate polarization. At the state level, supermajority rules are often used for budgeting matters, veto overrides, and constitutional amendments. At the federal government level, the U.S. Senate uses supermajority votes to end filibusters on judicial/executive confirmations and policy votes (although, unlike some states, not for budget votes).

Filibusters are now more common than in the past and are applied more widely, including to judicial nominations. As Casella, Turban and Wawro (2013, 3) point out, the median delay for uncontroversial circuit court nominees has increased from 44 days during the Reagan years to 218 days under Obama, and the proportion of those waiting more than 200 days has increased from 5% to 64%. The problem is that the vote to close debate requires a supermajority cloture vote, even if only one senator objects to a nominee. Although the Senate was able to reach a compromise and avoid elimination of the filibuster in 2005, the controversy surrounding its use continues.

There is virtue in requiring a supermajority vote for important decisions such as appointments to the judiciary because such a vote normally implies some degree of bipartisan support. This seems reasonable given that federal judges are meant to be impartial. But partisan extremists can use the supermajority rule to obstruct the appointment of moderate judges or can use their vote on a judicial appointment to gain leverage in policy votes. The core institutional flaw is that there is no budget constraint on the ability to obstruct federal judicial appointments. There is also no budget constraint with Senate-confirmed political appointees.

One way to compromise between the virtues of minority veto and majority rule would be to consider a storable vote system (Casella 2012). This would allow senators to express their preference intensity by casting multiple votes on those they strongly prefer or oppose while not allowing them to veto nominees as will. The specifics of the Casella, Turban, and Wawro (2013) proposal are as follows:

1. After normal vetting, nominees for federal district and circuit court would be presented to the full Senate as a slate of nominees at fixed intervals during the year.

2. Each nominee would be up for confirmation for a specific position and would not be competing with other nominees for that position; the only question to be voted on is whether he or she would be confirmed.

3. The slates would alternate at different times between district and circuit court slates.

4. Each senator would have a number of votes equal to the number of positions on the slate. When the motion to proceed to the final vote is called for each candidate, a senator can cast any number of votes in favor or against, with the constraint that the total number cast cannot exceed the number of positions on the slate.

5. If the motion to proceed with a given candidate is negative, the nominee is withdrawn; if positive, it moves forward to a simple majority confirmation vote.

Modeling different preference intensity distributions for the majority and minority and using simulation methods, the Columbia University group studying this approach maintains that storable votes under a number of assumptions prevents the minority from blocking preferences more than half the time. And when there is high polarization within the parties and agreement across the parties as to the most important nominations (as often happens in polarized situations), the minority success rate is closer to 20% to 30%. They also claim that the system is reasonably robust to majority attempts to manipulate the outcome through decoy appointments.

The storable votes idea illustrates a second type of approach to strong partisanship: namely, the creation of new rules that allow for minority protection where it is called for, but within a framework that preserves the principle that the majority should prevail a majority of the time.

CONCLUSION

If the United States is to manage polarization in a way that preserves its ability to aggregate preferences and negotiate outcomes effectively and fairly, we need to consider rule changes that empower the voices of the more moderate and less engaged voters and that compromise between majority and minority factions in the legislature. The main challenge for both approaches is that there is an inherent aversion to creating new rules in American political culture. The question is whether conditions have deteriorated sufficiently in the United States that there might be a greater openness to institutional innovations than is normal.

Money has become so dominant in American politics and the donor class is so small that voters may be interested in new approaches to public finance that give them more say in the allocation of public funds for political campaigns. It might make sense to try vouchers in a city or small state setting first to prove that the system can work. Similarly, if congressional polarization stymies the legislative process to a significant degree, leaders may be looking for new compromise solutions. District court appointments, which tend to be the least controversial federal judicial appointments, might be the best arena in which to test the storable votes procedure.

References

Ackerman, Bruce A., and Ian Ayres. 2002. *Voting with Dollars: A New Paradigm for Campaign Finance*. New Haven: Yale University Press.

Abramowitz, Alan I., and Kyle L. Saunders. 2008. "Is Polarization a Myth." *Journal of Politics* 70(2): 542–555.

Cain, Bruce E. 2014. *Democracy More or Less: The Quandary of American Political Reform*. New York: Cambridge University Press.

Casella, Alessandra. 2012. *Storable Votes: Protecting the Minority Voice*. New York: Oxford University Press.

Casella, Alessandra, Sébastien Turban, and Gregory Wawro. 2013. "Reforming Senate Rules for Judicial Nomination." Working Paper. New York University School of Law.

Fiorina, Morris P. 1999. "Extreme Voices: A Dark Side of Civic Engagement." *Civic Engagement in American Democracy* 395: 405–413.

Fiorina, Morris P., Samuel J. Abrams, and Jeremy Pope. 2005. *Culture War? The Myth of a Polarized America*. New York: Pearson Longman.

Hasen, Richard L. 1996. "Clipping Coupons for Democracy: An Egalitarian/Public Choice Defense of Campaign Finance Vouchers." *California Law Review* 1–59.

Empowering and Informing Moderate Voters

12

Data Science for the People

Adam Bonica

Reformers concerned about the rise of partisan polarization often advocate reforming institutions, reducing the influence of political actors believed to have a polarizing effect on politics, or simply adopting a cynical "throw the bums out" mentality. In this chapter I propose that, rather than seek to improve our institutions, we seek to inform and empower voters by combining recent advances in political science and technology. Just as Amazon has made smarter consumers and Netflix has made it easier to discover movies and television shows we like, data and technology can similarly transform the political marketplace. The marvels of the big data revolution that helped campaigns learn about voters and to predict their behavior have been widely lauded following the 2012 elections. However, I believe that the true potential of the big data revolution for politics will be realized by harnessing its power to help voters learn about candidates in an engaging and efficient way.

Much of the unease concerning the rise in partisan polarization relates to the perceived incongruence between the ideological extremity of elected politicians and the relative centrism of the electorate they are sent to represent. Although the mass public has become more polarized in recent decades, it has done so much more slowly than politicians (Fiorina, Abrams, and Pope 2005; Theriault 2008; Abramowitz 2010). This disconnect has fueled concerns about the health of our democracy and that broken electoral and representative institutions have prevented voters from electing the types of representatives they want or deserve. However, others push back, arguing that a flawed electorate, rather than flawed institutions, is to blame.

Scholars have struggled to reconcile the disconnect between the ideological dispositions of voters and those of the politicians elected to represent them. This debate has identified two general lines of explanation, one relating to candidate entry and the other to voter competence. The first arises from a system that gives voters the final say in elections, but much less control over the set of candidates that appear on their ballot. This is primarily a problem of getting the right types of candidates to run for office and helping them survive the early stages of their campaigns, a process that is heavily influenced by political elites and political money. The second relates to the general lack of political sophistication among voters. Even if voters faced choices between candidates where one was clearly more in step with their preferences on issues, voters would still not be competent or knowledgeable enough to actually make an informed decision about which candidate to support. Even the most sophisticated voters appear to rely on crude informational shortcuts, such as partisanship or candidate personality, neither of which tell us much about ideological extremity, especially in the context of partisan primaries and nonpartisan elections.

Ultimately, these two lines of explanation are interrelated. When considering a bid for elected office, candidates have been shown to be very strategic about entering a race. If voters, starved of the types of information needed to distinguish between candidates on the basis of ideology, fail to sufficiently reward candidates for their centrism and fail to punish others for their extremism, moderates become less likely to bear the cost of entry and less likely to win when they do. Many have placed blame on partisan primary systems designed in ways that advantage extremists. Primary systems certainly matter, and there are strong theoretical reasons to believe that some may be more friendly to moderates than others. But the problem persists even when primary systems are designed to be friendly to moderates (Ahler, Citrin, and Lenz 2013; Masket et al. 2014).

Rather than view political donors as part of the problem, I see them as a key part of the solution – but not for the reasons one might expect. Federal and state election agencies collect and disclose contribution records with the stated goal of safeguarding our democracy through increased transparency. However, these databases double as vast repositories of observational data on revealed political preferences. By carefully seeking out candidates to support who share their policy preferences from among the multitudes of the political marketplace, donors offer a way to learn about candidates and predict how they would behave if elected to office. In doing so, they provide valuable information regarding their personal ideology and the ideology of the candidates they support.

In what follows, I discuss the problem motivating the proposal and how it relates to the problem of political polarization, how to alleviate the problem, and what would need to be done to put it into action. The first step is determining what information and tools would benefit voters. The second step is figuring out how to present this information in an easily understandable and digestible format. The third, and least complicated, step is implementing the idea in the field.

VOTER COMPETENCE

There is a well-established literature in political science that addresses whether ordinary citizens are capable of reasoning coherently about politics. To say that most experts on the subject doubt the competence of voters would be somewhat of an understatement. There is extensive evidence that portrays voters as woefully ignorant about matters of politics. One line of evidence comes from survey research that demonstrates widespread ignorance about political institutions and public affairs. Further findings suggest the prevalence of non-attitudes, when survey respondents behave as if they were flipping a coin when expressing position stances on major issues or support for lesser known candidates. Taking the literature at face value, it is hard to argue that most voters are sufficiently knowledgeable to be up to the task. But a lingering question is whether voters actually lack the skills necessary to reason coherently about politics or simply lack the information needed to do so.

More recently, several studies have explored the effect of reforming primary elections in California by adopting a top-two system. Most of these studies find that the reforms had little to no effect. One conclusion that can be drawn is that voters have little interest in electing moderates. Another interpretation is that voters have difficulty determining who the centrist candidates are. Perhaps the key study in this group is by Ahler, Citrin, and Lenz (2013), who show that voters are incapable of distinguishing moderate candidates from the rest.

In an important contribution to the literature, Sniderman and Stiglitz (2012) tackle the question of voter competence from a different angle. They asked whether respondents were able to apply spatial reasoning skills when choosing between candidates if the ideological positioning of candidates were taken as known, hence essentially abstracting away the knowledge deficit from the equation. The study revealed that voters are very capable of selecting the candidates most proximate to their personal preferences after being shown a simple visual cue about the positions of candidates. The main implication of this finding is that the lack of voter competence is mostly a symptom of a lack of information rather than any inherent reasoning skills.

As long as voters have readily available informational cues, they are able to choose candidates who best represent their views. However, in the real world such cues are rarely available. The evidence from empirical studies on the effect of candidate positioning in actual elections suggests that candidate ideology does matter, but that the effect is quite small. Furthermore, the effect of candidate positioning appears to have declined with time. The estimated change in vote share associated with moving the midpoint two standard deviations to the right fell from 5.1% during the 1980s to just 1.96% during the 2000s (Bonica 2014). In other words, the advantage related to being moderate has declined drastically. Moreover, these results apply to races with the highest level of information available; in down-ballot races, it is likely that most voters are all but lost.

MEASURING AND FORECASTING IDEOLOGY

To much fanfare, a great deal of effort has been devoted to forecasting the outcome of congressional elections. However, although it is nice to know the partisan composition of Congress, that is generally not seen as the main quantity of interest. Political scientists instead tend to focus on the inputs of policy relating to the distribution of legislative preferences, such as gridlock intervals, pivots, and partisan polarization, which have all been shown to be closely related to legislative productivity. They also provide clear predictions about what types of policies can realistically be passed through legislation, and which are off the table, during a given Congress.

To forecast how these metrics change from one session of Congress to the next based on the outcomes of elections, we need to know more about candidates than just their partisan affiliation. We need to be able to forecast their ideological preferences before entering office. Congressional scholars have long gone beyond using partisan seat shares as the primary quantity of interest for understanding Congress. It is about time our forecasting models caught up – not just for the sake of researchers but for voters. The problem thus far has been that methods to measure ideology have predominantly relied on legislative voting records, which exclude the ability to capture the ideology of non-incumbent candidates before they take office. As a result, we have been limited to tracking polarization only after it has occurred, which has precluded the possibility of providing much-needed guidance to reformers and voters.

Fortunately, recently developed methods for measuring ideology offer a way forward. For instance, in an analysis I performed with Howard Rosenthal after the 2012 elections, we demonstrated the viability of forecasting changes in polarization from the 112th to the 113th Congress.Rather than base legislators' ideology on how they vote, we instead inferred ideology scores from the patterns of contributions made by their supporters (Bonica and Rosenthal 2013). In deciding which candidates to support, the typical donor is strongly influenced by his or her own ideological views. As a result, donors give almost exclusively to like-minded candidates with similar voting records. Using contributions through any period before an election, we can then predict the expected changes to polarization following an election based on the estimated ideological positions of outgoing – and importantly – incoming members. Figure 12.1 shows how closely the predicted changes in congressional polarization, as measured by DW-Nominate, track the actual changes. There is

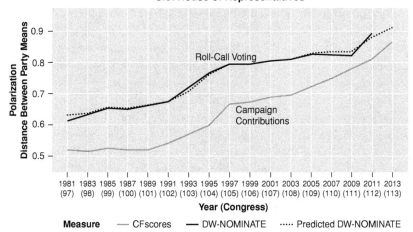

FIGURE 12.1. Forecasting Aggregate Changes in Polarization Based on Campaign Finance Based Ideal Point Measures. *Source*: Database on Ideology, Money in Politics and Elections.

a near-perfect correspondence between the predicted and actual outcomes. Furthermore, in addition to predicting aggregate changes in polarization, this technique is able to provide race-by-race predictions of the expected change in polarization. Figure 12.2 provides an example of how this can be shown for the Senate.

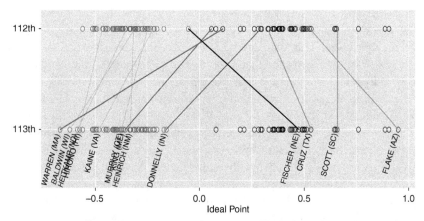

FIGURE 12.2. Effect of the 2012 Senate Elections on the Ideological Distribution of the Senate. Each line traces the change from the sitting senator during the 112th Congress to his or her replacement in the 113th Congress. *Source*: Database on Ideology, Money in Politics and Elections.

Perhaps the most promising feature of this technique is that it applies much more generally to electoral politics, reaching down to state and local races. These lower level offices are important in the long run because they are the feeders to higher offices, the path through which most congressional candidates travel. See Bonica (2013) for an overview of the expansive list of candidates.

The more important implications of these technological and methodological advances are not how they can aid researchers but rather how they can be used to help voters make more informed decisions about candidates in the ballot booth. The measures can accurately predict how candidates would vote if they were elected to office. As such, they offer a jumping-off point for determining which candidates will be most likely to serve as moderates and which will be most likely to serve as extremists.

A DATA-DRIVEN VOTER GUIDE

Currently, in the best scenario, voters are able to rely on partisan labels or endorsements as informational cues about candidates. In low-information elections and down-ballot races, the most important players are typically not the voters but rather a small group of knowledgeable political elites who have disproportionate influence over who runs and even the eventual winner. Moreover, this small group of political elites also tends to be more extreme than the average voter.

A few ideas to help voters become more informed about candidates have been tried in the past with limited success. Project Votesmart, for example, has attempted to address this problem by compiling policy positions through candidate surveys. This approach had little success for two reasons: the low response rate, which means that only a small percentage of the candidate pool is included, and the fact that reading through the candidate surveys is an extremely time-consuming (and often confusing) activity that few voters would actually do.

For a voter guide to truly be useful to voters, it needs to involve both a comprehensive set of measures and a convenient way to deliver information to voters quickly and effectively in a digestible format. A little bit of information can go a long way in helping voters make informed choices. Unlike many other proposed solutions, putting better information in the hands of voters would not require passing legislation or pushing for electoral reform. The proposal made here is actionable now. All that is needed to test its effectiveness are resources to get it in the field.

We have seen in laboratory experiments that voters do respond to simple spatial cues (Sniderman and Stiglitz 2012). This seems to be an easy starting point to present information to voters. One way to put this idea into action would be through randomized field experiments to see if it is possible to change voting behavior through "information injections." In theory, this could come in the form of direct mail fliers with the breakdown of every race on the ballot showing the estimated positions of the candidates.

To provide a rough sense of how the informational cues could be presented to citizens for use as a supplemental voter guide, I include two series of graphs along with a sample prompt written with the intention of priming readers to focus on partisan polarization. Each set of graphs shows the estimated ideological positions of all candidates running for a given seat in California. Figure 12.3 displays the positions of Californian congressional candidates running in primary elections for several high-profile races during the 2012 election cycle. Figure 12.4 does the same for candidates for state legislative office in California in 2012, as well as for candidates for attorney general in 2010. Figuring out how best to present the model results in a succinct but effective format would require careful thought and would likely benefit from user testing.

EXAMPLE PROMPT

"Campaigns have spent large sums learning to acquire and analyze data on the preferences and behavior of voters. You have been randomly selected to take part in an experiment to explore the potential of using similar statistical techniques to aid voters to learn about candidates.

The model, which was developed by researchers at Stanford University, makes use of data from millions of publicly disclosed campaign finance records to infer the policy positions of candidates. The ideological leanings of the donors who fund a candidate's campaign reveal a great deal about how a candidate is expected to behave if elected to office. Candidates who raise funds primarily from ideologically extreme donors are much more likely to establish ideologically extreme voting records after entering office, whereas those who primarily fundraise from more centrist donors are, on average, more moderate.

By observing patterns of who gives to whom, the model identifies positions for each candidate along an ideological spectrum (from most liberal to most conservative) that best summarize his or her policy views. Although a single dimension cannot offer a complete characterization of a candidate's policy preferences, it provides a very informative signal of how candidates will vote and behave if elected to office. Importantly, this provides a tool for voters like you to help distinguish between moderate candidates and those who are more extreme.

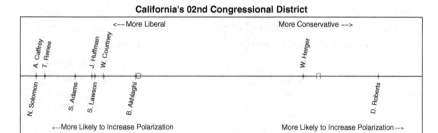

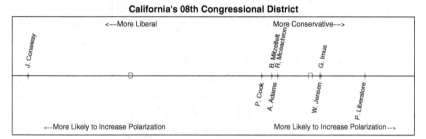

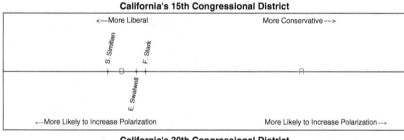

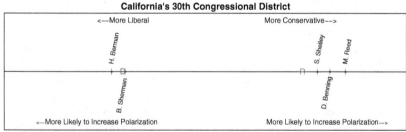

FIGURE 12.3. Example Format for Presenting Voters with Spatial Cues about the Ideological Positions of Congressional Candidates. *Source*: Database on Ideology, Money in Politics and Elections.

The graphs below show the estimated position for each candidate who appears on your ballot relative to their opponents. Candidates who are placed furthest to the left on the scale are more likely to vote with the most liberal Democrats. Likewise, candidates who are placed furthest to the right on the scale are more likely to vote with the most conservative Republicans. To aid

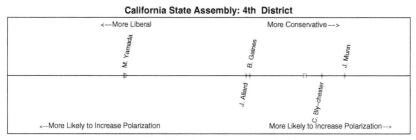

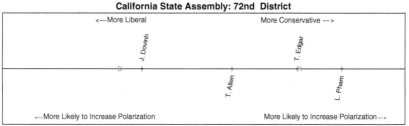

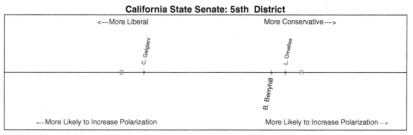

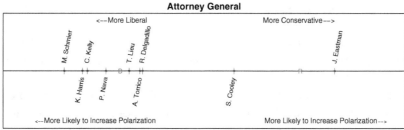

FIGURE 12.4. Example Format for Presenting Voters with Spatial Cues about the Ideological Positions of Candidates for State Office. *Source:* Database on Ideology, Money in Politics and Elections.

interpreting the scale, tokens of the letters D and R are used to indicate the average positions for Democrats and Republicans who are currently serving in Congress. The anticipated effect of electing candidates who are more extreme than their party average is to move the parties in Congress further from the political center and more toward the ideological extreme, resulting in a more polarized Congress. Electing moderate candidates who have positions nearer the center of the scale is expected to have the opposite effect."

CONCLUSIONS AND FURTHER CONSIDERATIONS

The true promise of data science when applied to politics is taking large amounts of publicly available data on revealed political preferences and summarizing the information into bite-size morsels that are easily interpreted and incorporated into decisions. Thus far, the thrust of big data and politics has been an effort by campaigns to learn about and target voters, but as political scientists are well aware, the information available on political elites – through what they say, how they vote, and how they network and fundraise – is much greater and richer than the information we have about the mass public; thus there is an enhanced potential to learn about them and discern their preferences.

In the same way that Amazon and countless other Silicon Valley firms have used collaborative filtering to make savvier consumers, and TurboTax has simplified filing a tax return, data science can help transform citizens into more sophisticated voters by simplifying the daunting process that otherwise justifies rational ignorance. Ideological measurement offers a tool to systematically simplify complex phenomena in order to better understand political processes. For the same reasons that this helps researchers, it can aid voters.

Another potential consequence of providing better informational cues about candidates to voters is making candidates more accountable with respect to their fundraising activities. As it stands, candidates are more or less free to actively court donors from the ideological extremes with little to no repercussions at the polls. Were these types of informational cues to become important features in defining candidate ideology for voters, it could very well create incentives for candidates to cultivate a more moderate donor base, similar to existing incentives to moderate their voting records (Canes-Wrone, Brady, and Cogan 2002).

There are, of course, potential limitations to this approach. First and foremost, we face the fact that often the predictions made by our models are wrong. However, we have to remember that the bar, which is currently set by the knowledge of the typical voter, is set quite low. Even people who consider themselves knowledgeable about politics have a hard time learning about the dozens of candidates and ballot measures in any given election, which is exactly why the crude informational tools we rely on are so powerful.

Second, if it is the case that voters actually prefer more extreme candidates, then we would need to abandon the search for an electoral solution to the problem of polarization and instead refocus our efforts on reforming institutions.

Thus far we have been content in assuming that our system is broken in part because voters are inept. However, part of the reason that voters have so little information about candidates is that candidates actively suppress the supply of information to voters because it is rarely advantageous to provide it. This proposal is one way of forcing candidates into the open and making them become more transparent about what type of representative they would be if elected to office. Our goal should be to get to the point whereby improving our models improves the politicians elected to office.

References

Abramowitz, Alan. 2010. *The Disappearing Center: Engaged Citizens, Polarization, and American Democracy*. New Haven: Yale University Press.

Ahler, Doug J., Jack Citrin, and Gabriel Lenz. 2013. "Do Open Primaries Help Moderate Candidates? An Experimental Test on the 2012 California Primary." *Working paper.*

Bonica, Adam. 2013. "Database on Ideology, Money in Politics, and Elections: Public version 1.0." Computer file.

Bonica, Adam. 2014. "Mapping the Ideological Marketplace." *American Journal of Political Science* 58(2): 367–386.

Bonica, Adam, and Howard Rosenthal. 2013. "A History (and Future) of Congressional Polarization." Retrieved from http://blogs.reuters.com/great-debate/2013/02/04/a-history-and-future-of-congressional-polarization/.

Canes-Wrone, Brandice, David W. Brady, and John F. Cogan. 2002. "Out of Step, out of Office: Electoral Accountability and House Members Voting." *American Political Science Review* 96: 127–140.

Fiorina, Morris P., Samuel J. Abrams, and Jeremy Pope. 2005. *Culture War? The Myth of a Polarized America*. New York: Pearson Longman.

Masket, Seth, Nolan McCarty, Eric McGhee, Steven Rogers, and Boris Shor. 2014. "A Primary Cause of Partisanship? Nomination Systems and Legislator Ideology," *American Journal of Political Science* 58(2): 337–351.

Sniderman, Paul and Edward Stiglitz. 2012. *The Reputational Premium: A Theory of Party Identification and Policy Reasoning*. Princeton: Princeton University Press.

Theriault, Sean M. 2008. *Party Polarization in Congress*. New York: Cambridge University Press.

13

Using Mobilization, Media, and Motivation to Curb Political Polarization

Markus Prior and Natalie Jomini Stroud

The impact of party identification in U.S. elections has grown since the 1970s (e g., Bartels 2000; Abramson, Aldrich, and Rohde 2010, 197–207). This trend has two components: The proportion of voters who consider themselves Democrats or Republicans (rather than independents, moderates, or something else) has increased, and partisan voters are more likely than in the past to vote for candidates of their party. There are several possible explanations for this trend. Increased partisan voting may reflect the presence of clearer signals about where the parties stand on issues, which in turn allow voters to better act on their preferences (Fiorina 2006). Stronger partisan voting patterns also could result from more automatic endorsement of one's own side and the reflexive dismissal of alternatives (Taber and Lodge 2006). And more partisan voters are turning out to vote at increasingly higher rates while moderates turn out less often (Prior 2007).

Whether attributable to fewer moderates voting or more partisan habits of mind, increased partisan voting likely has contributed to greater partisan polarization among elected representatives. Reflexively partisan voters inspire elite polarization when they routinely give their party's candidate the benefit of the doubt no matter how extreme her positions and when they automatically dismiss the opposition no matter how much the opposition proposes to compromise. When moderates are unlikely to turn out and the voting public is composed predominantly of partisans, candidates may have incentives to take more extreme positions to engage the base and to ward off more partisan primary challengers.[1]

---

[1] It remains unclear if the behavior of elected representatives is more responsive to electoral incentives in primaries or the general election. There is no consistent evidence linking primary voting to polarization. Hirano, Snyder, Ansolabehere, and Rodden (2010) find that the ideological extremeness of congressional representatives is not systematically related to the presence of primaries, turnout in primaries, or the ideological composition of primary voters.

In this chapter, we outline four citizen-focused and communication-based interventions to combat partisan polarization among the voting public. We first explain why turnout among moderates has declined and describe two solutions aiming to get them back to the polls. Next, we detail the rationale for tackling reflexively partisan decision making and propose a strategy for combating its prevalence. Finally, we explain why it may be effective and cost efficient to intervene with youth to motivate political interest and discourage reflexive partisanship. All of our proposed interventions can be readily tested in the field using randomized trials.

BRINGING MODERATE VOTERS TO THE POLLS

Relative to Americans who consider themselves Democrats or Republicans, voter turnout among independents and moderates has declined in recent decades. Figure 13.1 uses survey data from the American National Election Study (ANES) to illustrate the different levels of partisanship among voters and nonvoters. The top graph plots the share of strong partisans among voters and nonvoters over the last six decades. (The dotted extensions of both lines for recent elections are based on the new ANES turnout question, which lowered aggregate overreporting of turnout by about five percentage points.) In recent elections, about 40% of voters were strong Democrats or strong Republicans, a level that was last surpassed in the 1960s. Strong partisanship among nonvoters has dropped below 20% recently.

The bottom graph in Figure 13.1 uses a different measure of partisanship: the absolute difference in thermometer ratings that respondents assign to the two parties. Larger differences indicate stronger (affective) partisanship and a more polarized evaluation of the two parties. The time series clearly shows that American politics became less partisan in the late 1960s. This depolarization was followed by a widening gap between voters and nonvoters. Today, voters are as partisan as the public as a whole was in 1964, the first time ANES used this question. Nonvoters, in contrast, are barely more partisan than in the relatively moderate 1970s.

One explanation for these turnout changes, detailed in Prior's (2007) *Post-Broadcast Democracy*, is that changes in the media environment have contributed to the polarization of American elections. In the 1960s and '70s, more people routinely watched television news than in any other period. Even people with little interest in news and politics watched network newscasts because they were glued to their television set and there were no real alternatives to news in many markets during the dinner hour. News exposure motivated some less politically interested viewers to go to polls. And because their

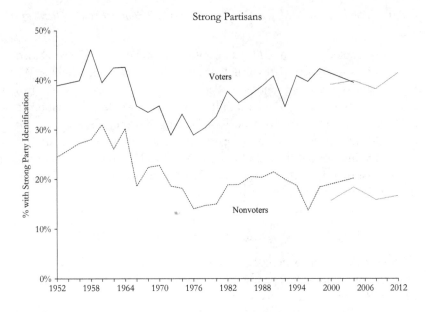

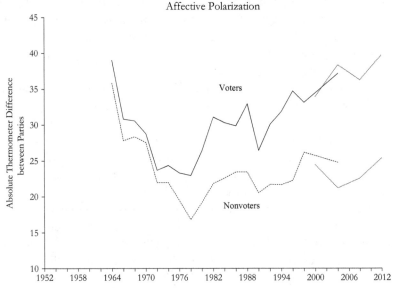

FIGURE 13.1. Partisanship among Voters and Nonvoters, 1952–2012. *Note*: Turnout is defined as turnout in House elections. Dotted line extensions starting in 2000 use the new ANES turnout question. In the late 1970s, the ANES changed its thermometer rating questions from asking respondents to rate "Republicans" and "Democrats" to asking about the "Republican Party" and the "Democratic Party." In 1980 and 1982, both versions of the question were asked. Comparisons reveal that the wording change affected the difference between ratings of the two parties. The increase due to the new wording averages 5.4 points in those two years. To remove this distortion from the times series, 5.4 was added to the difference in all years that used the old wording. *Source*: American National Election Study, face-to-face interviews only.

political views were not particularly ideological or partisan, their votes reduced the aggregate impact of party identification, so elections were less partisan in the broadcast era.

Beginning in the 1970s, the growth of cable television and later the internet created an escape for this inadvertent and nonideological audience segment. With greater media choice, individual content preferences became increasingly important in determining who would watch the news and who would abandon it. Without inadvertent news exposure, fans of entertainment programming lacked the occasional push to the polls. The turnout gap widened between these entertainment fans and people who prefer news (at least occasionally). And because entertainment fans are less partisan, their decreasing turnout rates led to more partisan elections.

Perhaps the most straightforward demonstration of the link between media choice and electoral polarization comes from an analysis of vote returns at the media market level (Prior 2007, 239–244), which found that partisan voting increased as a function of cable penetration rates. A rise in the share of cable households in a media market was followed by an increase in the correspondence between presidential and House voting patterns in the media market and by the correlation between consecutive presidential election results. These aggregate patterns are evidence for greater partisan polarization based on the premise that vote shares for candidates of the same party at different electoral levels will be more similar if people's voting behavior is strongly influenced by partisan considerations because partisans are less likely to split their ticket. Hence, the more partisan the voters, the greater the correlation between party vote shares for different offices or the same office over time (e.g., Jacobson 2000).

Figure 13.2 illustrates the magnitude of cable's impact on electoral polarization. It plots the strength of the relationship between House and presidential elections for election years between 1972 and 1988 for three different scenarios. The solid line shows the actual relationship in this period during which cable penetration rose nationally from 9% to 50%. The dotted line estimates what the relationship would have been if cable penetration had remained constant at its 1970 level of 6%. The correspondence between House and presidential elections barely would have changed in the absence of rising cable penetration. The dashed line graphs the relationship we would have observed if the 55% of households that had cable access in 1990 had already had cable in 1970 and if cable penetration had stayed at that level. The correspondence of House and presidential voting behavior would have been much higher to begin with, but it would not have changed much over time.

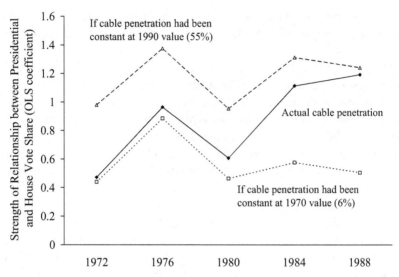

FIGURE 13.2. The Effect of Cable Television on the Correspondence of Presidential and House Elections, 1972–1988. *Note:* This figure appears in Prior (2007, 243). It shows predicted values based on the first model in Table 7.2 (Prior 2007, 241).

When less partisan entertainment fans do not go to the polls and news junkies, a good number of them well-informed ideologues, turn out at higher rates, ticket splitting declines, party affiliation becomes a more important determinant of vote choice, primary challenges to moderate candidates become more promising, and incumbents have greater incentives to appeal to their base. Therefore, because current nonvoters are less partisan, getting them to turn out could attenuate the role of partisanship in elections.

Intervention #1: GOTV to Mobilize Moderates

The technological changes that reduced turnout among less interested moderates by making it easier for them to follow entertainment programming instead of the news cannot be reversed. Instead, we propose to restore the functional equivalent of news exposure in order to counteract the effect of greater media choice on turnout levels among moderates.

One way to give less interested moderates the motivational push they used to get from news exposure is to target them for voter mobilization. One possible intervention, brainstormed with a group of scholars at the Hewlett Foundation, is to mobilize moderates using get-out-the-vote (GOTV) efforts.

GOTV efforts, including face-to-face canvassing, phone calls, text messaging, and mail, have been successful in increasing voter turnout (e.g., Gerber and Green 2000; Green and Gerber 2008; Dale and Strauss 2009). The goal of political parties, campaigns, and many other political organizations in using GOTV is to mobilize citizens who will support them. To avoid wasting resources, partisan GOTV efforts therefore identify and target people who are likely to vote for a particular party, would not have voted without GOTV, and will vote after being contacted (Alvarez, Hopkins, and Sinclair 2010; Hersh 2011, 2012).

By design, partisan GOTV efforts thus exclude precisely the kind of people whose voting decisions would be least influenced by reflexive partisan considerations. Less interested, entertainment-focused moderates are unlikely to be contacted by partisan GOTV. Recent research has shown that GOTV can exacerbate inequality in political involvement (Enos, Fowler, and Vavreck 2014).

We suggest that this intervention use voter files and commercial databases to determine mobilization targets, but modify the algorithm to identify moderates who are unlikely to turn out in the absence of mobilization. In some states, individuals can register as independents. Registered independents, are, *ex ante*, less likely than partisans to rely on reflexive partisanship in their vote decision. In many states, primary participation and changes in party registration allow for rough predictions of ticket splitting and swing voting. Predictions of swing voting and turnout propensity make it straightforward to identify mobilization targets. (With greater resources and access to commercial databases, it would be possible to extend a GOTV intervention to moderates who have a low-turnout propensity or are not even registered.)

Mobilization targets would receive information about the date of the election, their polling place, and options for early voting as well as an encouragement to vote. Targets would be randomly assigned to either receive the GOTV treatment or serve as a control group of individuals who are not contacted. It is possible to randomize at the individual level and use posttreatment surveys and updated voter files to measure participation rates. To link the treatment to aggregate vote totals (e.g., party vote across different offices in general elections and vote share for moderate candidates in primaries) without relying on (expensive) surveys, randomization at the lowest geographical unit would be preferable. Geographical randomization also can be used to link the treatment to subsequent roll-call votes and position taking by the election winners.

Intervention #2: Pairing GOTV of Moderates with Information Treatments

There are risks in increasing turnout among registered independents and individuals with a spotty and cross-party record of past turnout. First, some of them will refer to themselves (and register as) independents, but behave like partisans (Keith et al. 1992; Petrocik 2009). Second, many of the targeted individuals will have little information about their electoral choices and little interest in obtaining this information. They thus will be susceptible to information shortcuts, of which party labels are probably the most prominent. As a result, even mobilized voters with weak partisan predispositions might make their vote decision on the basis of undifferentiated party cues. Third, moderate, low-information voters who are not receptive to party cues may use other, misleading information shortcuts or cast essentially random votes. To the extent that these risks materialize, increasing turnout among moderates may have no effect on reducing polarization among elected officials.

Our second intervention reduces these risks by pairing the GOTV treatment with information about the candidates. This intervention is closer to a functional equivalent of news exposure that greater media choice replaced among relatively uninterested moderates. When these individuals watched local or network news because they could not find anything more entertaining at the dinner hour, they learned not only that an election was imminent, but they also received basic information about candidates (more so for presidential primary contenders and congressional candidates, less so for candidates in down-ballot elections).

There are a variety of conceivable information treatments. The content could vary from an interactive online platform for citizen engagement such as the Living Voters Guide (Freelon et al. 2012), to candidate statements collected by Project Vote Smart or e.thePeople, to expert ratings of candidates' ideological positions such as the scores proposed by Bonica in Chapter 12 in this volume, to media coverage of the candidates. Brief information can directly accompany the GOTV message. The GOTV message also can link to more detailed and interactive information available on the Web.

We expect two differences between Interventions #1 and #2. First, Intervention #2 will have a greater mobilizing effect than Intervention #1 because it not only reduces the cost of participation by informing recipients how to vote but also provides information about the candidates. Intervention #2 would help citizens better differentiate between candidates, which in turn will raise their motivation to cast a vote. Second, Intervention #2 reduces the likelihood of reflexive partisan voting among mobilization targets (even those who would have voted in response to Intervention #1 alone) by providing reliable, nonpartisan information about the candidates. To evaluate these expectations, Intervention #2 can employ the same design features for randomization and outcome measurement as Intervention #1.

DISCOURAGING REFLEXIVE PARTISANSHIP

Unlike politically uninterested moderates, many partisan voters need no encouragement to go to the polls. Yet partisanship can lead to reasoning habits and decision-making routines that disregard alternative views and impede compromise. In this section, we therefore propose an intervention aimed at partisan voters. If successful, this intervention would lead partisans to give some consideration to information and arguments that do not reflect the party line. This, in turn, would strengthen the incentives for elites of both parties to consider policies based on their merits because representatives seeking reelection could expect greater electoral benefits from taking moderate positions and entertaining compromise.

For many voters, their political party affiliation is an emotional, deeply ingrained part of their identity, often bolstered by shared values and important issue preferences (Campbell, Converse, Miller, and Stokes 1960; Green, Palmquist, and Schickler 2002). It would be unrealistic, and arguably undesirable, to create interventions aiming to weaken partisan identities in order to dampen partisan voting and polarization. Instead, this intervention aims to lessen the deleterious consequences that partisan identification has for the consideration of counter-attitudinal information and the treatment of political opponents. The goal of the proposed intervention is not to make people less partisan, but to discourage them from reflexively accepting their party's perspective and dismissing the other side.

Partisan identity has a number of worrisome consequences that can lead to departures from the ideal of unbiased information processing. As Lane and Sears (1964, 73) note, "to be rational a man must expose himself to congenial and uncongenial matters alike; he must be able to look at both and perceive them as they are, not merely as what he would like them to be, and he must be able to retain this information in an undistorted form." Contrary to this ideal, partisans often prefer likeminded over counter-attitudinal information and interpret counter-attitudinal information more critically than information matching their beliefs.

In terms of exposure, partisans seek out political information that is consistent with their predispositions to a greater extent than engaging with the views of the political opposition, a behavior known as selective exposure. In *Niche News*, Stroud's (2011) survey results demonstrate that people's political leanings are related to the outlets that they report using for news and information. Conservatives and Republicans are more likely than liberals and Democrats to report reading newspapers endorsing Republican presidential candidates, listening to conservative talk radio programs like Rush Limbaugh, watching

Fox News on cable, and turning to conservative websites such as the Drudge Report. Just the opposite, liberals and Democrats report turning to newspapers endorsing Democratic presidential hopefuls, liberal-leaning radio hosts like Randi Rhodes, MSNBC, and websites like the Huffington Post. Adding to this evidence, a lab-based study of which political magazines partisans select in a waiting room, or for a free subscription as a reward for participating in academic research, shows that participants gravitate toward magazines that correspond with their partisan views (Stroud 2011, 67–72). In addition to selecting partisan media matching their beliefs, people tend to discuss politics with others holding similar viewpoints, which can inflame partisan tendencies and reduce tolerance for alternative political perspectives (Mutz 2006).

When they do encounter counter-attitudinal information, partisans often interpret it more critically than information matching their beliefs. Interpreting like-minded information more charitably than information expressing a counter-attitudinal point of view is common. It happens when people watch sporting events (Hastorf and Cantril 1954), judge scientific research (Lord, Ross, and Lepper 1979), think about biases in the media (Vallone, Ross, and Lepper 1985), and encounter political messages (Taber and Lodge 2006). People's own views seem more correct and to require less scrutiny than oppositional perspectives. Given the extensive partisan media options available in the media environment and partisans' biased processing of political information, figuring out ways to encourage diverse exposure and openness to alternative political viewpoints seems critical.

Intervention #3: Designing News to Discourage Reflexive Partisanship

Although partisans often display a preference for likeminded over counter-attitudinal media, many also use mainstream sources (Garrett 2009; Gentzkow and Shapiro 2011; Prior 2013). Our third intervention therefore targets partisan voters as they visit mainstream news outlets. We propose to work with newsrooms to develop tools and strategies that encourage thoughtful engagement with diverse views. Work on this component already has begun as part of Stroud's Engaging News Project. In this section, we first offer a few concrete examples of how this intervention can work in practice and then describe the incentives for newsrooms to get involved in this research.

First, newsrooms could build on what academics have learned about encouraging more balanced consideration of different viewpoints. Scholars have shown that, under some conditions, partisans are willing to give alternative perspectives a fair hearing and substantively engage with information that favors another view. Research on self-affirmation suggests that the experience of seeing one's self positively can make one more open to conflicting views (Steele and Liu 1983). In one study, a random half of the participants were given the opportunity to self-affirm by reflecting on a value that was important to them and had affected their lives. The other half of study participants did not engage in this self-affirming activity. Those who engaged in self-affirmation had more positive assessments of the presidential candidate from the opposite side of the political aisle compared to those who had not had the opportunity to reflect on important values. Affirmed participants also evinced greater openness to opposing viewpoints (Binning, Sherman, Cohen, and Heitland 2010). Other research shows that appeals to accuracy can reduce partisan reasoning (Kim 2007; Prior, Sood, and Khanna 2013).

Results such as these could be adapted for news outlets by identifying slogans and phrases that help people process discrepant views more even-handedly. Manosevitch (2009), for instance, analyzed whether news site visitors would be influenced by different news slogans. For some topics, she found that people who saw a reflective cue ("Committed to thinking about issues with readers") accompanying a news article thought more about the article and perceived the media to be more important than people who saw the same article without the reflective cue. Prompts similar to those developed by Manosevitch could be designed to trigger self-affirmation, accuracy, or other such responses and, ideally, decrease biased information processing. They could be tested in news environments, appearing next to controversial articles or preceding a series of hyperlinks (see Stroud, Muddiman, and Scacco 2013a).

Second, experimentation with online deliberative spaces could analyze how to produce more substantive exchanges and promote more tolerance for other views. Practices such as moderating which submitted comments appear on a site, having journalistic involvement with site visitors, eliminating anonymous comments, modifying the interaction tools available, and displaying strong comments more prominently are among the many innovations that have the potential to reduce uncharitable and polarizing exchanges. In a lab experiment, Stroud, Muddiman, and Scacco, (2013b), for instance, show the democratic benefits of using a "Respect" button instead of a "Like" button in comment sections. In several instances, "Respect" generated more cross-partisan clicking in comparison to "Like."

Third, newsrooms could experiment with tools and widgets designed to decrease political polarization. For example, online quizzes created with the objective of informing citizens about various political facts may be a way to encourage substantive engagement with counter-attitudinal information. The quizzes could challenge participants to guess what percentage of the public holds a political opinion (e.g. what percentage of the public favors the

Affordable Care Act?) and then report the results based on reliable public opinion data. Questions also could ask people to guess facts (e.g. how many Americans are uninsured?) and then provide correct information.

This idea has roots in the fact-checking movement, which revolves around providing correct information to help citizens sort through misleading claims (e.g., Jamieson 1992; Kuklinski et al. 2000). Kuklinski et al. (2000) find some evidence that misinformation can be corrected by providing valid information after someone has incorrectly stated what was thought to be a political fact. Tremayne (2008) reports that interactive features, including political quizzes, can help people learn about politics. Mutz (1997) suggests that hearing about preelection poll results can lead people to think about why others intend to vote for different candidates. Harnessing these research findings, providing fact-based information in engaging quiz formats holds great potential. A laboratory test of this idea illustrated greater learning from quizzes than from information presented statically and without an interactive feature, and learning that occurred across partisan divides. The quiz feature also increased time on page relative to the same information presented in text formats (Stroud, Scacco, and Muddiman 2013).

The tools and strategies outlined here can serve as a starting point for newsrooms interested in using social-scientific methods to identify ways of engaging audiences to reduce political polarization and partisan reasoning habits. Experimental testing by randomizing the content to which audiences are exposed provides a way to test these ideas, both in lab settings and by partnering with interested news organizations. For instance, in some tests, the Engaging News Project worked with a news organization to randomize which quiz was shown to site visitors to examine differences in rates of quiz participation and time on page. Geographic-based tests, such as those proposed in the previous section, also could be employed. News interventions in some media markets could be contrasted with those in other, similar media markets to see if the intervention produces evidence of decreased polarization in the aggregate.

Ideas such as these take advantage of changes in the news ecosystem. News media, such as hard-copy newspapers, have seen declining circulations over the past several decades. At the same time, the percentage of the public using the internet for news has increased. Although the opportunity to innovate online is tremendous, many news organizations are not taking full advantage of these possibilities. As newsrooms move into digital spaces, there seems to be an opportunity to influence news practices. Curbing political polarization is reason enough for some newsrooms to consider new strategies or tools, but it is insufficient for others. Another important consideration for newsrooms is profit. Revenues from online news have not come close to making up for the losses that newsrooms have accrued as traditional advertising dollars have declined (Pew Research Center 2013). If ideas for reducing polarization also made business sense for news organizations, their adoption rate should increase. Business benefits could be immediate, such as increases in the number of clicks or time on page. Longer term benefits, secured by becoming a hub for innovative news presentations online, also could accrue.

In sum, the strategies proposed here tackle polarization by working with newsrooms to identify tools and strategies that combat partisan habits of mind. This intervention aims to create opportunities for respectful exposure to diverse views.

CURBING POLITICAL POLARIZATION IN THE NEXT GENERATION

The interventions we have described thus far address the symptoms of a citizenry characterized by great heterogeneity in political involvement and partisanship. We believe that it is worthwhile to rigorously test the potential for GOTV to bring more moderates to the polls and for media to discourage reflexive partisanship. Longer term solutions would address the issue of polarization at its source, in addition to dealing with the consequences of an already polarized voting public. We conclude this chapter by discussing more ambitious proposals designed to make desired changes self-sustaining and long term.

Reaching out to citizens when they are forming their political habits and identities represents an opportunity to change the course of political polarization. The primary reason why many Americans abstain from voting is their lack of political interest. Because for most people political interest becomes stable some time in adolescence or early adulthood (Prior 2010), an intervention to increase electoral participation in a sustained way would most effectively target young people. Likewise, partisan beliefs become established in early adulthood (Jennings and Markus 1984; Green, Palmquist, and Schickler 2002). To create less reflexively partisan reasoning habits, targeting young citizens with interventions seems promising.

For many children, substantive encounters with news and politics used to occur via television (e.g., Chaffee and Yang 1990; Delli Carpini 2000; McLeod 2000). But changes in the media environment affect young people just as they influence all citizens. Today, childhood and adolescence involve much less "politics by default" than in the past. Patterson (2000, 13) has suggested that growing up with broadcast news at the dinner hour is a reason why older generations pay more attention to news and are more interested: "The current generation of young adults was raised on cable television. Entertainment programming was readily available at all hours, and it dominated their TV exposure." If the challenge is to inculcate sustained political interest and openness to diverse information, it is important to figure out a new way to reach these audiences.

Intervention #4: Engaging Youth in Politics through Media Exposure

If the key to reducing partisanship in elections is to raise the participation of moderates and change the reasoning habits of partisans, then the most promising way to do so in a lasting fashion is to increase civic motivation among younger citizens without encouraging reflexive partisanship. A sustained change in motivation that does not need to be maintained through ongoing interventions would be a cost-effective way to curb polarization in the long run. The main challenge is to identify balanced news content and presentations likely to generate sustained political interest and make young people return for more. To address this challenge, we propose a two-part research program that includes both short- and long-term components.

In the short term, research can identify news content and formats that attract and engage younger audiences. Emerging research in the area suggests that there are strategies that can prove beneficial (e.g., Iyengar and Jackman 2004; Knobloch-Westerwick, and Hastall 2006), but more work needs to be done. Exploratory analyses would first inductively identify the types of news that attract youth audiences. Subsequent experimental testing would analyze the effect of these types of news on youth political interest and appreciation for different political perspectives. Such a systematic research program can inform more sustained interventions by identifying media content with a reasonable chance of inspiring political interest and motivating critical reasoning habits among youth audiences.

The longer term project, which would provide far greater insight, would involve longitudinal data. It can be accomplished through a panel study that first measures participants' natural baseline motivation to follow news and politics and then randomly assigns panelists to different streams of news content. By the time people turn 18, individual differences in partisanship and political interest already exist. A suitable research design must assess political interest and habits as they form by repeatedly interviewing a sample of minors and young adults.

Different conditions would compare the effects of exposure to mainstream news and to news tailored to be of particular interest to young people. We anticipate that exposure to youth-oriented news may have more substantive effects than exposure to mainstream news for several reasons. First, youth may opt out of news exposure because they are not well represented in news coverage. Research by Knobloch-Westerwick and Hastall (2006) showed that young people are more likely to select news about young people. If young people and their interests are not represented in the news media, then this age group has little incentive to seek news exposure. Second, previous research suggests that political interventions tailored to youth are more effective at motivating participation than content not modified to target this age group (Iyengar and Jackman 2004). By failing to tailor news products to younger citizens, newsrooms may exacerbate youth ambivalence about politics – and conversely by understanding how to effectively target this age group, newsrooms could expand their reach. This would be a desirable outcome with significant revenue implications for newsrooms.

For youth who are not particularly interested in politics and the news, both treatments amount to an encouragement to do something they might rarely be motivated to do otherwise. The experiment will establish if this kind of intervention can raise political interest among young people and thus increase the likelihood that they will seek out news content and go to the polls in the future. The longitudinal design is very important to answer this question because effects on political interest may not be instantaneous, but rather gradual and cumulative. Assessing the cumulative effects of repeated news exposure over time requires repeated measurement of political interest. To establish if experimentally induced effects become self-sustaining, measurement needs to continue after the treatment has ended.

A demanding test would assess if the intervention leads to lasting political interest, a preference for news content, and an appreciation for different viewpoints so that young people continue to seek out diverse political information even after the stimulus of experimentally induced news exposure has faded. If successful, such an intervention would generate not only more widespread political involvement but also lower levels of electoral polarization.

SUMMARY

The four interventions proposed in this chapter share three important characteristics. First, they all focus on citizens as a way to affect political polarization. Citizens provide a check on the behaviors of elected officials when they cast their ballots. An electorate that privileges partisan purity and intransigence elects representatives that eschew compromise and create gridlock. Whether increasing tolerance for partisans from across the political aisle or changing the partisan makeup of the electorate, the interventions proposed in this chapter look to curb polarization by engaging citizens. Second, the interventions all share a focus on communicative strategies for creating change. To effectively reach citizens, careful attention to the messages used is critical. Even subtle wording changes can affect how message recipients react. By analyzing message effectiveness, these studies will provide important insight into how to decrease polarization. Third, the proposed interventions involve experimental research. Without testing the messages used to engage citizens, interventions can backfire, sometimes even amplifying the problems they were designed to reduce. Using randomized experimental testing, all of the communication-based strategies proposed in this chapter can be evaluated for their effectiveness. Overall, the solutions and approach in this chapter provide, in our opinion, a promising start for combating political polarization.

References

Abramson, Paul R., John H. Aldrich, and David W. Rohde. 2010. *Change and Continuity in the 2008 Election*. Washington, DC: CQ Press.

Alvarez, Michael, Asa Hopkins, and Betsy Sinclair. 2010. "Mobilizing Pasadena Democrats: Measuring the Effects of Partisan Campaign Contacts." *Journal of Politics* 72: 31–44.

Bartels, Larry M. 2000. "Partisanship and Voting Behavior, 1952–1996." *American Journal of Political Science* 44(1): 35–50.

Binning, Kevin R., David K. Sherman, Geoffrey L. Cohen, and Kirsten Heitland. 2010. "Seeing the Other Side: Reducing Political Partisanship via Self-Affirmation in the 2008 Presidential Election." *Analyses of Social Issues and Public Policy* 10(1): 276–292.

Campbell, Angus, Philip Converse, Warren E. Miller, and Donald Stokes. 1960. *The American Voter*. New York: Wiley.

Chaffee, Steven H., and Seung-Mock Yang. 1990. "Communication and Political Socialization." In *Political Socialization, Citizenship Education, and Democracy*, ed. Orit Ichilov. New York: Teachers College Press: 137–157

Dale, Allison, and Aaron Strauss. 2009. "Don't Forget to Vote: Text Message Reminders as a Mobilization Tool." *American Journal of Political Science* 53(4): 787–804.

Delli Carpini, Michael X. 2000. "Gen.Com: Youth, Civic Engagement, and the New Information Environment." *Political Communication* 17(4): 341–349.

Enos, Ryan D., Anthony Fowler, and Lynn Vavreck. 2014. "Increasing Inequality: The Effect of GOTV Mobilization on the Composition of the Electorate." *Journal of Politics* 70(1): 273–278.

Fiorina, Morris P. 2006. *Culture War? The Myth of a Polarized America*. 2nd ed. New York: Longman.

Freelon, Deen G., Travis Kriplean, Jonathan Morgan, W. Lance Bennett, and Alan Borning. 2012. "Facilitating Diverse Political Engagement with the Living Voters Guide." *Journal of Information, Technology, & Politics* 9(3): 279–297.

Garrett, R. Kelly. 2009. "Politically Motivated Reinforcement Seeking: Reframing the Selective Exposure Debate." *Journal of Communication* 59: 676–699.

Gentzkow, Matthew, and Jesse M. Shapiro. 2011. "Ideological Segregation Online and Offline." *Quarterly Journal of Economics* 126(4): 1799–1839.

Gerber, Alan S., and Donald P. Green. 2000. "The Effects of Canvassing, Telephone Calls, and Direct Mail on Voter Turnout: A Field Experiment." *American Political Science Review* 94(3): 653–663.

Green, Donald, and Alan S. Gerber. 2008. *Get Out the Vote: How to Increase Voter Turnout.* Washington, DC: Brookings Institution.

Green, Donald, Bradley Palmquist, and Eric Schickler. 2002. *Partisan Hearts and Minds.* New Haven: Yale University Press.

Hastorf, Albert H., and Hadley Cantril. 1954. "They Saw a Game: A Case Study." *Journal of Abnormal and Social Psychology* 49(1): 129–134.

Hersh, Eitan. 2011. "At the Mercy of Data: Campaigns' Reliance on Available Information in Mobilizing Supporters." Unpublished manuscript, Yale University.

Hersh, Eitan. 2012. "Persuadable Voters in the Eyes of the Persuaders." Unpublished manuscript, Yale University.

Hirano, Shigeo, James M. Snyder Jr., Stephen Ansolabehere, and John Mark Hansen. 2010. "Primary Elections and Partisan Polarization in the U.S. Congress." *Quarterly Journal of Political Science* 5(2):169–191.

Iyengar, Shanto, and Simon Jackman. 2004. "Technology and Politics: Incentives for Youth Participation." *CIRCLE.* Working Paper 24.

Jacobson, Gary C. 2000. "Party Polarization in National Politics: The Electoral Connection." In *Polarized Politics: Congress and the President in a Partisan Era*, eds. Jon R. Bond and Richard Fleisher. Washington, DC: CQ Press: 9–30.

Jamieson, Kathleen Hall. 1992. *Dirty Politics: Deception, Distraction, and Democracy.* New York: Oxford University Press.

Jennings, M. Kent, and Gregory B. Markus. 1984. "Partisan Orientations over the Long Haul: Results from the Three-Wave Political Socialization Panel Study." *American Political Science Review* 78(4): 1000–1018.

Keith, Bruce E., David B. Magleby, Candice J. Nelson, Elizabeth Orr, Mark C. Westlye, and Raymond E. Wolfinger. 1992. *The Myth of the Independent Voter.* Berkeley: University of California Press.

Kim, Young Mie. 2007. "How Intrinsic and Extrinsic Motivations Interact with Selectivity: Investigating the Moderating Effects of Situational Information Processing Goals in Issue Publics' Web Behavior." *Communication Research* 34(2): 185–211.

Knobloch-Westerwick, Silvia, and Matthias R. Hastall. 2006. "Social Comparisons with News Personae: Selective Exposure to News Portrayals of Same-Sex and Same-Age Characters." *Communication Research* 33(4): 262–284.

Kuklinski, James H., Paul J. Quirk, Jennifer Jerit, David Schwieder, and Robert F. Rich. 2000. "Misinformation and the Currency of Democratic Citizenship." *Journal of Politics* 62: 790–816.

Lane, Robert Edwards, and David O. Sears. 1964. *Public Opinion.* Englewood Cliffs: Prentice-Hall.

Lord, Charles G., Lee Ross, and Mark R. Lepper. 1979. "Biased Assimilation and Attitude Polarization: The Effects of Prior Theories on Subsequently Considered Evidence." *Journal of Personality and Social Psychology* 37(11): 2098–2109.

Manosevitch. 2009. "The Reflective Cue: Prompting Citizens for Greater Consideration of Reasons." *International Journal of Public Opinion Research.* 21, 187–203.

McLeod, Jack M. 2000. "Media and Civic Socialization of Youth." *Journal of Adolescent Health* 27(2): 45–51.

Mutz, Diana C. 1997. "Mechanisms of Momentum: Does Thinking Make It So?" *Journal of Politics* 59: 104–125.

———. 2006. *Hearing the Other Side: Deliberative Versus Participatory Democracy.* New York: Cambridge University Press.

Patterson, Thomas E. 2000. *Doing Well and Doing Good: How Soft News and Critical Journalism Are Shrinking the New Audience and Weakening Democracy-And What News Outlets Can Do About It.* Cambridge, MA: Joan Shorenstein Center.

Petrocik, John Richard. 2009. "Measuring Party Support: Leaners Are Not Independents." *Electoral Studies* 28(4): 562–572.

Pew Research Center's Project for the Excellence in Journalism. 2013. *The State of the News Media 2013.* Retrieved from http://stateofthemedia.org/.

Prior, Markus. 2007. *Post-Broadcast Democracy: How Media Choice Increases Inequality in Political Involvement and Polarizes Elections.* New York: Cambridge University Press.

———. 2010. "You've Either Got It or You Don't? The Stability of Political Interest over the Life Cycle." *Journal of Politics* 72(3): 747–766.

———. 2013. "Media and Political Polarization." *Annual Review of Political Science* 16: 101–27.

Prior, Markus, Gaurav Sood, and Kabir Khanna. 2013. "The Impact of Accuracy Incentives on Partisan Bias in Reports of Economic Perceptions." Unpublished manuscript, Princeton University.

Steele, Claude M., and Thomas J. Liu. 1983. "Dissonance Processes as Self-Affirmation." *Journal of Personality and Social Psychology* 45(1): 5–19.

Stroud, Natalie Jomini. 2011. *Niche News: The Politics of News Choice.* New York: Oxford University Press.

Stroud, Natalie Jomini, Ashley Muddiman, and Joshua M. Scacco. 2013a. "Linking to Alternative Views." Unpublished manuscript, University of Texas at Austin.

———. 2013b. "Like, Recommend, or Respect: Social Media Buttons as Partisan Cues." Unpublished manuscript, University of Texas at Austin.

Stroud, Natalie Jomini, Joshua M. Scacco, and Ashley Muddiman. 2013. "Interactive Poll Features and Political Learning." Unpublished manuscript, University of Texas at Austin.

Taber, C. S., and M. Lodge. 2006. "Motivated Skepticism in the Evaluation of Political Beliefs." *American Journal of Political Science* 50(3): 755–769.

Tremayne, Mark. 2008. "Manipulating Interactivity with Thematically Hyperlinked News Texts: A Media Learning Experiment." *New Media & Society* 10: 703–727.

Vallone, Robert P., Lee Ross, and Mark R. Lepper. 1985. "The Hostile Media Phenomenon: Biased Perception and Perceptions of Media Bias in Coverage of the Beirut Massacre." *Journal of Personality & Social Psychology* 49(3): 577–585.

Lowering Barriers to Policy Making

14

Beyond Confrontation and Gridlock

Making Democracy Work for the American People

Alan I. Abramowitz

The government in Washington is dysfunctional. That is one of the few things that Democrats and Republicans agree on these days. Our nation faces major challenges in dealing with such problems as continuing high unemployment, growing inequality, an aging population, climate change, deteriorating infra-structure, poorly performing schools, lack of access to affordable health care, and gun violence. Yet Congress and the president seem incapable of agreeing on policies to address these challenges or even carrying out basic functions such as producing a budget; indeed repeated confrontations over the budget and the debt ceiling in recent years have threatened to undermine an already fragile economic recovery (Mann and Ornstein 2012). But although there is widespread agreement that our national government is not working well and has not been working well for some time, there is considerable disagree-ment about the causes of this problem and what, if anything, can be done to remedy it.

Some scholars and observers of American politics place the blame for grid-lock almost entirely on the nation's political leaders (Fiorina and Abrams 2009). According to this view, what is happening in Washington is a break-down of representative democracy: elected officials are primarily concerned about protecting their own power and positions in Washington and fear a backlash from party leaders, talk show hosts, large financial contributors, and ideologically extreme primary voters if they are seen as cooperating with mem-bers of the opposing party (Eilperin 2006). The solution, according to this theory, is to change the rules of Congress and/or the electoral process to reduce the incentives for partisan behavior and increase the incentives for bipartisan compromise (Edwards 2012).

I believe that this elitist theory of government dysfunction is deeply flawed. Although party leaders, talk show hosts, financial contributors, and primary voters have played a role in the development of gridlock, they are not the main causes of dysfunctional government in Washington, and reforms that focus mainly on changing primary rules or congressional procedures are unlikely to be effective in reducing gridlock. The main cause of dysfunctional government and confrontational politics is the deep ideological divide that exists between Democrats and Republicans in Washington, and that ideological divide is itself based on deep divisions within American society. To be effective, proposed solutions to polarization need to recognize this reality, which is unlikely to change any time soon and may even worsen.

EXPLAINING GRIDLOCK: THE CHANGING ELECTORAL ENVIRONMENT

When we examine trends in election results and survey data on the changing characteristics and attitudes of voters, we find that over the past four decades the parties in the electorate have become increasingly divided along geographic, racial, cultural, and ideological lines. The fundamental cause of polarization in Washington is that the types of constituencies and voters represented by Democratic and Republican elected officials are much more distinctive now than in the past (Stonecash, Brewer, and Mariani 2003; Jacobson 2012; Abramowitz 2013).

One of the most striking changes in American elections over the past four decades has been a growing partisan divide among the nation's states and congressional districts. This shift can be seen very clearly in Figure 14.1, which compares presidential vote margins in states and House districts in two elections: 1976 and 2012. I chose these two elections because they are separated by 36 years and because they were both highly competitive at the national level. But although both elections were highly competitive at the national level, the results at the state and congressional district level were very different.

The results displayed in Figure 14.1 show that there were far more closely contested states in 1976 than in 2012. In 1976, 20 states with a total of 298 electoral votes were decided by a margin of less than five percentage points. This group included the nation's six most populous states: California, New York, Texas, Illinois, Ohio and Pennsylvania. Only 10 states with a total of 63 electoral votes were decided by a margin of 15 points or more. In contrast, in 2012, only four states with a total of 75 electoral votes were decided by a margin of less than five percentage points, whereas 27 states with a total of 286 electoral votes were decided by a margin of 15 points or more.

The congressional district results show an even more dramatic shift between 1976 and 2012. There were far more competitive districts in 1976 than in 2012 and far more landslide districts in 2012 than in 1976. In 1976, 186 House districts

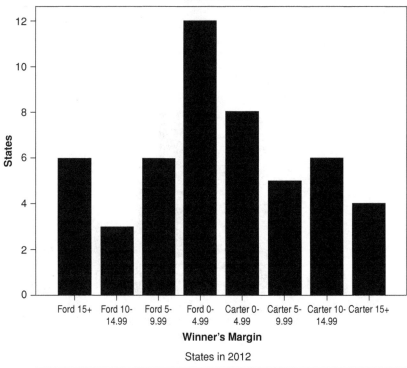

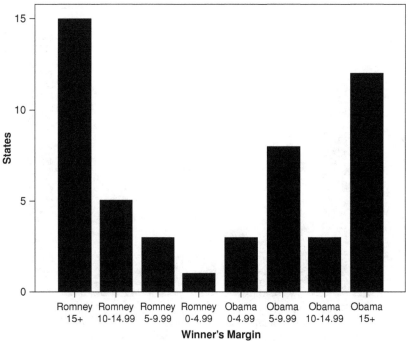

FIGURE 14.1. The Changing Electoral Environment: Presidential Vote Margins in States and House Districts in 1976 and 2012. *Source*: State results from http://www .uselectionatlas.org. House results compiled by David Nir for DailyKos elections.

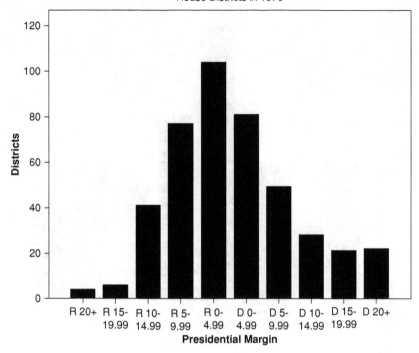

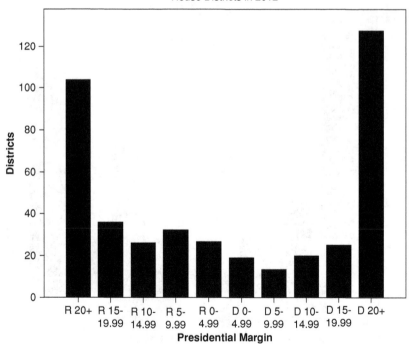

FIGURE 14.1 (*continued*)

were won by a margin of less than five percentage points, and only 26 were won by a margin of more than 20 percentage points. In contrast, in 2012, only 47 districts were won by a margin of less than five percentage points, whereas 232 were won by a margin of more than 20 percentage points.

A growing proportion of deep red and blue states and House districts, along with increasing party loyalty in voting, means that there are far fewer members of the Senate or the House who are concerned about winning the support of voters in the opposing party and far more whose only real concern is maintaining the support of voters in their own party. In many of these one-party states and districts, the primary election of the dominant party is the only election that matters because the opposition party has no chance of winning a general election.

One of the forces contributing to the geographic divide between the parties is a deep and growing racial divide between the Democratic and Republican electoral coalitions. According to national exit poll data, between 1992 and 2012, the nonwhite share of Republican voters increased from 5% to 11%, while the nonwhite share of Democratic voters increased from 19% to 44%. As a result, Democratic elected officials at all levels are much more dependent on overwhelming support from African Americans, Hispanics, and other non-white voters than in the past. Meanwhile, Republican elected officials at all levels continue to receive the overwhelming majority of their support from white voters. This growing racial divide, in turn, contributes to the growing ideological divide between the parties because nonwhite voters generally have much more liberal views than white voters on a wide variety of issues, involving the role of government in U.S. society. As the nonwhite share of the electorate continues to grow over the next few decades, the racial divide between the Democratic and Republican electoral coalitions is likely to widen (Frey 2008).

In addition to a growing racial divide, the past 30 years have been marked by a growing cultural divide between supporters of the two major parties in the United States, especially between white supporters of the two major parties. Since the 1970s, however, with the emergence of culturally divisive issues such as abortion and gay rights and efforts by Republican leaders to appeal to religiously conservative voters, a new religious divide has emerged in American politics – a religious commitment divide (Leege et al. 2002; White 2003).

White Republicans today are much more likely to attend religious services regularly than white Democrats. They are also much more likely to identify themselves as born-again or evangelical Christians. Thus, in 2008, according to data from the American National Election Study, white born-again or evangelical Christians made up 54% of Republican congressional voters compared with only 24% of Democratic congressional voters. And these highly religious

TABLE 14.1. *The policy divide in 2012: opinions of democratic and republican congressional voters on domestic issues*

	Democratic voters	Republican voters
Favor Activist Government	74%	17%
Favor Keeping Health Care Law	81%	14%
Favor Raising Income Taxes	83%	44%
Favor Same-Sex Marriage	73%	29%
Favor Legal Abortion	82%	43%

Source: 2012 National Exit Poll.

white voters are much more likely to hold conservative opinions on a wide range of issues, especially cultural issues such as abortion and gay rights.

Democratic and Republican elected officials today represent electoral coalitions with sharply diverging policy preferences across a wide range of economic and cultural issues. This is clearly evident in Table 14.1, which compares the preferences of Democratic and Republican congressional voters in the 2012 national exit poll on the role of government along with four specific policy issues: health care reform, taxes, abortion, and same-sex marriage. On every one of these questions, a majority of Democratic voters were on the liberal side, whereas a majority of Republican voters were on the conservative side. The divide between supporters of the two parties was especially stark on the issue of health care. In 2012, as in 2010, the vast majority of Democratic voters wanted the recently passed Affordable Care Act to be preserved or expanded, whereas the vast majority of Republican voters wanted it to be partially or completely repealed.

IS GRIDLOCK INEVITABLE?

Regardless of the outcomes of future presidential and congressional elections, the deep ideological divide between the two major parties will remain a major obstacle to any meaningful bipartisan compromise on major policy issues for the foreseeable future. Moreover, unless the rules governing debate in the Senate are modified, even under unified party control it is almost certain that the minority party in the Senate will hold considerably more than the 41 votes needed to block legislation by using the filibuster, a tactic that has become routine in recent years (Sinclair 2009; Smith 2012).

The fundamental problem is that the American political system, based on the Madisonian principles of separation of powers and checks and balances, was not designed to work under conditions of intense partisan polarization. Political parties in their modern form did not exist at the time of the founding, of course. Indeed, the founders viewed parties as dangerous fomenters of conflict. But modern political parties quickly developed during the first half of the nineteenth century with the expansion of the franchise and the need to mobilize a mass electorate. Today, parties are generally considered essential for the effective functioning of representative democracy, providing a link between candidates and elected officials and the public and clarifying the choices for voters in elections.

Within government, parties also play a vital role in the American political system by organizing the legislative process and helping bridge the separation of powers by creating a bond of self-interest between the president and members of his party in the House and Senate. For the bond of self-interest to work, however, the president and both chambers of Congress must be controlled by the same party. When that is not the case, the result is either bipartisan compromise or confrontation and gridlock. In an earlier era of less polarized parties, bipartisan compromise was much easier to achieve, and divided government worked reasonably well (Mayhew 1991). In an era of deeply polarized parties, however, divided government almost inevitably leads to confrontation and gridlock as we have seen since the 2010 midterm election resulted in a takeover of the House of Representatives by the most conservative Republican majority in modern times.

There are two main approaches to overcoming gridlock. One involves bipartisan compromise, which is the preferred solution of many editorial writers and pundits. They wonder why Democrats and Republicans cannot get together and move past their parties' entrenched positions to "do what is in the best interest of the country." The answer is that Democrats and Republicans today profoundly disagree on what is in the best interest of the country. In fact, their ideas about what should be done to address the nation's biggest problems are fundamentally incompatible. As long as these fundamental differences between Democrats and Republicans continue to exist, and there is little reason to expect them to disappear any time soon, bipartisan compromise is going to be very difficult or impossible. Simply urging an end to partisan in-fighting, as many pundits and editorial writers have done, is not going to accomplish anything. As we have seen, the diverging positions of Democratic and Republican elected officials and candidates reflect the diverging positions of those who put them in office. Partisan confrontation and gridlock do not reflect a failure of representation – they reflect effective representation of diverging constituencies.

PARTY DEMOCRACY AS AN ALTERNATIVE TO BIPARTISAN
COMPROMISE: PROMISE AND PITFALLS

A more plausible formula for overcoming gridlock under these circumstances is party democracy. Under party democracy, a system that exists in some countries with a parliamentary political system such as the United Kingdom, the party that wins an election gets to carry out the policies it campaigned on until the next election, at which point the voters get to choose whether to keep that party in power or replace it with the opposition party. Of course, the situation gets more complicated, and electoral accountability becomes more difficult, when one party does not have a majority of seats in the legislature and a coalition government must be formed.

The American system of checks and balances and separation of powers was clearly not designed with party democracy in mind. Effective party democracy would require unified party control of the executive and legislative branches for a long enough time period to allow the majority party's policies to be enacted and implemented, a requirement that midterm elections frequently interfere with. Two years simply may not be enough time for major changes in the direction of public policy to be adopted and implemented. In the case of health care reform, for example, many of the key provisions of the Affordable Care Act, which was passed by Congress and signed into law in early 2010, were not even scheduled to be implemented until 2014. Four of the last six presidential elections produced unified party control of the executive and legislative branches: 1992, 2000, 2004, and 2008. In three of these four cases, however – 1992, 2004, and 2008 – the midterm election two years later resulted in the opposition party regaining control of one or both chambers of Congress.

Divided government has been the rule rather than the exception in Washington since the end of World War II. Midterm elections are a major reason for this. Of the 34 elections between 1946 and 2012, 21 resulted in divided-party control of the executive and legislative branches, including 8 of 17 presidential elections and 13 of 17 midterm elections. In the current era of polarized politics since 1992, four of six presidential elections have produced unified party control compared with only one of five midterm elections.

Of course, divided party control is not the only obstacle to party democracy in Washington. Effective party democracy would also require an end to anti-majoritarian rules such as the Senate filibuster that allow the minority party to frustrate the will of the majority – as occurred frequently even when Democrats enjoyed unified control of the executive and legislative branches during 2009 and 2010. During that period, the frequency of filibusters soared as Republican leaders saw their use as their last line of defense against legislation supported by President Obama and congressional Democrats.

Effective party democracy would require major reforms of the American political system. I suggesting five such reforms that have the potential to increase collective accountability and reduce the chances of confrontation and gridlock.

1. *Redistricting reform* to ensure that the results of House elections reflect the preferences of a majority of the American electorate. This was not the case in 2012 – Democratic candidates received about 1.4 million more votes than Republican candidates across the nation, but gained only a handful of seats in the House largely as a result of Republican control of redistricting in key states such as Ohio, Pennsylvania, Michigan, and Florida. Nonpartisan redistricting probably would not greatly increase the number of competitive House districts in most states, but it should make the overall results more reflective of the preferences of the electorate. Ideally, districts lines should be drawn with an eye toward producing aggregate outcomes that reflect the preferences of a state's voters, even if this requires some creative line drawing.

2. *Filibuster reform* to end the ability of the minority party to permanently block legislative action. The Senate is already the most malapportioned national legislature in the world, giving sparsely populated, rural, and mostly Republican states disproportionate influence in the policymaking process. The minority does not need even more protection against the will of the majority in the Senate. Recent reforms enacted by the Senate have eliminated the 60-vote requirement for ending debate on executive branch nominations and on judicial nominations except to the Supreme Court. But this rule change still would allow the minority party to block legislation that falls short of the 60-vote threshold. The Senate should eliminate the undemocratic filibuster entirely. At a minimum, it should require those conducting a filibuster to actually hold the floor and produce at least 41 votes to extend debate.

3. *Abolishing the debt ceiling* to remove the temptation for the minority party to engage in political extortion, potentially undermining the full faith and credit of the United States. The debt ceiling serves no useful purpose because the money owed by the federal government has already been committed by Congress, but it has regularly been used by both parties to engage in political gamesmanship. In today's polarized political environment, however, these political games have become much more dangerous.

4. *Expanding the American electorate* by providing an expedited path to citizenship for immigrants and automatic voter registration for all citizens.
Expanding the electorate would increase the likelihood of election outcomes reflecting the preferences of a majority of the public. In the short
term this would most likely benefit Democrats. According to data from
the 2012 American National Election Study, nonvoters are disproportionately nonwhite and are more supportive of activist government than
voters. They preferred Barack Obama to Mitt Romney by a 22-point
margin in the 2012 preelection survey. In the longer term, though, it
could encourage Republican leaders to moderate their parties' positions
in order to appeal to an increasingly diverse electorate, thereby reducing
ideological polarization.

5. *Concurrent election of members of Congress and the president* to decrease
the likelihood of divided government, increase the sense of shared fate
among members of both the majority and minority parties, and allow
enough time for the policies of a newly elected majority party to be fairly
evaluated. Electing all members of Congress in presidential election
years would also ensure that they are chosen by a larger, more diverse,
and more representative electorate than that which turns out in midterm
years.

The reforms that I am proposing will not be easy to implement. Although
ending or weakening the filibuster in the Senate could be accomplished
through a simple majority vote to change the rules, implementing concurrent
terms for members of Congress and the President would require amending the
Constitution – something that is very difficult under any circumstances and
almost impossible in today's polarized political environment. And expanding
the electorate through an expedited path to citizenship and universal voter
registration, along with meaningful redistricting reform, would in many cases
require overcoming intense opposition from national and state political leaders
with a vested interest in preserving the status quo.

Party democracy would be risky for supporters of both parties because it
requires the minority party to accept the right of the majority party to implement its policy agenda no matter how much the minority party dislikes those
policies. This may explain why members of the majority party in the Senate
have been unwilling to eliminate the filibuster – they fear losing the ability to
block the majority's policies when they are again in the minority. But the fact
that members of the majority party are likely to find themselves in the minority
at some point in the near future can act as a check on abuses of power or ideological overreach, as would collective accountability for results. A governing

party that tried to implement extreme or unpopular policies would almost certainly find itself replaced in the next election. And in a polarized political system, the alternative to party democracy is not bipartisan compromise – it is continued confrontation and gridlock.

References

Abramowitz, Alan I. 2010. *The Disappearing Center: Engaged Citizens, Polarization and American Democracy*. New Haven: Yale University Press.

Abramowitz, Alan I. 2013. *The Polarized Public: Why American Government Is So Dysfunctional*. New York: Pearson Longman.

Binder, Sarah A. 1999. "The Dynamics of Legislative Gridlock, 1947–96." *American Political Science Review* 93(September): 519–533.

Edwards, Mickey. 2012. *The Parties Versus the People: How to Turn Republicans and Democrats into Americans*. New Haven: Yale University Press.

Eilperin, Juliet. 2006. *Fight Club Politics: How Partisanship is Poisoning the House of Representatives*. Lanham, MD: Rowman & Littlefield.

Fiorina, Morris P., with Samuel J. Abrams. 2009. *Disconnect: The Breakdown of Representation in American Politics*. Norman: University of Oklahoma Press.

Frey, William. 2008. "Race, Immigration and America's Changing Electorate." In *Red, Blue and Purple America: The Future of Election Demographics*, ed. Ruy Teixeira. Washington, DC: Brookings Institution Press: 79–108.

Jacobson, Gary C. 2012. "The Electoral Origins of Polarized Politics: Evidence from the 2012 Cooperative Congressional Election Study." *American Behavioral Scientist* 56(12): 1612–1630.

Leege, David C., Kenneth D. Wald, Brian S. Krueger, and Paul D. Mueller. 2003. *The Politics of Cultural Differences: Social Change and Voter Mobilization in the Post-New Deal Period*. Princeton: Princeton University Press.

Mann, Thomas E., and Norman J. Ornstein. 2012. *It's Even Worse than It Looks: How the American Constitutional System Collided with the New Politics of Extremism*. New York: Basic Books.

Mayhew, David R. 1991. *Divided We Govern: Party Control, Lawmaking and Investigations, 1946–1990*. New Haven: Yale University Press.

Sinclair, Barbara. 2009. "The New World of U. S. Senators." In *Congress Reconsidered*, eds. Lawrence C. Dodd and Bruce I. Oppenheimer. 9th edition. New York: CQ Press: 1–22.

Smith, Steven S. 2012. "The Senate Syndrome." In *The U.S. Senate: From Deliberation to Dysfunction*, ed. Burdett A. Loomis. Washington, DC: CQ Press: 132–158.

Stonecash, Jeffrey M., Mark D. Brewer, and Mack D. Mariani. 2003. *Diverging Parties: Social Change, Realignment and Party Polarization*. Boulder: Westview Press.

Tesler, Michael, and David O. Sears. 2010. *Obama's Race: The 2008 Election and the Dream of a Post-Racial America*. Chicago: University of Chicago Press.

White, John K. 2003. *The Values Divide: American Politics and Culture in Transition*. New York: Chatham House.

15

American Political Parties

Exceptional No More

David Karol

To understand polarization we must understand political parties. Polarization is often considered abnormal and even pathological. Yet this assumption is questionable. Polarization is typically defined as growing cohesion in the policy stands of parties' officials, activists, and voters and divergence in parties' policies (Fiorina and Abrams 2008). A comparative and historical perspective reveals that cohesive parties with divergent policy positions are common in stable democracies. Parties draw support from different societal interests, taking on divergent policy positions as a result (Karol 2009). Party competition also generates "teamsmanship" (Lee 2009), as politicians seek to discredit the other side while claiming credit for themselves. As a result, clear divisions between parties are the norm.

In countries other than the United States, however, strong parties do not produce the dysfunction now visible in Washington. The problem is the mismatch between polarized parties and the U.S. Constitution's separation of powers. This tension was obscured for decades when parties were atypically divided and, earlier still, when the American state did little. The parties' increasing cohesion was unplanned, as was their mid-twentieth-century eclipse. Polarization may abate again, but there is little reason to believe such a development is imminent or that tinkering with redistricting, primaries, and campaign finance law will hasten it. Recognition of polarization's durability could eventually produce openness to reforms that are now beyond reach, such as a move toward a parliamentary system. In the medium term, however, abolishing the filibuster is a more realistic goal.

AMERICAN PARTIES: PAST AND PRESENT

Traditionally, political scientists have seen American parties as pragmatic and election oriented. For some leading party scholars, parties and interest groups were competing forms of political organization. E. E. Schattschneider saw the American political system plagued by "pressure groups" that he thought disproportionally represented the wealthy. For him strong parties were the solution. In *Party Government* (1942, 192) Schaatschneider asserted that "if the parties exercised the power to govern effectively, they would shut out the pressure groups." The famous 1950 American Political Science Association report, "Toward a More Responsible Two Party System," produced by a team led by Schattschneider, also reflected this view.

Schaatschneider (1960) later conceded that lobbies were often aligned with parties. However, he still insisted that lobbies' influence within parties was limited, because individual groups typically made a modest contribution to a party's total vote. Even specifying the percentage of a party's vote accounted for by members of a pressure group overstated its importance in his view, because many of the group's members would have voted for a party even without the lobby endorsing it.

Schattschneider's distinction between interest groups and parties was long accepted; for example, Schlozman and Tierney (1986, 201) state that "party and organized interest strength are proportional where parties are strong, organized interests are weak and vice-versa." A more recent authoritative study (Aldrich 1995) also sees "parties in service" to elected officials and candidates.

A different perspective emerges in what has been termed the "UCLA School" of party scholarship. In these studies (Cohen et al. 2008; Karol 2009; Masket 2009; Bawn et al. 2012) parties are seen *not* chiefly as formal structures dominated by office seekers, but as coalitions of "policy demanders." These groups dominate the nomination process, ensuring the choice of candidates more faithful to them than the notional median voter. However, politicians still play an important role as coalition managers (Karol 2009) who encourage the movement of groups into the party by taking new stands on issues and who play a coordinating role, balancing the concerns of disparate elements of the party.

Yet the key aspect of a party for those seeking to understand governance is the coalition and not the candidates it supports. The stakes in this debate are not merely academic. Models of parties as politician dominated can still allow for divergence from the median voter by incorporating the value of a "party brand" for candidates. Yet group-centered parties that care about policy will diverge more from each other and from the wishes of the public than candidate-centered ones. Parties will support extreme policies in order to please constituent groups to the extent that they can exploit the "blind spot" (Bawn et al. 2012) of voter ignorance.

In reality, the relationship between groups and parties has varied. The low-polarization period in American political history (roughly the late 1930s through the mid-1980s) was anomalous and marked by large regional variation in party coalitions. It stemmed chiefly from the dominance of Democrats in the South, itself a result of the disenfranchisement of African Americans in the former Confederate states. Southern Democratic politicians long represented a very different constituency from that of their Northern co-partisans, especially after the New Deal brought labor union members and African Americans into the party outside the South. Ideological pluralism within the Republican Party, although less marked, was also significant in this period. Into the late twentieth century, split-ticket voting was common. Many members of Congress represented states or districts that voted for presidents from the other party (Jacobson 2013). The presence of these "cross-pressured" legislators often allowed chief executives to find allies across party lines.

The heterogeneity of the two parties had important consequences for governance. Often the working majority in Congress was a bipartisan "conservative coalition" comprising most Republicans and Southern Democrats. Congresses "controlled" by Democrats could seldom enact the Democratic platform. Shifts in formal party control on Capitol Hill, uncommon after the New Deal, did not typically have a large impact on policy.[1] Likewise, whether control of Congress and the presidency was unified in the hands of one party or divided between Democrats and Republicans did not have enormous policy consequences during this low-polarization era (Mayhew 1991).

This period, so different from the pattern in other countries as well from other eras in U.S. history, was also the time when the American state greatly expanded at home and abroad. A vast peacetime military with bases dotted around the globe was created for the first time in the postwar years. Federal revenues grew enormously, and a welfare state of sorts was established from the 1930s through the 1960s. Regulation of industry increased. Earlier state growth in the Progressive Era (Skowronek 1982) also occurred at a time when traditional patronage-based party organizations had begun to decline, even if voting in Congress was still relatively polarized.

The parties' limited cohesion during the period when the state grew mitigated the tensions between the logic of partisanship and American political institutions. Epstein (1986) described "parties in the American mold" as only moderately cohesive, just strong enough to lend some coherence to elections and build linkages among elected officials without overpowering the

---

[1] An exception to this rule was the enactment of the Taft-Hartley labor law in the Republican-controlled 80th Congress. Yet even that measure passed with substantial Democratic support.

political structure. Although many contemporary observers, including political scientists, deplored such weak parties, Epstein found them appropriate for our political institutions. Yet if so, this was merely a happy accident and not something inherent in the Democrats and Republicans.

In the decades before the depolarized mid-twentieth century the American political system saw polarized parties more similar to those active today. How did it cope? Some say that these parties had few policy differences. Yet that view is overstated (Gerring 1998). Another answer is that the filibuster, unimpeded by any cloture procedure until 1917, was seen as an extreme tactic and used sparingly. Controversial major legislation passed the Senate by narrow margins (Wawro and Schickler 2006). Yet there were other forms of parliamentary obstruction including the "disappearing quorum" in the House of Representatives during much of this period.

The short answer is that the consequences of extreme partisanship were less severe in the late nineteenth century than they are now because the state took a much less active role in society in the earlier period. The federal government could have shut down for quite a while before anyone noticed.[2] Partisan strife is more damaging under our current political arrangements precisely because the government is far more pervasive than it was during the nineteenth century.

In any case, the unpolarized parties some remember fondly are history. Southern Democratic legislators' constituencies became more similar to those of their Northern co-partisans following the passage of the Voting Rights Act, narrowing the gap between the preferences of the two groups of Democrats on Capitol Hill. Eventually the number of Southern Democrats in Congress greatly declined as well. Although the realignment of the South is the most dramatic change, other developments have combined to produce the parties we now see. Since the 1970s new constituencies have been drawn into parties (Karol 2009, 2012): gun rights supporters and religious conservatives in the GOP, feminists and LGBT rights advocates in the Democratic Party. Anti-tax activists have become organized in the GOP in the form of the Club for Growth and Americans for Tax Reform. These groups join the traditional party constituencies just as labor unions joined the Democratic Party. Collectively these groups fuel polarization. Ambitious politicians are compelled to be responsive to such groups or risk their renominations. Few members of Congress now are elected from districts or states that supported the other party's presidential candidate (Jacobson 2013), so fewer face depolarizing cross-pressures.

---

[2] The Post Office was perhaps the one part of the nineteenth-century government that was visible to people.

PARTIES AND THE MADISONIAN SYSTEM

The Founders famously did not seek or anticipate political parties. Their frequent use of the term "faction" denoted both parties and interest groups as we now understand them. James Madison was mistaken about some important things, at least in his incarnation as the *Publius* of Federalist 10 and Federalist 51. Separation of powers is undermined – ambition does not reliably check ambition – when elected officials see themselves as partisans first and tenants of the Congress or the presidency second. The extent to which the legislative branch investigates the executive branch now depends on whether one party controls both ends of Pennsylvania Avenue. This dynamic was unanticipated by the Madison and other framers.

An "extended republic" in which no single church or economic interest would comprise a majority was Madison's second solution to factional tyranny. Yet an extended republic – even one far more extensive and diverse than Madison imagined – has proved no bar to factional influence, because factions do not need to be majorities to affect policy. By entering coalitions with other intense policy demanders that care about different policy areas, interest groups can gain much influence through the institutionalized logroll that is party politics.

Yet if U.S. political institutions do not impede the formation of parties, they do combine with them to frustrate policy making. No other advanced industrialized country has so many institutional veto points: a powerful presidency and two chambers of a legislature with nearly equal powers elected in very different ways, and a Supreme Court armed with the power of judicial review. Moreover, Senate rules, although not in the Constitution, are difficult to change and ensure that a sizable minority party in that chamber can also block most legislation.

This multiplicity of veto points in the American political system typically ensures that each party can thwart action if it sticks together. Since 1980 one party has controlled all of these veto points (not including the Supreme Court) for only a portion of a single Congress. As Dahl (2003) observes, this political system has always been exceptional among stable democracies. We used to have exceptional parties to go with it. They did *not* stick together consistently. Now our parties resemble those in parliamentary democracies, but our political system still does not. So instead of responsible party government, in which one party (or a party coalition in multiparty systems) can be judged by voters on conditions since the previous election, we get gridlock and finger pointing.

The ubiquity of polarized parties abroad suggests that it is our unusual political institutions that require reform, rather than our party system. Yet many resist this diagnosis. Our constitutional scheme has lasted more than two centuries and the filibuster is almost as old, whereas within living memory American parties have been weak. Understandably, many assume that the more recent condition should be easier to remedy. For older observers, bipartisan cooperation is still an expectation. Deviations from it are seen as pathologies to be treated. There is a great temptation to blame gridlock on a lack of leadership or to believe that tweaking election laws will be effective. The strategies of many older foundations, think tanks, and media outlets presuppose elected officials free to build bipartisan coalitions and voters prepared to listen to voices from outside their partisan tribe.

There is no reason to expect polarization to decline anytime soon, however. The trends in American political parties, toward division and incoherence from the 1930s through the 1970s, and toward polarization more recently, were largely unplanned. The issue agenda of national politics and the changing composition of party coalitions rather than electoral or procedural reforms have been the key drivers. Cross-cutting issues could again arise, but none appear imminent. So the clash between American political institutions and parties needs to be addressed.

COPING STRATEGIES

If Madison overestimated (or perhaps oversold) the constitutional order's ability to tame factions, he was right that the *causes* of faction are ineradicable in a free society. The challenge is how to cope with them. In the decade since polarization has become a major concern among political observers, many "solutions" have been proposed. Some of these reforms (e.g., independent redistricting commissions or open primaries) may have their own merits. I think the normative case is much stronger for the former, but studies indicate that we should not expect either redistricting reforms (McCarty, Poole, and Rosenthal 2009) or opening primaries (McGhee et al. 2014) to have much impact on polarization. The case for these reforms, such as it is, lies elsewhere.

More radical reforms such as the imposition of nonpartisan ballots – which are common at the municipal level and are used in some county and state elections – might make more of a difference. Some polling suggests this proposal would be popular (Wright 2008). Yet not only would it be resisted but if implemented it would also come at a great cost: turnout is lower in nonpartisan elections (Schaffner, Streb, and Wright 2001; Trounstine 2013). This effect may be greatest among voters of lower socioeconomic status, for whom the informative value of the party cue is greatest (Wright 2008). In an era of rising inequality nonpartisan ballots might demobilize low-income voters.

Moreover, any measure that would reduce voters' information about candidates should be approached with caution. Absent the party cue, voters are likely to fall back on other cues, including incumbency (Trounstine 2013) and candidate ethnicity and gender (Matson and Fine 2006). The importance of campaign contributions would grow. Groups would still organize to influence elections and shape policy, but they would be even less accountable, as demonstrated by both existing nonpartisan elections and the initiative process, filled with shadowy groups that have misleading names financing campaigns.

Once it is accepted that parties will not and should not be reformed away and that polarization is normal and natural, prospects for institutional reform may improve. Even moves toward a parliamentary system may begin to seem less fanciful. This prospect remains remote, of course. Reformers have long recognized the difficulty of even broaching this topic. Even the authors of the 1950 American Political Science Association report "Toward a More Responsible Party System," who gazed longingly across the Atlantic at Westminster, did not advocate a parliamentary system. Instead they made do with a recommendation for four-year terms for U.S. Representatives, elected at the same time as the president, in hopes of reducing the incidence of divided government. Yet discussion of constitutional reform is a prerequisite to change, and educating Americans about the unusual nature of our system and its attendant dysfunctions is a worthwhile activity for scholars and public-minded foundations.

Even in the medium term, the Constitution will not change, and polarization will not abate. These sobering realities make developing coping strategies more urgent. One promising candidate is filibuster reform. Ideally, the filibuster would be abolished, but senators have been reluctant to go so far. In November 2013, however, Democratic senators changed the rules to allow a simple majority to reach cloture on executive branch and judicial nominations except for the Supreme Court. Under divided government, which is likely to persist at least until the end of the Obama administration, abolishing the filibuster on legislation is less urgent, because the partisan divide is the main impediment to legislation. Yet the move to majority cloture on most nominations breaks a taboo and makes eventual abolition of the filibuster seem more plausible.

Some reforms short of abolition have been suggested. Requiring obstructionists to speak on the floor, the so-called talking filibuster, would achieve little. Forty-one or more Senators using the filibuster as a partisan tactic could easily take turns holding the floor. A return to single-tracking of the Senate agenda, customary before the mid-1970s, would make obstruction more costly by blocking all other legislation when a minority is filibustering a bill. Yet this cost would be borne by both parties, not just the obstructionists.

A more promising rule change would allow one senator seeking action to call for a vote and require the 41 or more obstructionists to vote against this action. This would greatly increase the costs of obstruction for the minority without hurting those in the majority.

Another tactic that might facilitate a move toward majoritarianism in the Senate is to abolish the filibuster, but to delay this change for four to six years. This delay could advance the cause of reform in two ways. First, it could reduce concerns about partisan advantage. At any given time a minority might fear losing the power to block legislation. Often there is agreement about which party is likely to be in the majority after the next election as well. However, there is more uncertainty as to which party will enjoy majority status four or six years hence. Second, it is often older, more senior senators who are most attached to the current rules. A change scheduled to occur some years in the future might seem less threatening to such legislators. The reform might also be made more palatable to minorities by adding a provision allowing them to offer at least a couple of amendments on bills.

Unlike the redistricting or primary reforms often advocated, abolishing the filibuster would have an important impact on policy making. In contrast to moving the United States toward a parliamentary system, filibuster abolition would not require constitutional amendments. Nor is it a doomed effort to block factions from forming or a heavy-handed attempt to keep voters from using party as a cue to navigate the political world. It may not be easy, but it is imaginable in the medium term, especially after the reform voted in November 2013.

It is important to recognize that allowing the Senate to function via majority rule would probably *increase* party-line voting. Sixty-vote majorities would no longer have to be cobbled together routinely. Since winning votes from the other side often requires watering down legislation or, historically, wooing Senators with "side payments," bills would probably pass by narrower margins along party lines in a post-filibuster Senate. In that sense abolition or weakening of the filibuster could be seen to *increase* polarization.

Yet bipartisanship should not be an end in itself. Filibuster abolition would not make separation of powers and polarized parties fully compatible, but it would allow a cohesive party to govern when it controlled both Capitol Hill and the White House. The recent reform has reduced the delays in the present confirmation process and the resulting vacancies in the executive and judicial branches. While seen as revolutionary by senators who jealously guard their personal prerogatives, this change, and even the total abolition of the filibuster is really a modest reform from the standpoint of the system as a whole. The United States would still retain more veto points than other advanced democratic countries.

CONCLUSION

Political parties exist in all stable democracies. They commonly work as teams, stake out distinct policy positions, and seek to discredit their rivals for control of political institutions. Today's Democrats and Republicans are not exceptional in this respect. However, U.S. political institutions, established at a time when parties did not exist and were not sought, do not work well with cohesive parties. This conflict was long obscured by the anomalous weakness of our parties and, earlier still, by the very limited activity of the national government.

These conditions no longer obtain and are unlikely to return, so we are faced with a chronic problem. Discussion about constitutional reform should be advanced, even though this is not a realistic prospect in the short or medium term. A more attainable goal, itself not achievable without struggle, is filibuster abolition. Other coping strategies may also be possible, but the first step is a more clear-eyed understanding of the situation. Polarization is "the new normal." Recognition of this fact may advance efforts to cope effectively with it.

References

Aldrich, John R. 1995. *Why Parties? The Origin and Transformation of Party Politics in America.* Chicago: University of Chicago Press.

Bawn, Kathleen, Martin Cohen, David Karol, Seth Masket, Hans Noel, and John Zaller. 2012. "A Theory of Parties: Groups, Policy Demands and Nominations in American Politics." *Perspectives on Politics* 10(3): 571–597.

Cohen, Marty, David Karol, Hans Noel, and John Zaller. 2008. *The Party Decides: Presidential Nominations Before and After Reform.* Chicago: University of Chicago Press.

Dahl, Robert. 2003. *How Democratic Is the American Constitution?* New Haven: Yale University Press.

Epstein, Leon D. 1986. *Political Parties in the American Mold.* Madison: University of Wisconsin Press.

Fiorina, Morris P., and Samuel J. Abrams. 2008. "Political Polarization in the American Public." *Annual Review of Political Science* 11: 563–598.

Gerring, John. 1998. *Party Ideologies in America, 1828–1996.* New York: Cambridge University Press.

Jacobson, Gary. 2013. "How the Economy and Partisanship Shaped the 2012 Presidential and Congressional Elections." *Political Science Quarterly* 3(1): 1–38.

Karol, David. 2009. *Party Position Change in American Politics: Coalition Management*. New York: Cambridge University Press.

———. 2012. "How Does Party Position Change Happen? The Case of Gay Rights in the U.S. Congress." Working paper.

Lee, Frances E. 2009. *Beyond Ideology: Politics, Principles and Partisanship in the U.S. Senate*. Chicago: University of Chicago Press.

Mann, Thomas E., and Norman J. Ornstein. 2012. *It's Even Worse than it Looks: How the American Constitutional System Collided with the New Politics of Extremism*. New York: Basic Books.

Masket, Seth. 2009. *No Middle Ground: How Informal Party Organizations Control Nominations and Polarize Legislatures*. Ann Arbor: University of Michigan Press.

Matson, Marsha, and Terri Susan Fine. 2006. "Gender, Ethnicity and Ballot Information: Ballot Cues in Low-Information Elections." *State Politics & Policy Quarterly* 6(1): 49–72.

Mayhew, David R. 1991. *Divided We Govern: Party Control, Lawmaking and Investigations: 1946–1990*. New Haven: Yale University Press.

McCarty, Nolan, Keith T. Poole and Howard Rosenthal. 2009. "Does Gerrymandering Cause Polarization?" *American Journal of Political Science* 53(3): 666–680.

McGhee, Eric, Seth Masket, Boris Shor, Steven Rogers, and Nolan McCarty. 2014. "A Primary Cause of Partisanship Nomination Systems and Legislator Ideology." *American Journal of Political Science* 58(2): 337–351.

Schaffner, Brian F., Matthew Streb, and Gerald Wright. 2001. "Teams without Uniforms: The Nonpartisan Ballot in State and Local Elections." *Political Research Quarterly* 54(1): 7–30.

Schattschneider, E. E. 1942. *Party Government*. New York: Farrar and Rinehart.

———. 1960. *The Semisovereign People: A Realist's View of Democracy in America*. New York: Holt, Rinehart and Winston.

Schlozman, Kay Lehman, and John T. Tierney. 1986. *Organized Interests and American Democracy*. New York: HarperCollins.

Skowronek, Stephen. 1982. *Building a New American State: The Expansion of National Administrative Capacities, 1877–1920*. New York: Cambridge University Press.

Trounstine, Jessica. 2013. "Turnout and Incumbency in Local Elections." *Urban Affairs Review* 49(2): 167–189.

Wawro, Gregory, and Eric Schickler. 2006. *Filibuster: Obstruction and Lawmaking in the U.S. Senate*. Princeton: Princeton University Press.

Wright, Gerald C. 2008. "Charles Adrian and the Study of Nonpartisan Elections." *Political Research Quarterly* 61: 13–16.

16

Partisan Polarization and the Senate Syndrome*

Steven S. Smith

The rise of the Reagan coalition of economic and social conservatives, with the associated rightward movement of national Republicans across the country, is the proximate cause of partisan polarization among members of Congress and other political elites in the period since the 1970s (Sinclair 2006).[1] The emergence of the Reagan coalition siphoned Southern conservative Democrats from the Democratic coalition that had dominated national politics from the 1930s through the 1970s. In time, the northeastern states lost moderate Republicans who were replaced by Democrats. The net effect was to make congressional Democrats more uniformly liberal and the congressional Republicans more uniformly conservative. This realignment has made control of federal institutions highly contested in most elections and, step by step, has produced the most polarized congressional parties at any time since the Civil War.

This partisan polarization in policy and ideological outlook was accompanied by a radicalization of legislative strategies and tactics, first on the part of the minority-party Republicans and then in the majority-party response. This process affected both houses of Congress and continued when party control of the two houses changed in the 1990s. The character of House policy making changed first, but the character of Senate policy making changed the most.

In the House, the "Gingrich Republicans," a combination of neoconservative, supply-side, and religious-right conservatives, expanded their ranks in the 1980s. They eventually gained election to top party posts and adopted a variety

---

* This chapter draws from Smith (2014). Additional detail, literature, and academic arguments about the Senate are available there.
[1] The rise of that coalition may in part reflect and promote the polarization of the electorate, rising income inequality in America, the antigovernment shift in public mood, and public policies that have shifted in the pro-market direction. These are consequential developments for congressional policy making, but I do not address them in this chapter.

of parliamentary guerrilla tactics to challenge the majority-party Democrats. The more aggressive minority strategies were met with adjustments in the way Democrats managed committees, structured the floor agenda, and named conference delegations, which further marginalized the role of minority-party Republicans in policy making and aggravated interparty grievances. In the years since the 1980s, the procedural warfare has intensified, but the House majority party, whether the Democrats or the Republicans, has had the weapons to win most battles.

The Senate is a different story and is the subject of this chapter. Since the 1980s, minority-party senators have more vigorously pursued obstructionist strategies to block the majority party's efforts to gain floor action on important bills and presidential nominations to executive and judicial posts. The majority party has responded with efforts to circumvent obstruction, restrict the minority's options, and change the rules by unorthodox means. The Senate's traditional informal, civil, and slow decision-making process has evolved into a full-blown case of the "Senate syndrome" – a pattern of obstruction and restriction that often produces deadlock on major issues. The syndrome became so severe in the fall of 2013 that the majority-party Democrats took strong action in one important category of Senate business: they imposed simple majority cloture on presidential nominations.

In this chapter I address solutions to polarization from the perspective of the Senate and make three recommendations. Creating a larger middle in the Senate's ideological spectrum is a matter of restructuring the electoral coalitions of senators. This cannot be done directly, but *changes in election processes* can increase the incentives to build coalitions in the political middle. Holding senators accountable for uncompromising behavior requires that the media more accurately and fully report Senate activity. The *media must be educated about the pro-minority bias* in much of its Senate reporting. Removing the camouflage of parliamentary complexity requires that *the Senate alter its rules to prevent unrelenting obstructionism.*

THE SENATE SYNDROME

Over most of the twentieth century, filibusters of legislation and nominations were rare events. That has changed. Figure 16.1 reports the frequency with which cloture motions have been filed from 1961–2010. Cloture motions are usually filed by the majority leader in response to a minority threat to prevent a vote on a bill or nomination. They have other purposes, such as barring nongermane amendments, but there is little doubt that a large increase in minority obstruction has driven the general pattern evident in the figure.

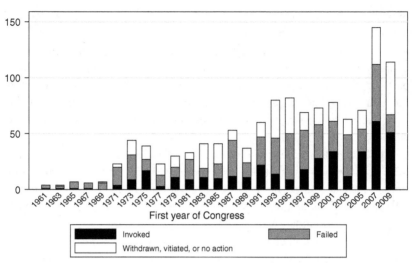

FIGURE 16.1. Number of Cloture Petitions, by Disposition, 1961–2010

The pattern is reconfirmed when we look at major legislation, as in Figure 16.2. In this figure, I take advantage of *Congressional Quarterly*'s annual listing of "key votes," which are the 20 or so votes that are judged to be the most critical on the most important legislation, nominations, and treaties in each session of Congress. The figure shows that most major legislation in recent

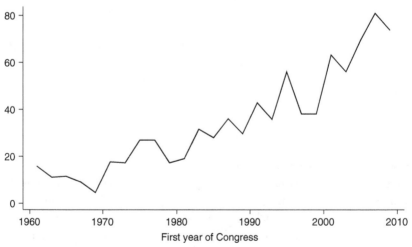

FIGURE 16.2. Percentage of Key-Vote Measures Subjected to Cloture Petitions, 1961–2010

Congresses has been subject to a cloture motion (and some form of minority obstruction).

The pattern in Figure 16.1 shows a step increase in cloture motions in the early 1970s, another in the 1990s, and yet another at the end of the first decade of the twenty-first century, after the Republicans lost majority control in the 2006 elections. The pattern of increasing obstruction is smoother for major measures, but the same general trend is evident. The figures do not separate cloture motions related to legislation from those associated with presidential nominations, but obstruction has been on the rise in both cases. In fact, 82 (49%) of the 168 cloture motions ever filed on nominations have occurred since January 2009 when President Barack Obama took office.

The trend in these figures is only the most conspicuous feature of the record of obstruction, which has affected a wide range of legislation and numerous executive and judicial nominations (Smith 2014, chapters 4 and 5). It extends to the use of holds (objections to taking up measures on the floor), the use of dilatory amendments, and efforts to block the naming of conference committees. It has created a "60-vote Senate," an explicit view of the Senate Republicans that any legislation or nomination of modest significance must be approved only after acquiring the three-fifths majority required for cloture.

Majority parties have tolerated much of the delay and obstruction, but, on many occasions, they have attempted to change the rules and precedents to get Senate action on legislation and nominations. In 1975, the threshold for cloture was reduced from two-thirds of senators voting to three-fifths of elected senators. Over the years, majority parties have forced adoption of precedents that limited barriers to moving into executive session, allowed dilatory motions and amendments during post-cloture debate to be set aside expeditiously, and allowed for quick disposal on nongermane amendments to appropriations bills. And statutory debate limits – often labeled "fast track" procedures – have been enacted for a variety of measures. Debate limits on budget resolutions and reconciliation measures are best known and have been exploited by majority parties in new ways after the turn of the twenty-first century.

Majority leaders have innovated in the everyday procedural strategies, too, creating a kind of procedural arms race between the parties. Innovations include quicker use of cloture, filling the amendment tree, more frequent use of motions to table, tracking legislation so that more than one measure can be pending at one time, more elaborate unanimous consent agreements, 60-vote thresholds for amendments, and use of side-by-side amendments. The threat of filibusters has encouraged majority leaders to package more legislation as reconciliation bills and other kinds of omnibus bills and to avoid conference committees and the associated stages at which filibusters could be conducted.

Leaders of both parties have, when in the majority, threatened the "nuclear option," which involves forcing a change in precedents or rules through a parliamentary ruling about the ability of a simple majority to invoke cloture on a change in the rules.

These developments represent a fundamental change – a change in kind, not just degree – in the way the Senate operates. The Senate was never easy for the outsider to understand, but it was once properly known for its civility and informality. Over recent decades, minority strategies and the majority-party response have created a Senate that often is tied into parliamentary knots, bound by the application of formal rules and precedents, impermeable to public scrutiny, and unable to meet the expectations of the vast majority of Americans.

In November 2013, after years of frustration, Democratic Majority Leader Harry Reid acquired enough support from fellow Democrats to support his point of order that a simple majority may invoke cloture on a presidential nomination to executive and judicial branch positions, with the exception of the Supreme Court. By employing the "nuclear option" as they did, a majority of senators ignored the plain text of the cloture rule and changed the effective rule by merely declaring the rule to be something else. The move was radical by Senate standards, but it was not precipitous. It followed years of minority obstruction and only modestly effective majority-party responses to the intensifying Senate syndrome.

Reid's move will make it much easier for a Senate majority to act on nominations. The move does not affect legislation, at least for the foreseeable future. Moreover, the move keeps in place the cumbersome cloture process that involves filing a cloture petition; waiting two days to vote on cloture, which now can be decided on a simple majority vote; and then conducting debate on the nomination, which remains up to 30 hours for a circuit court judge or a cabinet officer. The Senate syndrome remains real and severe.

ACCOUNTABILITY, THE MEDIA, AND THE SENATE

The media make matters worse. Consider this case: on March 29, 2012, *The Hill*, one of a few high-quality publications that cover Capitol Hill, reported the outcome of Senate action on a controversial tax bill. The headline was "Senate defeats Democrats' measure to kill off 'Big Oil' tax breaks, 51–47." The story continued: "The Senate on Thursday thwarted Democratic plans to strip billions of dollars in tax breaks from the largest oil companies, just an hour or so after President Obama urged the chamber to kill off the deductions. Lawmakers voted 51–47 to move forward with Sen. Robert Menendez's

(D-N. J.) bill. Sixty votes were needed to advance the measure" (German and Ryan 2012).

The average reader might infer that there was a special 60-vote requirement for bills on tax breaks and that the majority-party Democrats failed to reach that threshold. A not-so-careful reader might even conclude that there were only 47 votes for the bill. Actually, 60 votes were required to invoke cloture, because Republicans refused to allow a vote or agree to a unanimous consent request to provide for a final vote on the bill. Fifty-one senators voted to invoke cloture, presumably because they favored the bill. Minority obstruction, not the regular procedure or the lack of a majority for the bill, killed the bill that day. Essential detail did not make it into the story.

If *procedural ambiguity* were the only problem, we might readily correct it by asking the media to add a sentence of additional detail where required. Unfortunately, the problem of procedural ambiguity is compounded by the problem of *false equivalence*. Some coverage treats minority obstruction to Senate action on legislation as equivalent to a mere logjam or stalemate associated with a partisan divide on issues. Even when the outcome is the result of deliberate blocking actions taken by one side, the reports often treat each party as equally to blame. It represents an artificial neutralism about the parties' actions. This false equivalence, journalist James Fallows emphasizes, places the media in a position of offering rhetorical camouflage for the Senate minority. It reduces the public relations costs that obstructionists pay and may actually shift the costs to the majority party, which, after all, is in the majority.

Shortcuts to reporting on the Senate are inevitable. Shortcuts reflect (1) the pressures to be brief and avoid being boring and (2) ignorance of or impatience with the facts of Senate policy making on the part of reporters. Unfortunately, much of the reporting appears to reflect the acceptance of minority obstruction and majority restrictions as routine, even traditional and normal.

Minority senators understand and exploit this state of affairs. The minority obstructs with impunity, and the majority party may even get blamed for its incompetence at governing. Responsibility is confused. With changes in party control of the Senate, senators freely shift from espousing pro-filibuster to anti-filibuster procedural principles with little attention from the media or the public. The accountability of senators and their parties for both their policy moves and their procedural tactics suffers.

THE PUBLIC'S VIEW OF PARLIAMENTARY PROCEDURE

What does the public think of the Senate's procedure? With a colleague, I conducted a survey experiment to gauge Americans' attitudes about how the principles of majority rule and minority rights should be balanced in a generic legislature and in the U.S. House and Senate (Park and Smith 2013). A national sample of Americans was asked whether they agreed or disagreed with each of these statements about majority rule and minority rights in a legislature:

1. The majority party should be able to pass legislation that is supported by a majority of legislators.
2. The majority party should be able to limit or prohibit amendments to its legislation.
3. The minority party should be able to delay or block action on legislation supported by the majority party.
4. The minority party should be able to get a vote on its amendments to legislation.

The respondents were randomly assigned to three groups. For Group 1, a single set of questions about legislatures in general was asked. For Groups 2 and 3, in which the House and Senate were mentioned, the four questions were asked about each house. For Group 3, but not for Group 2, the identity of the majority and minorities parties was included.

The survey found that the large majority of Americans favor both the right of the majority to gain a vote on its legislation and the right of the minority to have its amendments considered. Whatever the group, a large majority is opposed to allowing the minority to delay or block a vote on legislation – this is the least popular of the four propositions. Furthermore, the American public makes little distinction between the House and Senate when expressing a view about majority rule and minority rights. Elite arguments about the importance of preserving minority blocking power in the Senate have hardly registered with the general public.[2]

WHAT SHOULD BE DONE?

It is unrealistic to think that procedural fixes or more elaborate media coverage of the Senate will materially affect the partisan polarization that has shaped the Senate in the last quarter-century. Forces outside of the Senate – those that affect who gets elected and reelected – far outweigh internal decision-making processes and the nature of media coverage as influences on the polarization of the parties within Congress. Nevertheless, changes in Senate procedure and media coverage that might enhance accountability and speed the development of a larger middle in Senate politics are desirable.

[2] Party matters only for the respondents with high level of political sophistication.

Senators, Behave

Observers sometimes hope that senators would behave in a civil, collegial, and deliberative manner that defuses partisanship, builds trust across party lines, and focuses on solving problems. In fact, senators make this appeal to each with some frequency. The problem is not bad rules but rather bad senators. After all, the argument goes, the cloture rule has not been changed for decades, and yet the Senate is struggling with far more turmoil than ever. Willpower – not the Senate rules, political alignments among senators, or even a poisoned political environment – is the problem.

A variation of the argument is that procedural tactics cause intensified partisanship. It is common for legislators to claim that the procedural tactics of the other side contribute to interparty alienation and increase the incentive for procedural counter-punches. For this reason, the suggestion is often made that Congress's problems could be ameliorated by a return to traditional norms and procedures – a return to the "regular order."

Another variation of the argument is that the Senate would be a different place if it had more effective leadership. The claim is that the Senate needs leaders who are less tolerant of their colleagues' selfish behavior, who are willing to call the bluffs of senators who threaten to filibuster, and who demand that filibustering senators pay a high price in the commitment of time and effort to floor debate. With such a leader – the argument is really about the majority leader – the Senate could operate under "regular order," and stronger incentives for good behavior would be in place.

These are not persuasive arguments. The claim that senators' political personalities contribute to the functioning of the Senate is reasonable, but the argument understates the strength of the incentives that have emerged for obstructive and partisan behavior. The demands for senators to fully exploit their parliamentary rights are real, frequent, intense, and often unforgiving. Again and again, direct appeals to senators' sense of responsibility have failed.

Senate Reforms

No reform of Senate rules is going to make a dent in partisan polarization in the near future in either the Senate or elsewhere. Instead, let me propose reforms that enhance the transparency of senators' behavior and improve accountability. The hope is that these reforms, if adopted, will hasten a return to more deliberative and less partisan processes in the Senate when conditions external to the Senate permit.

I would not argue that the public's view of parliamentary procedure should necessarily guide senators' procedural preferences. However, I do insist that

accountability should be a high-priority value in designing democratic institutions. When we can improve accountability in a manner consistent with
public views of procedural propriety, we should take that possibility seriously.
I therefore propose to bring the Senate more in line with public expectations
about good parliamentary procedure.

The spirit of desirable reform is to guarantee parliamentary rights to conduct
debate and offer policy alternatives, but also to give a majority of senators the
ability to bring a matter to a vote. Senators have proposed a variety of plans to
move in these directions. Only one plan, championed by Tom Harkin (D-IA)
since the early 1990s, captures the full dimensionality of the required majority
rule and minority rights.

On the side of majority rule, Harkin proposed that the Senate's Rule XII
be amended so that the cloture threshold be reduced from the current level
(three-fifths of senators duly chosen and sworn) by three votes in a series of
steps until only a simple majority was required. If all current Senate seats
were filled, the threshold would be reduced from 60 to 57 to 54 to 51 over a
matter of two or three weeks, so that ample time for debate would be available
and, eventually, simple-majority cloture would be available to a majority of
senators. In recent Congresses, this proposal has attracted the support of some
of the most liberal Democrats.[3]

On the side of minority rights, Harkin modified his original proposal to
guarantee the consideration of germane amendments before each cloture
vote. From the perspective of writing an effective formal rule, this is a tricky
proposition. To prevent the majority leader from filling the amendment tree
after cloture is invoked, Harkin and others advocate a rule that allows a majority
to set aside pending amendments so that amendments that have majority
support, even those opposed by the majority leader, can be considered.

For at least a handful of his fellow Democrats and most Republicans,
Harkin's approach to balancing majority rule and minority rights goes too
far in the direction of majority rule. The result is that in recent years leading reformers have advocated more modest reforms, including reducing the
number of motions that can be filibustered, disclosing the identity of senators
placing holds, and limiting debate on presidential nominations to low-level
executive branch posts.

The Senate majority has forced adoption of simple majority cloture for
presidential nominations to executive and judicial positions, except for the
Supreme Court. An open question is whether a future majority will extend
simple majority cloture to Supreme Court nominations, legislation, and rules

---

[3] A variation on the theme is to require that, rather than requiring a three-fifths majority for
cloture, debate be terminated.

changes, using legislative brute force again. The temptation will be strong, although, in late 2013, it appeared that at least a few senators who supported Majority Leader Reid's move on nominations would not favor a similar move for regular legislation.

For the time being, the Senate syndrome is just as severe as ever. If anything, early Republican reaction to Reid's move indicates that Republicans will obstruct and delay Senate action even more than before, which will encourage the Democrats to respond with more cloture motions and more resistance to the consideration of minority amendments to legislation.

Journalists, Behave

Without improvements in the coverage of the Senate by journalists, the general public will not, or will incorrectly, hold senators and their parties accountable for their floor behavior. It may not be possible to counter the economic pressures on modern journalistic organizations or to expand the audience for Senate news, but the ignorance and impatience of today's journalists seem correctable. Moving away from the he said/she said reportorial style, as the evidence-based journalism movement demands, and providing a little more context will enhance the quality of reporting. It is incumbent on scholars and informed reporters to show how to provide the necessary detail and avoid the false balance that permeates most reporting on Congress. However, I am pessimistic about the possibilities of moving journalists to provide more sophisticated reporting on the Senate.

New Election Rules

We cannot expect the partisan polarization of our national legislators – rooted in their electoral coalitions, driven by organized activists, and enabled by low turnout in primary elections – to give way without being forced to do so by more moderate political competitors. Those competitors have proven weak. Two proposals for reforming election rules hold some hope to alter the electoral coalitions of winning candidates for Congress and create incentives for the emergence of stronger moderate candidates.

The first proposal is the nonpartisan primary. California used a version of a nonpartisan primary for the first time in 2012. In that case, candidates of all parties run a single primary election, and the top two vote getters run in the general election. In contrast, the most common primary system – each party has its own primary, in which only people registered with that party may vote – has facilitated more extreme activists by limiting the playing field to half of the political spectrum. The promise of the nonpartisan primary is that a candidate is more likely to fashion a winning primary coalition (that is, become one of the top two vote getters) from middle-of-the-road voters. The theory is that, if two candidates from the same party move to the general election, the more centrist candidate is advantaged. It is too early to determine whether this is the bias of the California system.

The second proposal is instant runoff voting (IRV) for the general election, which might eliminate primaries and encourage multicandidate general elections.[4] A centrist candidate who is not the first ranked candidate for Democratic or Republican voters may nevertheless win by being the second- or third-ranked for many of those partisans. Advocates of IRV argue that the need to avoid alienating middle-of-the-road voters will temper partisan, uncivil, negative campaigning and governing.

Both systems encourage centrist candidates to emerge by improving their competitiveness, at least relative to their competitiveness under the current two-election, plurality winner system. Of course, candidates of all political stripes are more likely to emerge, so the details of each race and electorate are essential to more precise predictions. IRV has potential problems of its own, such as the defeat of a candidate who could beat each of two other candidates in two-way contests, and it is less likely to be adopted than the California primary.[5] The California primary holds greater hope, at least for the near term, for restructuring incentives for candidates to make centrist voters the core element of their electoral coalitions.

CONCLUSION

Partisan polarization streams into the Senate through its membership and is reinforced by the polarized structure of the political environment in which

---

[4] In IRV systems, voters rank all candidates. If there are four candidates, each voter specifies a first choice, second choice, etc. The winner is determined as follows. A candidate receiving a majority of first-place votes is an immediate winner. If no candidate receives such a majority, then the candidate with the fewest first-place votes is eliminated. On the ballots where this candidate was top ranked, the ranks of all the other candidates are upgraded one step. The first-place votes for the remaining candidates are counted again, with the new first-place votes included. As before, a candidate receiving a majority of first-place votes is declared the winner, else the process is iterated.

[5] Both systems, like all systems, are imperfect. The nonpartisan, open primary creates the possibility that a major party moves no candidates to the general election. It creates a strong incentive for a party to avoid, if it can, the dilution of having multiple candidates. In the more common two-stage, plurality system, multiple candidates of the same party may run in the primary without creating the possibility of the party having no candidates in the general election. For a good review of the IRV system's strengths and weaknesses, see www1.cs.columbia.edu/~unger/articles/irv.html.

senators operate. The Senate's inherited rules give the alienated minority party ample strategies for obstructing the majority party, which responds with its limited procedural tools. The result is a Senate that is frequently incapable of acting even when compromise policies are available. This obstruct-and-restrict syndrome is not readily ameliorated – the same parliamentary procedures that are used to block legislation and nominations can usually block reform.

In this chapter I proposed three approaches to the problem. Creating a larger middle in the ideological spectrum is a matter of restructuring the electoral coalitions of senators. Changes in election processes provide some hope. Holding senators accountable for polarizing behavior requires that the media more accurately and fully report Senate activity. Removing the camouflage of parliamentary complexity promises to reduce the incentives for obstructionism. However, I am not optimistic.

References

German, Ben, and Josiah Ryan. 2012. "Senate Turns Back Sweeping Oil-Drilling Amendment." *The Hill*, March 13. Retrieved from http://the hill.com/blogs/floor-action/senate/215787-senate-turns-back-sweeping-oil-drilling-amendment.

Park, Hong Min, and Steven S. Smith. 2013. "Public Attitudes about Majority Rule and Minority Rights in Legislatures: A Survey Experiment." Paper presented at the Annual Meeting of the Midwest Political Science Association, Chicago.

Sinclair, Barbara. 2006. *Party Wars: Polarization and the Politics of National Party Making*. Norman: University of Oklahoma Press.

Smith, Steven. S. 2014. *The Senate Syndrome: The Evolution of Parliamentary Warfare in the Modern U.S. Senate*. Norman: University of Oklahoma Press.

17

Finding the Center

Empowering the Latent Majority

Russell Muirhead

Although many today long for the ideologically amorphous parties of the mid-twentieth century, those parties gave no opportunity to citizens who wanted a change – not simply a change of elites but also a change in policy, program, and the general orientation of government. As Woodrow Wilson said in his first Inaugural Address given on March 4, 1913, "The success of a party means little except when the nation is using that party for a large and definite purpose." Mid-century bipartisanship, predicated as it was on the erasure of ideology, brought real benefits, especially in equipping the United States to pursue a coherent foreign policy across four decades. But it also came at a price, most notably in the bipartisan consensus to keep racial equality off the national agenda.

Yet today's parties, which offer voters a real choice, also exact a cost, one that hardly needs to be detailed amid repeated threats of national default and government shutdowns. As Mann and Ornstein argue, parliamentary parties – disciplined and devoted to convictions about public policy – can bring a separation-of-powers system to its knees (Mann and Ornstein 2012). But the intensified partisanship of the moment also has its benefits, which have been too little noted. Parties can clarify important public choices that cannot easily be avoided. Expanding entitlements, maintaining the Defense Department at present levels, cutting taxes, and balancing the budget do not form a coherent package. Today's parties are presenting the choice between additional entitlements and additional taxes (among other choices) more rigorously than they have since the resurgence of partisanship with Reagan's first election. It may be an unwelcome choice, but is a necessary one.

Partisanship itself is not the problem – not even vigorous, passionate partisanship that engages real differences. Partisanship has important purposes to serve. Yet today, the parties too often betray their great purposes. Although the parties are clarifying important public choices – especially the choice between using the government to solve national problems or containing its cost by restricting its mission – they are obscuring other choices, especially ones that would address acute problems in a manner that is broadly popular. And they are at risk of obstructing popular government rather than facilitating it. In the process, they threaten to incapacitate government to a degree that may qualify as a constitutional crisis.

The solution should not aim to overcome party and partisanship – first, because partisanship has a role to play in a vital democracy, and second, because partisan polarization is likely to continue for some time. Rather, the solution should use partisanship to solve some of the problems currently caused by partisanship. It will depend on a party – perhaps a new party – that empowers the latent majority that is now incapacitated by party polarization.

BETRAYING THE PURPOSES OF PARTY

Parties have crucial purposes to serve in any healthy democracy. Perhaps the most important purpose is constructing a governing majority (Rosenblum 2008; Muirhead 2014). The observation that parties "aggregate" opinion is a staple of twentieth-century political science. What goes less noticed is that this aggregation is not automatic. Majorities are not already there in the electorate, waiting as stable entities to be represented. They need to be created. Partisans have an interest in creating a durable majority, because this is the path to power.

What gets lost too often amid the high-stakes maneuvering of the parties under conditions of divided party control is the deeper fact that each party is trying to build a durable governing majority around its central policy commitments. At the moment, neither of the major American parties has succeeded, and the tendency to split elections almost evenly makes consensual governing very difficult. That difficulty is exacerbated by the fact that, with each election cycle, each party can reasonably hope to assemble a governing majority. Yet neither party has been quite successful enough to construct a majority that governs, because neither can reliably command both houses of Congress and the executive. In addition, compromise is difficult because the ideological space between the parties is substantial. As a result, rather than facilitate governing, the parties incapacitate it.

One might think the solution lies in reducing the ideological space between the parties. In some sense, this is right. But the disagreement between the parties is in many respects both understandable and healthy. It is understandable because the translation of general positions into concrete policies forces one to ask tough questions, the answers to which will necessarily cause one to take a stand that is closer to the extreme than to the center. And it is healthy because polarized elites help frame political questions for the rest of us.

Take the classic polarizing issue of contemporary politics: abortion. Morris Fiorina and his colleagues argue that people generally agree on the broad contours of the issue, which seems to be the issue most dependent on non-negotiable values. Most Americans agree that abortion should be legal when pregnancy poses a threat to a mother's life, and most agree that abortion should not be permitted when parents prefer their fetus to have a different gender. Other circumstances – financial distress, fetal defect, threat to a mother's health (not life) – elicit middling levels of agreement. On these questions, the differences between red states and blue states are not striking. As Fiorina says, "When given a stark choice between classifying themselves as 'pro-choice,' or 'pro-life,' Americans divide fairly evenly, with a slight edge to pro-life. But... those simple labels make a mockery of the nuanced views that Americans actually hold" (Fiorina and Abrams 2009, 35).

The question for legislators and political elites, however, is how to translate nuanced views into legislation. A majority, for instance, thinks that abortion should be legal in the case of incest; a majority also does not think that abortion should be legal in the case of financial distress (Fiorina and Abrams 2009). One might imagine a nuanced piece of legislation that could differentiate the two circumstances. If the nuanced legislation is drawn in a manner that minimizes the chance that someone in financial distress will successfully procure an abortion, the restrictions in the legislation might also prevent *some* victims of incest from getting access to abortions. Conversely, if the legislation were drawn to ensure that no victim of incest were denied access, it might be impossible in practice to exclude those seeking abortions out of financial difficulty.

What matters with legislation is which kind of errors one finds more tolerable. Would one rather have legislation that prevents access to some incest victims, in order to be sure that absolutely no one who feels her fetus has the 'wrong' gender gets access? Or would one rather be more certain that no incest victim is denied access, even if this means that the policy will be broad enough to permit some people who think their fetuses have the 'wrong' gender to get access? The answer to questions such as these tends to push one away from the nuanced middle toward policies like those favored by the more extreme pro-choice and pro-life positions.

Legislation cannot always reflect all of the nuanced considerations that inform moral judgment; a law is a clumsy thing because it applies general rules to tens of millions of people in acutely different settings across long spans of time. If political elites are more polarized than ordinary citizens, some of the difference may arise from the fact that political elites focus on legislation, whereas citizens' opinions reflect the moral nuances of issues.

THE LATENT MAJORITY

The solution is not to diminish partisan disagreement, even if we could. Although the parties disagree on important matters, there remains a range of policies that would be broadly popular and that could plausibly elicit support from a majority of those in office – yet that cannot be passed. In the context of the 113th Congress (2013–2015), which was notorious for shutting down the government in October 2013 and producing one of the least productive legislative sessions in U.S. history, it often seemed as if approximately 80 purists in the House dominated 150 more pragmatic types and, in the process, succeeded at wedding their party to all sorts of legislative possibilities that had no realistic chance of passing the Senate (Lizza 2013; Cillizza 2014).

Ordinarily, one might expect that the democratic process should contain, if not cure, the disease. Extremists, if they are unpopular, should be punished at the polls. Or if the "extremists" more accurately reflect popular opinion than the centrists, pragmatists will be punished and the extremes, in time, will not look so extreme. The problem with the democratic cure is that congressional districts more often than not reward the extremes even when they are broadly unpopular. The geographical distribution of partisans combined with the perfection of the gerrymander means that only a small proportion of members of Congress have to worry about facing a strong challenger in the general election. But they *do* have to worry about a primary election challenger. Because the broad (and more centrist) electorate pays less attention to primary elections, even legislators of a pragmatic or centrist temperament will be more concerned about satisfying the extremists who dominate primary elections than about tending to the concerns of the broad center.

As a result, party polarization often renders the government unable to legislate even with respect to issues that command broad support within both parties. That there are such issues may seem obvious, but it is worthwhile to canvass what constitutes the core of "centrism": ready examples include reliably raising the debt ceiling so as to maintain confidence in the creditworthiness of the U.S. government, containing health care inflation, effectively addressing acute environmental problems, and comprehensively addressing immigration.[1] These are not small issues, but a "latent majority" likely exists that would support a prudent and perhaps comprehensive legislative attempt to address them.

In the 113th Congress, there were intimations of a latent majority in the House of Representatives consisting of a majority of Democrats and a minority of Republicans. However, some of the data on polarization in Congress can obscure the possibility of such a latent majority. DW-NOMINATE scores, for instance, show increasing divergence in party means (Hare, Poole, and Rosenthal 2013). Yet because the majority will not allow bills that would split its conference to see a floor vote, and because DW NOMINATE relies on roll-call votes, there might be a "latent majority" that the DW-NOMINATE picture of congressional polarization obscures.

But this latent majority is almost completely disempowered. The solution should aim to empower the latent majority, and the most direct way to do this is to focus on the legislature. In the House, it should aim to diminish the power of the extreme wing of the majority party and, correspondingly, to move the decisive force in the legislature closer to the center. In the Senate, reform should aim to diminish the power of the minority to use the filibuster to obstruct legislation.

Some might think that electoral reform is the most obvious remedy. Two reforms in particular stand out: independent redistricting commissions that eradicate the partisan gerrymander and the top-two primary on the Washington/California model, which gives centrist voters more influence in districts dominated by one party.[2] One state – California – is presently experimenting with a version of both reforms simultaneously. These reforms may indeed relax polarization in the long run (though as numerous contributors to this volume have noted, the evidence to date is not promising). The problem with these reforms is that they conceive of the disagreement between the parties as an artifact of institutional design, rather than as actual disagreements about important questions. Party disagreement is real enough to overwhelm these reforms. Again, the problem is not simply that we disagree about critical matters; it is that this disagreement is preventing action on a range of other important questions about which we largely do agree. The best solutions will

---

[1] I would like to thank my colleague Charles Wheelan for identifying the issues that define the core of political centrism; for a more complete account, see his sensible and astute analysis in Wheelan (2013).

[2] Thirteen states have redistricting commissions that might be called "bipartisan" and that sharply constrain the legislature's power to draw maps in a manner that would benefit only the majority party; see www.ncsl.org/legislatures-elections/redist/2009-redistricting-commissions-table .aspx.

not try to displace party disagreement, but to moderate it, at least on certain issues.

A SPEAKER OF THE WHOLE HOUSE?

In the short run, it would be more effective to directly address the congressional forces that disempower the center. The mechanism of this disempowerment is crystallized in the so-called Hastert rule, by which legislation is not taken to the floor for a vote without the support of a majority of the majority. The Hastert rule is not a formalized rule adopted by the party conference (though some would like it to be) (Kane 2013): it is merely a reflection of the elemental incentives any Speaker faces. Speakers are elected by a majority vote of their party caucuses, and if they do things their caucuses do not like, the caucus can vote them out (Ball 2013). Although the rule is occasionally relaxed – 39 times between January 1991 and May 2014 – such instances are rare, especially when the majority party is ideologically unified (House Votes Violating the "Hastert Rule," 2014).[3] This is why Speaker of the House John Boehner, whatever he might have wished to do, was hostage to the most extreme wing of his conference.

Formally, the speakership is not a partisan property but a constitutional office: as House Speakers occasionally like to remind people, the Speaker is the Speaker of the *whole* House (Green 2010, 14; Muirhead 2012). It is natural for the majority party in Congress to desire to control the agenda, and capturing the speakership (as well as endowing the Speaker and the party leadership with agenda-setting power) is an obvious way to do that. But when the *party majority* obstructs the latent *bipartisan majority* and in the process renders the government incapable of governing, we might question whether it makes sense for the speakership to remain the property of the majority party.

There is an alternative: members of the minority party could join with a number of the majority party to elect a Speaker who could truly be said to be a Speaker of the whole House (this idea is similar to Elaine Kamarck's recommendation in Chapter 6 of "supermajority selection of the Congressional leadership"). This bipartisan Speaker would in some ways be less powerful than some recent partisan Speakers of the House; party leaders could

---

[3] By contrast, in Reagan's first term, Speaker Tip O'Neil led an ideologically diverse coalition of Democrats that included a number of Southern Democrats who supported Reagan's agenda; to hold the coalition together, he needed to allow Reagan's agenda to receive floor votes in spite of the fact that it was not supported by a majority of the majority.

retain power over staffing committees and negotiating for their support on legislation, for instance. The Speaker's distinctive power would merely be the capacity to admit legislation to the floor that has bipartisan majority support.

This change requires that a number of disaffected members from the majority party would prefer a Speaker less beholden to the extreme elements in their own party. Perhaps more crucially, it would require members of the minority party to join these disaffected members of the majority party to vote for a moderate speaker from the opposing party (in the context of the 113th Congress, Democratic members of Congress would have had to vote for a moderate Republican speaker over Nancy Pelosi). In theory, they should be willing to consider doing so because it would allow them (and the House) to pass a range of laws amenable to them, to the Senate, and to the president. That would seem preferable to voting for a Speaker of their own party. Both the majority and minority could continue to elect party leaders, neither of whom would be identical with the Speaker. The majority-party leader would continue to wield power over committee assignments.

Transforming the Speakership so the office reflects its constitutional stature may seem unlikely. But these are not ordinary times, and if the governing capacity of Congress diminishes any further, extraordinary change may become necessary for the Constitution to function. Most of all, this kind of transformation would require a change in the spirit of partisanship that presently dominates Congress; it would require building the "norms of moderation," as Jacob Hacker and Paul Pierson call for in Chapter 3. An outside effort by journalists and political scientists that imagines the Speakership in a new way might, under dire circumstances, prod the latent majority to reconceive it as well.

THE CENTRIST FRINGE

To the extent that petty partisanship within Congress overwhelms prospects of internal reform, it may be necessary to engage the electorate in order to change the partisan dynamics of the legislature. For example, Charles Wheelan suggests that even a small Centrist Party would transform the dynamic in Congress (Wheelan 2013, 121–131). Five to eight Centrist senators could offer one of the two major parties a filibuster-proof majority. For his part, Wheelan focuses his analysis on the Senate, but it applies just as emphatically to the House. The partisan breakdown in the 113th Congress was 233 Republicans and 199 Democrats; the election of 32 Centrist Party members, drawn equally from each party, would prevent either party from constituting a majority of the legislature – meaning that the Speaker and the House leadership would need to be elected by a bipartisan coalition. A Centrist Party minority would be essential to forming a majority in the House, which would move the decisive force in the legislature away from the extremes and toward the center. The Speaker would at that point be beholden less to the most ideological 50% of his caucus and more to the Centrist party members.

The Centrist Party would not need to be a national party, nor would it need to rival existing parties in organizational strength, electoral force, or geographical scope. Rather, it would focus on particular states and districts in which the dominant tendencies of the Democratic Party are too liberal to be broadly palatable, while those of the Republican Party are too conservative. We can get a sense of the potential size of a Centrist Party from the Republican Main Street Partnership, a group of moderate Republicans: 52 members of the Republican majority belonged to this group in 2014.[4] Many of these are from New York, New Jersey, the Midwest, and the Northwest: northern Republicans, in short. Of these, 16 were elected in 2012 with less than 55% of the vote; another 14 attracted less than 60%. Add to these the 15 Blue Dog Democrats (5 of whom were elected with less than 55%), and it is not implausible to suppose that a Centrist Party could elect 50 members to the House. That it might elect five members to the Senate is just as plausible: as it stands, Maine already has one senator who would fit the Centrist Party (Angus King, who caucuses with the Democrats).

While third parties in American politics face daunting obstacles, this idea is nevertheless realistic: because it would not be a national party, it would not need to focus on ballot access across the country, as Ross Perot's Reform Party did in the 1990s. The aim is not to contest the presidency nor to create a third party that vies to win a legislative majority. Although even the modest goal of electing 5 Senators and 35 members of the House would be ambitious, it would not require constitutional revision, a transformation of the existing parties, or structural reform of the electoral system. The resources it would require are significant, but not implausible: contesting 40 House seats and 10 Senate seats might cost about 200 million dollars.

The centrist project does not try to overcome partisanship altogether, but preserves the important disagreements and choices that the parties clarify. It simply aims to prevent these disagreements from disempowering the latent majority and in the process incapacitating government. Its goal is to elect a small but decisive number of representatives who would caucus with one or

---

4 See www.republicanmainstreet.org/members.

another of the established parties, thereby changing the calculus that prevents contemporary House Speakers from allowing legislation to reach the floor that would collect support from a bipartisan, centrist coalition.

The state of party polarization, especially in the House, prevents partisanship from serving its central purpose of creating a governing majority. Although partisanship is clarifying important public choices, it does so at the expense of governing with respect to those issues that command broad agreement. The party system today supplies Congress with rival majorities that can hope for little more than obstructing their opponents. The fundamental normative purposes of partisanship are correspondingly betrayed: rather than serving a "large and definite purpose," the parties aim for the petty purpose of blocking the other side. The distortion of party spirit constitutes a slow-motion constitutional crisis. A plan that activates and empowers the latent majority does not seek to cleanse politics of party spirit, but rather to restore those qualities that make partisanship admirable and constitutional democracy workable.

References

Ball, Molly. 2013. "Even the Aide Who Coined the Hastert Rule Says the Rule Isn't Working." *The Atlantic*, July 21. Retrieved from www.theatlantic.com/politics/-archive/2013/07/even-the-aide-who-coined-the-hastert-rule-says-the-hastert-rule-isnt-working/277961/.

Cillizza, Chris. 2014. "The Fix: Yes, President Obama Is Right. The 113th Congress Will Be the Least Productive in History." *Washington Post*, April 10. Retrieved June 13, 2014, from www.washingtonpost.com/blogs/the-fix/wp/2014/04/10/president-obama-said-the-113th-congress-is-the-least-productive-ever-is-he-right/.

Fiorina. Morris P., and Samuel J. Abrams. 2009. *Disconnect: The Breakdown of Representation in American Politics*. Norman: University of Oklahoma Press.

Green, Matthew N. 2010. *The Speaker of the House: A Study in Leadership*. New Haven: Yale University Press.

Hare, Christopher, Keith T. Poole, and Howard Rosenthal. 2013. "An Update on Political Polarization through the 112th Congress." *Voteview Blog*, January 16. Retrieved September 28, 2013, from voteview.com/blog/? p = 726.

"House Votes Violating the 'Hastert Rule.'" 2014. *New York Times*. Retrieved October 10, 2014, from http://politics.nytimes.com/congress/votes/house/hastert-rule.

Kane, Paul. 2013. "What the Hastert Rule Fight Tells Us About House Republicans." *Washington Post*, June 17. Retrieved from www.washingtonpost.com/blogs/the-fix/wp/2013/06/17/what-the-hastert-rule-fight-tells-us-about-house-republicans.

Lizza, Ryan. 2013. "Where the GOP's Suicide Caucus Lives." *The New Yorker*, September 26.

Mann, Thomas E., and Norman J. Ornstein. 2012. *It's Even Worse than It Looks: How the American Constitutional System Collided with the New Politics of Extremism*. New York: Basic Books.

Muirhead, Russell. 2012. "A Bipartisan Speaker of the House." *Balkinization*, December 26. Retrieved from http://balkin.blogspot.com/2012.

Muirhead, Russell. 2014. *The Promise of Party in a Polarized Age*. Cambridge, MA: Harvard University Press.

Rosenblum, Nancy. 2008. *On the Side of the Angels: An Appreciation of Parties and Partisanship*. Princeton: Princeton University Press.

Wheelan, Charles. 2013. *The Centrist Manifesto*. New York: W. W. Norton.

18

Making Deals in Congress*

Sarah A. Binder and Frances E. Lee

There is one unavoidable fact about legislating in a democratic system. No single person, faction, or interest can get everything it wants. Legislating inevitably means compromising, except in the rare circumstances when consensus is so strong that one dominant view can prevail with ease.

Robert Kaiser 2013, p. 174

Compromise may be the "unavoidable fact" about legislating in a democratic system. Yet, scholars have few systematic answers to this question: How do legislators "get to yes"? To put the question in language more familiar to students of politics: How do politicians with diverse, often-conflicting interests and policy preferences reach agreements on public policy in a legislative body of co-equals? In this chapter, we offer a perspective on deal making in the contemporary Congress, highlighting the impact of political and partisan considerations on lawmakers' abilities to secure policy agreements.

Negotiation in Congress is never solely about policy: politics and policy are always intertwined. Congressional negotiations thus differ from those in the private sector, in which actors seek to maximize benefits and minimize costs and the substantive terms of an offer are paramount. Congressional deal making occurs in a political context that shapes the willingness of party leaders and their "rank and file" to negotiate at all or to accept even favorable offers. Lawmakers must justify votes and policy compromises to their constituencies, whereas party leaders must attend to key groups in the party coalition and to the party's

* We thank former chair of the House Financial Services Committee, Representative Barney Frank, for his valuable insights on congressional negotiation. Frank's examples and analyses were most helpful in orienting our thinking from the outset. We also benefited from a discussion with Gary Andres, staff director of the House Energy and Commerce Committee. This chapter originally appeared in Jane Mansbridge & Cathie Jo Martin, eds., *Negotiating Agreement in Congress* (Washington, D.C.: APSA, 2013).

public image. Given the political context of congressional negotiations, we evaluate the tools and institutional arrangements that make deals in Congress more likely – emphasizing that conflicting incentives and interests place a premium on negotiating out of the public eye. We conclude with a broader assessment of the prospects for negotiation in a party-polarized Congress.

DISTRIBUTIVE VERSUS INTEGRATIVE MODELS OF NEGOTIATION IN CONGRESS

Negotiation theorists typically distinguish between distributive and integrative solutions to public problems (see Chapters 4 and 5). Distributive solutions involve zero-sum bargaining over extant benefits. As Riker (1962) emphasized in his work on political coalitions, what one party gains, the other must lose. Distributive models depict congressional bargaining as a matter of splitting differences over divisible policies. In contrast, integrative solutions emphasize expanding "the pie" rather than just doling out its pieces. Follett (1925/1942) first developed the logic of integrative solutions – that is, agreements that create value by taking advantage of differences in players' valuations of problems and solutions. Exploiting differences across players' priorities – achieved by "logrolling," vote trading, or crafting multidimensional agreements – allows negotiators to enlarge the pie, moving negotiators past narrow, distributive solutions.

Legislative scholars have developed a robust literature on bargaining and coalition building in Congress, almost all of which is predicated on a distributive model of politics. We suspect that congressional studies favor a distributive framework for both empirical and theoretical reasons. Readily available data and contemporary modes of modeling discourage a focus on integrative solutions. For decades, Sorauf's (1992, 164) "law of available data" has steered students to design their analyses of Congress at the level of the individual legislator. The entire floor roll-call record across congressional history is readily available, encouraging scholars to make congressional voting the focus of their studies. With the addition of Poole and Rosenthal's (1997, 2013) DW-NOMINATE data, which provide robust estimates of legislators' revealed preferences, proxies for legislators' policy positions over the full course of congressional history are also at scholars' fingertips.

Analyses of such data has yielded a wealth of knowledge about the forces that shape lawmakers' votes. Costs are also apparent: we know an enormous amount about the choices legislators face when they take positions on policy and procedural questions, but relatively little about the politics and processes that facilitate the underlying deals and terms of policy proposals. Arnold's

(1990) analysis of leaders' strategies for forming successful coalitions provided an important exception. Focusing on the substance and politics of winning coalitions, of course, is challenging: no comparable databases track the formation of legislative deals. To make matters more difficult, virtually all such deals are negotiated out of the public eye. Subsequent reporting about what terms were offered or refused is often contested; therefore, it may be impossible to construct a consensus account of what transpired. Even if we knew which alternatives were on the table during negotiations, we would still need to know how lawmakers crafted and chose among them.

The influence of formal modeling also has encouraged a focus on distributive policy making. For example, Baron and Ferejohn's (1989) foundational work in this area – "Bargaining in Legislatures" – focuses on divide-the-dollar games. Elaborations of such formal models include important work on vote buying, coalition formation, coalition sizes, and policy outcomes. These are significant contributions to our understanding of Congress. Still, these models emphasize a view of congressional bargaining as a matter of splitting differences rather than creating value. If successful negotiation often requires enlarging the pie, then existing formal models offer only a limited basis for understanding congressional deal making.

Congressional scholars' focus on the spatial model of politics also reinforces the primacy of distributive politics: players come to the table with exogenously fixed policy preferences, hold perfect information about fellow players' preferences, and either accept or reject proposals following a set of rules for play. This basic framework works well for reaching agreement on policy when bargaining occurs over who gets what at whose expense in splitting divisible benefits; for example, see Krehbiel and Rivers' exemplary (1988) study of changes to the minimum wage.

The key assumptions of the spatial model – especially fixed, exogenous preferences and complete information – are difficult to fit into models of negotiation that involve integrative solutions. The assumption of fixed preferences is incompatible with a view of politics that suggests lawmakers' preferences are endogenous to the legislative process (Evans 2011). Decades of research suggest that, although lawmakers hold a set of core beliefs, their policy preferences (and, hence, the deals to which they are likely to agree) develop as they weigh input from various constituencies and stakeholders. Assuming complete information about players' preferences also limits the reach of the spatial model in settings that entail expanding the number of available solutions. As Arnold (1990) argued, lawmakers with similar preferences might reach different conclusions about the policy and electoral consequences of competing alternatives, raising uncertainty for leaders in negotiating agreements with opponents and partisans alike.

Students of Congress recognize that spatial and formal models, by design, offer stylized accounts of legislative politics. The empirical literature on Congress is replete with accounts of the messy dynamics that underlie legislative politics. Here, we note only the tip of the iceberg: in addition to the study by Arnold (1990), Sinclair's (2006) work emphasizes how party leaders exploit procedural tools to construct multidimensional packages, allowing them to assemble complex bargains that meet competing demands. Smith's (2007) treatise on legislative parties in Congress encouraged more careful thought about how legislators' and leaders' multiple goals influence their strategic choices and shape policy outcomes. Evans's (2004) exploration of pork barreling explained how legislative "lard" can be used to buy votes for broad-based national legislation. Arguably, distributive bargaining is more often an instrument for crafting integrative solutions than an end in itself.

STARTING PREMISES

Politics and policy are tightly intertwined on Capitol Hill. Former Representative Barney Frank (D-Mass.) stated it well: "Nobody pushes for unpopular policies." This simple premise has important implications for understanding how coalition leaders build winning coalitions in Congress. Deal making is not merely a matter of finding the ideological "sweet spot" between competing coalitions. Instead, common ground is typically a joint function of lawmakers' policy views and political calculations. As we elaborate herein, three key political premises continually shape congressional negotiations over policy.

First, lawmakers represent constituencies. Stated more accurately, they represent political coalitions within the constituencies that elected them. Officeholders must manage these coalitions. These "intense demanders," who are critical to politicians' fundraising and activist base, often sharply constrain lawmakers' flexibility on key issues (Karol 2009). When legislators or their leaders negotiate over policy, they know that they will have to justify any deals to their active supporters. The catch, as Gilmour (1995, 25–37) explained, is that such constituencies often have little understanding of what is and is not possible in Congress. Constituents will not be happy to hear that they must settle for less than what they wanted or that they must make unpalatable concessions to achieve desired goals. Not being a party to the negotiations themselves, they must trust what their representative tells them about what was achievable. Rather than accept disappointment, they may prefer to listen to other voices – such as those of activist group leaders or congressional hardliners – who tell them that a better deal was possible. As a consequence, lawmakers must continually cope with constituencies, activists, and supporters who push them to take a tougher line and refuse compromise. "On both sides, the task is dealing with all the people who believe that insufficient purity is the reason why their party hasn't won more elections," observed Representative Frank.

Even if a particular deal is the best that can win sufficient support in Congress to pass – and would be an improvement, in their view, over the policy status quo – lawmakers still may conclude that they would be unable to defend it successfully with their constituencies. Lawmakers may well reject "half a loaf" and settle for nothing, if taking the half would be understood by constituents or denounced by important groups or activists as an unacceptable sellout. Pundits today call this a fear of being "primaried," although the electoral imperative to satisfy activist constituencies has deep roots in congressional politics.

Second, as Mayhew (1974) taught us, individual lawmakers are responsible for the positions they take (i.e., their votes), but not for the resulting policy outcomes. In almost all cases, blame or credit for the outcome of negotiations in Congress does not attach to individual lawmakers, largely because a single lawmaker's vote rarely decides an outcome. Lawmakers therefore weigh vote decisions for their effects on their reputations as politicians, not only for their effects on public policy. Lawmakers will not necessarily vote for a deal that they support on policy grounds if the vote could harm their public image; conversely, they might vote in favor of a deal to which they object on policy terms if the vote would be helpful to their image.

Third, lawmakers affiliate with political parties in a highly competitive, two-party system. Party leaders are responsible for stewardship of the party "brand" – that is, for protecting the party's public image on issues. Individual members, for their part, care about the party brand name to the extent that they perceive a favorable party image as important to their party's majority status in Congress or to their own electoral interests. In promoting a party's brand name, the question is often whether party leaders and members want a law or a political issue addressed. When a party perceives that it has an advantage with the public on an issue, it may prefer to keep its image unsullied by the compromises that are usually necessary to legislate. The party may see more political benefit in refusing to negotiate and in preserving the issue for future campaigns. Nearly two decades ago, Gilmour (1995, 9) termed this dynamic "strategic disagreement": parties to a potential deal "avoid the best agreement that can be gotten given the circumstances in order to seek political gain." In short, explicitly partisan political considerations condition the opportunities for deal making on policy issues.

The 2012 congressional negotiations over the so-called fiscal cliff offer an example of the complex interplay between politics and policy. With the tax cuts originally passed in 2001 under President George W. Bush set to expire at the end of 2012, Speaker of the House John Boehner (R-Ohio) sought support from his party's conference for legislation that would have made permanent all of the tax cuts for those with taxable incomes less than $1 million. Preserving the Bush tax cuts was unquestionably a consensus policy objective among congressional Republicans. Passage of Boehner's so-called Plan B proposal would have strengthened the House Republican leader's negotiating position vis-à-vis the Democratic-controlled Senate and President Barack Obama, who wanted to raise taxes on taxpayers at the much lower income level of $250,000. In addition, House passage of the bill would have enhanced the Republican public image by portraying the party as fighting for tax cuts that benefited those outside the richest 1% of Americans. Under circumstances in which the alternative was the imminent expiration of all of the Bush tax cuts, Boehner's proposal was a vast improvement over the status quo for all lawmakers who wanted low taxes; it also put the party more in tune with national public opinion. Nevertheless, Boehner could not win the support of a key contingent of Republicans who refused to cast a vote that allowed anyone's taxes to rise. As a result, Boehner was sidelined from further negotiation, with the eventual deal worked out between the White House and Senate leadership.

The Plan B episode illustrates that a proposal's policy effect is not the only matter at stake in congressional deal making. Members and party leaders continually take stock of political stakes as well. Moreover, congressional parties are not unitary actors, and party leaders have limited power to command followership from their rank and file. With respect to Boehner's Plan B, considerations of policy and the party brand pulled in the opposite direction from many lawmakers' political calculations. Regardless of the strength of the party leaders' case in favor of Plan B, a group of Republicans would simply not allow themselves to be personally associated with a compromise on the issue: their individual reputations as authentic, principled conservatives took priority.

The premise that policy and political choices are tightly interwoven has implications for how we explain the dynamics of negotiating in Congress. If politics always took a back seat to policy considerations, then deal making in Congress would consist of distributive and integrative bargaining to locate a common zone of policy agreement. However, if both policy and politics matter, then the players' willingness to negotiate or sign onto compromises becomes a threshold matter. In the following section, we explore the politics of crossing that threshold and the implications for negotiations that often ensue.

GETTING TO AGREEMENT: KEY ELEMENTS

In this section, we outline key elements of congressional negotiations on major public problems. We explore the central players, the terrain of potential policy solutions, and the dynamics of interparty and intraparty bargaining. Collectively, these elements of congressional deal making lead to the expectation that successful negotiations in Congress usually revolve around the task of building integrative (or at least partially integrative) solutions to policy dilemmas.

Players. Generally, party and committee leaders of the majority party take the lead in negotiating policy deals. The rise of party leaders as pivotal negotiators reflects the emergence of "unorthodox lawmaking," a term coined by Sinclair (2012) to capture the nature of lawmaking in a polarized and increasingly centralized legislative institution. There is certainly room for issue entrepreneurship in some cases (see Volden and Wiseman 2009; Wawro 2000). Recently we saw entrepreneurs emerging on the complex matter of immigration reform in 2013, although there seems to be more room for such activity in the Senate than in the House. Even when authority to negotiate deals devolves to committee or other coalition leaders and the involvement of party leaders is difficult to detect, in the contemporary Congress, those leaders are rarely left uninformed.

Negotiation terrain. One of the most important differences between private negotiations and deal making in Congress is the broad – perhaps limitless – reach of congressional jurisdiction. As Representative Frank framed it, "The key to understanding deal making in Congress is to remember that the ankle bone is connected to the shoulder bone. Anything can be the basis of a deal. . . . In Congress, the jurisdiction is universal." The omnicompetence of congressional authority makes possible frequent integrative solutions to policy problems. Congress's broad reach allows leaders to enlarge the policy pie and to secure positive-sum solutions to otherwise intractable problems. Unrelated or loosely related issues can be addressed simultaneously, giving different lawmakers alternative reasons to sign onto a package. "Different priorities across issues," Representative Frank noted, "are often the basis of an agreement."

In a book subtitled *How Congress Really Works*, Representative Henry Waxman (D-Calif.) views integrative, win-win negotiation as the basis of most successful congressional deals. "The greatest misconception about making laws is the assumption that most problems have clear solutions, and reaching compromise mainly entails splitting the difference between partisan extremes," he wrote (2009, 77). Waxman offered the Food Quality Protection Act of 1996 as one example. This law, a comprehensive new set of regulations governing pesticides in food, was passed during conditions of divided government, despite long-standing partisan stalemate over regulatory policy in this area. According to Waxman, he and Representative Tom Bliley (R-Va.), chair of the House Commerce Committee, were able to negotiate a deal that took advantage of their different priorities. Conservative Republican Bliley prioritized repealing a strict regulation of carcinogens in processed food – a regulation that experts expected would be more rigorously enforced in the wake of a court ruling. Liberal Democrat Waxman was most concerned with the lack of regulations on carcinogens in *raw* foods – to his mind, a greater problem given the impact of such pesticides on children. Waxman, Bliley, and representatives of the affected industries struck an accord that established a single standard governing pesticides in food – raw or processed – that required a reasonable certainty of "no harm" to consumers (including special considerations for infants and children). Their solution won unanimous approval in the House, verbatim acceptance in the Senate, and President Bill Clinton's signature.

The search for win-win solutions is labor-intensive, as this and other case studies recount. Information must be gathered from many sources – for example, interest groups, affected industries, policy experts, activists, and government agencies – before members and their staffs can understand the causes and dimensions of a policy problem and see a pathway to possible solutions. Lengthy discussions and negotiations are often needed for the different actors and stakeholders to understand one another's interests. Many, probably most, such negotiations fail. However, these processes of information gathering, consultation, and discussion lay the groundwork for creative problem solving that can address the concerns of all key interests at once. The result can be legislation that commands widespread support, even from players who initially saw their interests and preferences as opposed.

Interparty negotiations. In interparty negotiations, there is no default presumption of cooperation. Given the two parties' diametrically opposed electoral interests in winning and retaining control of Congress, members generally regard initiatives sponsored by the opposing party with suspicion and skepticism. In the contemporary Congress, there may even be a default presumption of opposition, such that the minority party will resist the majority's proposals unless it is actively courted and successfully co-opted. As one experienced congressional negotiator noted, "It is not uncommon for members of one party to oppose legislation merely because the other political party champions it" (Barry 2003, 434).

Before commencing negotiations across party lines, members and leaders of both parties ask: What are the political consequences of refusing negotiation? Who will suffer more politically from a deal not being done? The answers to those questions determine each side's bargaining power. The greater (lower) is the cost to the minority of saying no, the greater (lower) is the majority's bargaining leverage. Because both parties gauge the political fallout from a failure to produce a deal, Representative Frank explained, "It boils down to which side can message it better." Those who perceive themselves on the right side of public opinion will see themselves as having political leverage. A minority party that expects to win the message battle may disengage altogether. A majority party that expects to win the message battle will see less need for policy concessions to the opposition. In contrast, anticipation of losing the "blame game" can drive partisans to the negotiating table.

From the majority's perspective, coalition leaders must decide whether to try to include the minority. Given the differences in House and Senate rules, bipartisanship is typically more necessary in the upper chamber than in the House. A Senate majority party rarely can hope to legislate without at least some support from the minority. Reflecting on his long Senate career (1981–2011), former senator Chris Dodd (D-Conn.) observed that on every major legislative success, "I've always had a Republican partner, every time" (quoted in Kaiser 2013, 204). Strictly speaking, a House majority party that can hold its ranks together does not need support from the minority to get legislation through the chamber. Even so, House majority leaders may nevertheless prefer to seek support from the minority party. Having bipartisan support in the House sends signals that can be beneficial for winning the necessary support elsewhere in the legislative process. As Waxman (2009, 136) recounted about the Food Quality Protection Act of 1996, when his staffer called President Clinton's chief of staff, Leon Panetta, to inform him of the deal, Panetta stopped him, saying, "If Waxman and Bliley are together on this, I don't need to know any more. We're for it."

Bipartisanship can also confer political legitimacy on a majority party's legislative efforts. A majority party may well be prepared to pay for such legitimacy by making substantive policy concessions to the minority. Barry (2003, 442) described the many efforts that House Judiciary Chairman F. James Sensenbrenner Jr. (R-Wisc.) made to obtain bipartisan support for the USA-PATRIOT Act in 2001. "The [George W. Bush] Administration wanted and needed overwhelming bipartisan support for its anti-terrorism proposal," she described. "Thus, the proposal's opponents were aware that in making public their disagreement with many of the provisions – and threatening the legitimacy of the Administration's proposal – they would receive some degree of leverage in the negotiations." Sensenbrenner and the Bush administration made policy concessions that were not strictly essential for House passage in order to secure broad bipartisan backing. Recognizing a similar political logic, Senate minority leader Mitch McConnell (R-Ky.) explained the strategy behind systematically withholding Republican support across the board for health care reform legislation in 2009–2010: "It was absolutely critical that everybody be together because if the proponents of the bill were able to say it was bipartisan, it tended to convey to the public that this is O. K., they must have figured it out," said McConnell. "It's either bipartisan or it isn't" (quoted in Hulse and Nagourney 2010, A13). The minority party's ability to confer or withhold this kind of political legitimacy gives it leverage in interparty negotiations.

The majority must ask how much it has to give away to achieve its goals. As Representative Frank described the logic, "You start with the rational people. You order your preferences. You hope that you care more about more different things than they do, which gives you more flexibility in bargaining." A majority party may well decide that the price being demanded by the minority is too high. It may try to go it alone, even though it is rare that major legislation in the United States passes with support from only one party (Mayhew 2005). A majority party may eschew compromise altogether to keep an issue alive for the next election campaign, especially if it expects to gain additional seats in Congress.

At the same time, the opposition has its own calculations. As with the majority, the minority party also faces explicit tradeoffs between politics and policy. As Representative Frank stated it, "You think to yourself: 'They have the votes anyway. Am I better off making a deal and improving the policy? Or am I better off just opposing?'" In other words, does the minority party want to use the issue to draw clear political distinctions between the parties, even at the cost of diminishing its influence over the substantive policy outcomes? Or does it prefer to influence the policy by trading its support in exchange for concessions, recognizing that doing so comes at the price of not being able to campaign as forcefully against the majority party on that issue? The minority may well prefer to use an issue for campaign purposes, even when the majority is willing to offer favorable substantive concessions on policy. Kaiser (2013, 206–207), for example, reported that Senator McConnell was uninterested in a bipartisan deal on new Wall Street regulations in 2009–2010. Instead, he considered Democrats' reform efforts a major opportunity for the Republican Party to raise campaign funds from financial interests. In short, both parties must be willing to cross a threshold before any real bargaining is possible. When there are few or no political costs to saying no (or even benefits to saying no), then interparty negotiation will probably not even take place.

Party members will nevertheless sometimes reach different conclusions about the costs of saying no than party leaders. Consider, for example, the uncertain prospects for immigration reform in the summer of 2013. Many Republican elites and party strategists concluded that the electoral costs of blocking a deal on immigration reform are too great for the Republican Party over the long term. In this context, a bipartisan Senate "gang" was able to drive a comprehensive immigration reform to passage in the Senate Judiciary Committee and on the Senate floor. To be sure, less than a third of Senate Republicans signed on to the deal. However, the package safely cleared the Senate's supermajority requirements that in the past had blocked immigration reform. Given both parties' willingness to negotiate, the final Senate package was an integrative, win-win solution. Democrats cared the most about securing a path to citizenship for the nation's undocumented millions; the GOP cared most about securing the borders. A deal was reached when Democrats offered to *double* spending on border security. Even the prime GOP sponsor of the deal-making amendment called the border spending "almost overkill" (quoted in Blake 2013). Whether House GOP members reach the same conclusion about the costs of saying no remains to be seen. So far, rank-and-file Republicans in the House seem interested only in the parts of immigration reform that are popular with conservative constituencies and business interests back home. Can party elites convince their members that blame for blocking reform would be too costly for the party as a whole to shoulder? How Republicans answer that question will help determine when or if Congress will "get to yes" on immigration reform.

Intraparty negotiations. Rank-and-file members have many reasons to sign on to deals advocated by party and committee leaders. We might say that it is a default position for members to support their party leaders; they "go along to get along" and vote no only when they have a specific reason to do so. Members have a political interest in seeing the leaders of their party succeed. Party unity is usually seen as helpful to a party's brand-name reputation for competence and policy coherence. Substantive policy negotiation is also easier among party members because the barriers of mistrust and suspicion are lower than between the parties. Beyond the generalized trust and goodwill that are stronger within the political parties than between them, there are many extra-legislative favors that coalition leaders can provide to facilitate intraparty deal making.

First, leaders have procedural powers that can offer political benefits to members. As Representative Frank stated, "Members need protection." Sometimes such protection comes in the form of assurances that members will not have to face votes on controversial issues. Again, from Representative Frank:

> I'd often have members come to me to say, "Can you guarantee that a particular issue will not come up for a vote?" I'll say, "Well, it's kind of a crazy idea, and it won't come up." They'll respond, "If you can guarantee that it won't come up, I can announce I'm for it."

Smoothing the way for a member on a difficult issue helps leaders curry support on other issues. Similarly, party leaders can sometimes win support from recalcitrant members without making policy concessions to them. For example, they may grant a member a recorded vote on a favorite issue. The member may well be satisfied with winning political visibility as a "player" and a champion on that issue, even if his or her amendment fails in adoption. As Representative Frank explained with respect to House floor votes on Dodd–Frank financial regulatory reform,

> I would go to leaders to ask for an amendment from Walt Minnick or Melissa Bean. The leadership will permit it if it can be defeated.... If so, then it can be offered. It's like the situation in *Catch-22*: "Only schedule appointments when I'm not in the office."

Second, leaders' control of resources allows them to do favors for their rank and file that increase the likelihood of support from fellow partisans. Such favors include guaranteeing consideration of members' minor bills on the House floor, contributions from leadership political action committees (PACs) to members' campaign coffers, and even seemingly minor gestures such as showing up for members' fundraisers. "Always give people a vested interest in maintaining a good relationship with you," advised Representative Frank.

In summary, the prospects and likely outcomes of congressional negotiation are very different within and between the congressional parties. With rare exceptions, rank-and-file partisans willingly engage in negotiations with their own party leaders. After all, members usually have a political interest in seeing their party leaders succeed. Furthermore, party leaders possess many resources to please their rank-and-file members even without making substantive policy concessions on a pending issue. Interparty dealing is far more limited: the opposition must first weigh the political incentives to negotiate at all. If they are unwilling to cross that threshold, strategic disagreement kicks in. Under such conditions, legislative deals are out of reach except for unusual political circumstances (e.g., the short "window" running from 2009 into early 2010 when Democrats controlled both ends of Pennsylvania Avenue, bolstered by a filibuster-proof majority in the Senate). Under normal circumstances, interparty negotiations can begin and have a chance at success only when sufficient numbers of the opposition decide that they want to "get to yes."

SUCCESSFUL NEGOTIATING: INSTRUMENTS

This chapter identifies a set of institutional arrangements and policy tools that have facilitated successful negotiations in other contexts, including private meetings, penalty defaults, expertise, and repeated interactions (Martin 2013).

In this section, we explore the relevance and effectiveness of these factors in the congressional context, as well as other factors informed by the congressional literature.

Secrecy. The move toward greater transparency in congressional operations – starting in the 1970s with a burst of "sunshine" laws for committees and the House floor in particular – has proven to be a double-edged sword. Greater openness of a legislative body might be considered a normative good: it increases the ability of the public and organized interests to hold accountable individual lawmakers and the institution as a whole for its decisions. However, the more transparent the legislative process is, the more the public dislikes Congress (Hibbing and Theiss-Morse 1995). Most people prefer to be "out of the kitchen" when legislators "grind sausage." Transparency does not necessarily lead to greater institutional legitimacy; in some cases, it undermines it.

More worrisome, transparency often imposes direct costs on successful deal making. First, public attention increases the incentive of lawmakers to adhere to party messages, a step rarely conducive to setting aside differences and negotiating a deal. We consider, for example, what senators said as they emerged from the Senate's bipartisan retreat behind the closed doors of the old Senate Chamber in the summer of 2013, when Democrats were considering "going nuclear" to change the Senate's filibuster rule. "There was no rancor at all," Senator John Boozman (R-Ark.) noted about the closed-door session with 98 senators in attendance. "I think if the American people were watching, the whole tone would have been different. It's different when the TV cameras are on. That might be part of the problem" (quoted in O'Keefe and Johnson 2013). Along these lines, Bessette (1994, 221) contended, "The duty to deliberate well may often be inconsistent with attempts to conduct policy deliberations on the plane of public opinion." Public settings encourage members to posture before external audiences rather than engage directly with their congressional interlocutors.

Second, transparency interferes with the search for solutions. Conducting negotiations of multidimensional, integrative solutions behind closed doors gives lawmakers more freedom to explore policy options. The genius of integrative solutions is that negotiating parties care unequally about different parts of the deal, requiring enlargement of the pie to secure competing parties' consent. The common mantra surrounding such negotiations is "nothing is agreed to until everything is agreed to" (Yglesias 2011), which reflects the conditional nature of most integrative solutions. Support for a provision that might be unpopular with your side is contingent on including a provision about which your side cares more. Leaking a less popular part of a deal – without linking it to what your party really cares about – is likely to kill the viability of the leaked provision, weakening the prospects for a deal. Waxman (2009, 137) attributed his successful pesticide negotiations with Bliley to a good mutual relationship and a common commitment to secrecy: "We implicitly trusted one another not to go public, had things not worked out, with the details of what the other had been willing to concede." Keeping negotiations secret until the whole package is unveiled allows both sides to justify the broader deal to constituencies and, in theory, avoid blame for unpopular giveaways. "The only way this type of negotiation can succeed is to tackle the whole problem in one fell swoop so that news of the deal arrives concurrently with the endorsements of all the major interests" (Waxman 2009, 137). This is also why – Representative Frank reminds us – serious negotiations rarely take place until very late in the game: early negotiations risk leaks of the parts of an integrative solution.

Despite the costs of transparency, private negotiations in Congress are increasingly difficult to secure. Repeated efforts to negotiate grand bargains on deficit reduction in the 112th Congress (2011–2012) were undermined each time by successful leaks about potential elements of a deal. Democratic-affiliated activists rejected reworking how the government calculates inflation for federal benefits (i.e., the so-called chained Consumer Price Index proposal), whereas Republican-affiliated activists rejected any provisions that would raise revenue by increasing tax rates. Exceptions to the rule include the most recent bipartisan Senate gang on immigration reform, whose negotiations were shrouded in secrecy to the extent that participants could engineer it. The gang essentially made a pact to oppose deal-threatening amendments in committee and again during Senate-floor consideration. Critical to the deal's success was its initial crafting in secret: that move gave senators the space to knit separate dimensions of immigration reform into a single package, exploiting the variation in their weighting of key issues and making support of one another's priorities conditional on support for the whole. The rarity with which House and Senate leaders can secure privacy complicates negotiations in Congress.

Penalty defaults.[1] Congress rarely acts in the absence of a deadline. Congress seems to recognize this and therefore regularly builds deadlines into the design of policies. Such deadlines often take the form of "sunset dates," which are limited authorizations for public programs that force the parties to reconsider policies when an appointed time arrives (Adler and Wilkerson 2013). At times, Congress crafts temporary fixes, requiring reconsideration at a later date. Congress tries to "rig" many such penalty defaults to guarantee action from itself at a future date, such as when it agrees to only a small increase in the government's legal borrowing limit. Other times, penalty defaults are

---

[1] The origins of the concept of penalty defaults stem from contract law (Ayres and Gertner 1989).

beyond Congress's control: courts or states can impose policy changes that create an unacceptable status quo. Perhaps the most familiar penalty default is embedded in the U.S. Constitution: "No money shall be drawn from the Treasury but in consequence of appropriations made by law."[2] Failure to enact annual spending bills to fund the government's discretionary programs forces a government shutdown.

Regardless of the origin or structure of a penalty default, the underlying concept is the same. In the congressional context, such default provisions are expected to be action forcing. In theory, Congress will move to avert an unacceptable penalty imposed by the default. The default fallback provisions create "must-pass" bills because failure to legislate would produce what is deemed to be an extreme (and, thus, politically unacceptable) reversion policy. However, as we argue herein, policy and politics are always intertwined. When we think about the potential for penalty defaults to force lawmakers to make a deal, we must consider the political consequences of blocking an agreement.

At times, the penalty defaults engineered by Congress work. Hacker and Pierson (2005, 61–62) called them policy "time bombs." The fiscal cliff "worked" to get Congress to act on tax policy because the restoration of Clinton-era middle-class income tax rates was deemed a political nonstarter by both parties; neither party wanted to shoulder the blame for raising middle-class taxes. Other times, penalty defaults are a bust. The Joint Committee on Deficit Reduction (aka the "Supercommittee") of 2011 failed to produce a budget grand bargain even when the penalty default was *sequestration* – that is, blanket cuts across discretionary federal spending. Sequestration – at the time considered a "sword of Damocles" that would give both parties an incentive to cooperate – failed in practice as a penalty default. Lawmakers individually escaped blame for the draconian cuts, even as Congress came under fire for its failure to act. In short, there was little incentive for Republicans (and perhaps for Democrats) to avoid the penalty outcome. Congress did act to avert cuts at the Federal Aviation Administration but only after the well-organized air-travel industry (including pilots, flight attendants, passengers, and shippers) raised the political costs of saying no for both parties. The conditional success of penalty defaults keeps them from being an easy solution for securing major deals in Congress.

Expertise. Congress relies on information and expertise but not of a technocratic sort. Neutral expertise bodies established within the legislative branch, including the Government Accountability Office and the Congressional Budget Office, have limited impact on negotiating deals in Congress. Lawmakers

[2] Article I, Section 9, Clause 7.

cite these agencies when the experts produce favorable results for their own agenda; however, such expertise is heavily discounted when unfavorable.

That said, Congress is anxious for expertise of a more politicized sort. It seeks out input from affected interests on the possible effects of legislative proposals. It wants to know whether interest groups are "on board." Kaiser (2013, 166) wrote that the first responsibility of congressional staff in crafting major legislation is "to hear out and sometimes to seek out the opinions of every party that would be significantly affected by it." Information gathering (e.g., from groups, industry, and agencies) allows members to discern different valuations across issues that allow potential win-win deals to be made. If all affected groups can coalesce around a policy – and settle the controversies among themselves – Congress often will ratify the result.

Repeated interactions. Current and former members and staff testify to the importance of relationships and getting to know one another on a personal basis. Political scientists are often skeptical of such claims. However, a sizable literature shows that senior legislators are more legislatively successful (Cox and Terry 2008) and that their effectiveness in office increases across their careers in the House (Volden and Wiseman 2009). Lawmakers who have been in office longer have more specific human capital that enhances their legislative success. Female legislators in the minority party seem to outshine their male colleagues in legislative effectiveness (Volden, Wiseman, and Wittmer 2013), a function perhaps of their superior collaborative skills (see, e.g., Rosenthal 1998).

Institutional arrangements that encourage repeated interactions may thus promote successful deal making in Congress. The standing committees of Congress comprise the primary congressional institution fostering repeated interactions and expertise among members, although committee-chair term limits imposed by Senate Republicans and by House chamber and Republican Party rules have disrupted sustained relationships in both chambers. Most major legislative deals emerge from committee work. In the case of the Dodd–Frank financial regulatory reforms, the key committee chairs – Representative Frank and Senator Dodd, both long-time institutional loyalists – had built relationships of trust during their many years of service that assisted them in constructing durable coalitions (Kaiser 2013). All else equal, repeated interactions – across lawmakers, their staffs, and lobbyists for key organized interests – undoubtedly facilitate deal making.

The rise of partisanship, however, has weakened congressional committees and contributed to the breakdown of "regular order." For example, the Senate Finance panel's slow start in 2013 in getting tax reform off the ground testifies to the difficulties that committee leaders now face in tackling policy challenges without the support of party leaders (Lesniewski 2013). Lawmakers often resort to ad hoc or "unorthodox" procedures to achieve major deals in the contemporary context. Sometimes small bipartisan groups of legislators (or "gangs") assume responsibility outside of the formal committee system for generating bipartisan measures. Some of these are successful (e.g., the Finance Committee gang that worked to generate the Senate health care proposal in 2009); others are not (e.g., the Gang of Six that met in 2011 and 2012 to negotiate a grand bargain on debt and deficit reduction). Ad hoc arrangements sacrifice many of the negotiating advantages afforded by long-standing repeated interactions, but they are sometimes the only pathways to success under contemporary conditions.

Messaging and communications. The "messaging game" shapes the public's views of legislative battles in Washington (Sellers 2010; Malecha and Reagan 2012). Episodes of messaging and communication strategies more generally can put pressure on the opposition party to come to the table to negotiate a deal. However, messaging typically must be blunt and often becomes little more than an effort to demonize the opposition; it then can impede negotiations. This is yet another reason why secrecy often improves the prospects for a deal, although party messaging tends to continue right up to the eleventh hour, even when lawmakers find themselves cloistered behind closed doors in the final moments before an impending deadline.

Leadership from the president. The president unquestionably has a central role in setting the stage for congressional negotiations. When presidents focus on an issue, they can set the legislative agenda "single-handedly" (Kingdon 1995, 23). Presidents surpass any individual lawmaker in their ability to garner media attention. Strategic appeals from the president – which, in turn, are shaped partially by the disposition of public opinion on an issue (Canes-Wrone 2001) – can help a president win more in bargaining with Congress (at least with respect to budget battles over spending). At the same time, presidential appeals can be a double-edged sword: they potentially commit lawmakers to particular positions, a move that limits legislators' bargaining flexibility (Kernell 2006). More generally, Edwards (2003) in his book, *On Deaf Ears*, warns that presidential appeals almost always fail to move public opinion.

Presidential leadership is more helpful with members of the president's party than with the opposition. Members of the president's party have a political stake in the president's success, separate from their views on the underlying policy issues involved. As a consequence, a president who is publicly championing an issue undoubtedly puts pressure on members of his party in Congress. By the same logic, however, presidential leadership alienates the opposition party

(Lee 2009; 2013). After all, a president's policy successes are not politically beneficial to his party opposition. As one White House aide in the George W. Bush administration observed, "It seems like if the President is publicly 'for' something, the Democratic leaders [in Congress] are automatically against it" (quoted in Andres 2005, 764). Senator Pat Toomey (R-Pa.) observed this dynamic among his fellow Republicans during the Obama presidency: "There were some on my side who did not want to be seen helping the president do something he wanted to get done, just because the president wanted to do it" (quoted in Brandt 2013). Do quieter appeals make a difference for congressional negotiations? Perhaps, although it is a more difficult conjecture to evaluate, given the low visibility and traceability of an administration's behind-the-scenes role in deliberations over policy.

CONCLUSIONS

In tribute to one of his principal staff negotiators, Senator Mitch McConnell (R-Ky.) said, "I assure you it is rare in this business to come across somebody who combines a brilliant mind for policy and a brilliant mind for politics in one package."[3] McConnell's comment captures a truth about negotiation in Congress. The outcome of congressional negotiations depends on more than policy considerations. Negotiation in Congress is also driven by politics. Members and leaders negotiate with an eye to deals that they can defend successfully to constituencies outside of Congress. In this light, a good deal on the policy merits still may be judged too politically risky. Members and leaders also consider whether it is in their party's interests to strike a deal or whether it seems more politically advantageous to preserve the disagreement for electoral purposes. Politics will often lead members to reject compromises that would be acceptable if public policy were the only consideration. By the same token, members sometimes accede to undesirable policies when the politics of holding out becomes too difficult to sustain.

One obvious implication is that negotiation in Congress is far more complex than negotiation in the private sector. As Mansbridge argues in Chapter 19, many cognitive obstacles stand in the way of successful negotiation, including fixed-pie bias, self-serving bias, and general difficulties of perspective taking. All of these difficulties inevitably affect negotiation in Congress as well. Making success even more problematic, congressional negotiation also occurs in a political context, in which members must evaluate deals for their effects on their individual reelection efforts and political reputations, as well as for their

---

[3] *Congressional Record*, July 31, 2013, S6085.

party's broader interests in winning and maintaining institutional control. Members of Congress frequently confront tradeoffs between their political interests and their policy goals.

On the other side of the ledger, there is more room in Congress for integrative solutions than in most other negotiation settings. Congress's broad jurisdiction allows for a wide array of unrelated issues to be considered simultaneously, affording players with different priorities a reason to come together and shake hands on a deal. This basic fact suggests that scholars need to do more to investigate how integrative negotiation works in Congress rather than relying so heavily on a congressional literature that emphasizes models of "splitting the difference." Undoubtedly, splitting the difference can be the basis of agreement in Congress when the conflict is over divisible goods, such as budgets, appropriations, and taxes. However, many issues are not amenable to this kind of resolution. At the same time, the broad range of issues available to congressional negotiators gives wide scope for creative legislators to strike deals.

The contemporary Congress labors under remarkably high barriers to success in negotiations. As described by Barber and McCarty in Chapter 2, Congress today is strongly polarized by party in terms of members' policy preferences. During the 1950s, 1960s, and 1970s, the broader range of policy positions held by members of both parties in Congress facilitated interparty negotiation. In the contemporary Congress, there is far less overlap between the policy preferences of Republicans and Democrats. As the parties have moved further apart in policy terms, they also have tended to become internally more homogeneous. Increased party cohesion in the House can make intraparty negotiation in the House more efficient and successful. (Yet, since 2011, a House GOP majority increasingly *divided* between mainstream and hard-line elements has struggled to reach deals within its conference.) However, increased party cohesion can undermine deal making in the Senate. Given the Senate's supermajority procedures, increased intraparty homogeneity coupled with partisan conflict has rendered Senate obstruction rampant, with the minority party deploying the filibuster as a veto against the majority party's legislative agenda. Even parties under unified government rarely have a clear shot to legislative success. In short, party polarization has greatly complicated the task of legislating (Binder 2003; Sinclair 2006, 2012).

Today's political context is unfavorable for congressional negotiations. Political competition between the parties for control of national institutions creates electoral incentives for the parties to engage in "strategic disagreement." The United States is also in the midst of a ferociously party-competitive era, in which the two major parties stand at near parity in terms of their prospects for winning or holding control of national institutions. Since 1980, control of the Senate shifted seven times, with Democrats and Republicans each in the majority for nine Congresses. Control of the House of Representatives reversed three times, also with Democrats in the majority for nine Congresses and Republicans for eight. Between 1981 and 2017, Republicans will have held the presidency for 20 years and Democrats for 16 years. When control of Congress or the White House hangs in the balance, lawmakers weigh more heavily the partisan political consequences of negotiations. Such zero-sum competition fuels antagonism between the parties beyond the policy-based obstacles to agreement fostered by ideological polarization.

In the United States, both political and policy considerations complicate successful negotiation, especially in periods of polarized parties. Our political system's many veto points and extensive array of checks and balances demand considerable negotiating skill among officeholders to make government function. Yet, "Congress is becoming more like a parliamentary system," observed former Senator Olympia Snowe (R-Maine), "where everyone simply votes with their party and those in charge employ every possible tactic to block the other side" (quoted in Kaiser 2013, 398). The outcome is a Congress and a national government in which deals are more elusive than ever.

References

Adler, E. Scott and John D. Wilkerson. 2013. *Congress and the Politics of Problem Solving*. New York: Cambridge University Press.

Andres, Gary. 2005. "The Contemporary Presidency: Polarization and White House/ Legislative Relations: Causes and Consequences of Elite-Level Conflict." *Presidential Studies Quarterly* 35(4): 761–770.

Arnold, Douglas. 1990. *Logic of Congressional Action*. New Haven: Yale University Press.

Ayres, Ian, and Robert Gertner. 1989. "Filling Gaps in Incomplete Contracts: An Economic Theory of Default Rules." *Yale Law Journal* 99: 87.

Barber, Michael, and Nolan McCarty. 2013. "Causes and Consequences of Polarization." In *Negotiating Agreement in Politics*, eds. Cathie Jo Martin and Jane Mansbridge. Washington, DC: American Political Science Association: 19–53.

Baron, David, and John Ferejohn. 1989. "Bargaining in Legislatures." *American Political Science Review* 83(4): 1181–1206.

Barry, Mindy. 2003. "Principled Negotiating: Breeding Success and Protecting Public Interests behind Closed Doors." *Georgetown Journal of Law and Policy* 1: 431–444.

Bessette, Joseph M. 1994. *The Mild Voice of Reason: Deliberative Democracy and American National Government*. Chicago: University of Chicago Press.

Binder, Sarah A. 2003. *Stalemate: Causes and Consequences of Legislative Gridlock*. Washington, DC: Brookings Institution Press.

Blake, Aaron. 2013. "Corker: My Border Security Deal Is 'Almost Overkill.'" *Washington Post*, June 20. Retrieved July 31, 2013, from www.washingtonpost.com/blogs/post-politics/wp/2013/06/20/corker-my-border-security-deal-is-almost-overkill/?wprss=rss_politics&wpisrc=nl_wonk_b.

Brandt, Evan. 2013. "Toomey Doubts Second Senate Gun-Control Vote Any Time Soon." *The Times Herald* (Norristown, PA), May 1.

Canes-Wrone, Brandice. 2001. "The President's Legislative Influence from Public Appeals." *American Journal of Political Science* 45(2): 313–329.

Cox, Gary W., and William C. Terry. 2008. "Legislative Productivity in the 93rd–105th Congresses." *Legislative Studies Quarterly* 33(4): 603–618.

Edwards, George. 2003. *On Deaf Ears*. New Haven: Yale University Press.

Evans, C. Lawrence. 2011. "Congressional Committees." In *The Oxford Handbook of the American Congress*, eds. Eric Schickler and Frances E. Lee. New York: Oxford University Press: 396–425.

Evans, Diana. 2004. *Greasing the Wheels: Using Pork Barrel Projects to Build Majority Coalitions in Congress*. New York: Cambridge University Press.

Follett, Mary Parker. [1925]1942. "Constructive Conflict." In *Dynamic Administration: The Collected Papers of Mary Parker Follett*, eds. H. C. Metcalf and L. Urwick. New York: Harper: 30–49.

Gilmour, John B. 1995. *Strategic Disagreement: Stalemate in American Politics*. Pittsburgh: University of Pittsburgh Press.

Hacker, Jacob S., and Paul E. Pierson. 2005. *Off Center: The Republican Revolution and the Erosion of American Democracy*. New Haven: Yale University Press.

Hibbing, John, and Elizabeth Theiss-Morse. 1995. *Congress as Public Enemy*. New York: Cambridge University Press.

Hulse, Carl, and Adam Nagourney. 2010. "Senate G.O.P. Leader Finds Weapon in Unity." *New York Times*, March 16, A13.

Kaiser, Robert. 2013. *Act of Congress: How America's Essential Institution Works, and How It Doesn't*. New York: Knopf.

Karol, David. 2009. *Party Position Change in American Politics: Coalition Management*. New York: Cambridge University Press.

Kernell, Samuel. 2006. *Going Public*. 4th edition. Washington, DC: CQ Press.

Kingdon, John W. 1995. *Agendas, Alternatives, and Public Policies*. 2nd edition. New York: HarperCollins.

Krehbiel, Keith, and Douglas Rivers. 1988. "The Analysis of Committee Power: An Application to Senate Voting on the Minimum Wage." *American Journal of Political Science* 32(4): 1151–1174.

Lee, Frances E. 2009. *Beyond Ideology: Politics, Principles, and Partisanship in the U.S. Senate*. Chicago: University of Chicago Press.

Lee, Frances E. 2013. "Presidents and Party Teams: The Politics of Debt Limits and Executive Oversight." *Presidential Studies Quarterly* 43 (December): 775.

Lesniewski, Niels. 2013. "Reid Dismisses Baucus' Tax Overhaul Efforts." *CQ/Roll Call*, July 25. Retrieved July 31, 2013, from http://blogs.rollcall.com/wgdb/reid-dismisses-baucus-tax-reform-efforts/.

Malecha, Gary Lee, and Daniel J. Reagan. 2012. *The Public Congress: Congressional Deliberation in a New Media Age*. New York: Routledge.

Martin, Cathie Jo. 2013. "Conditions for Successful Negotiation: Lessons from Europe." In *Negotiating Agreements in Politics*, eds. Cathie Jo Martin and Jane Mansbridge. Washington, DC: American Political Science Association: 121–143.

Mayhew, David. 1974. *Congress: The Electoral Connection*. New Haven: Yale University Press.

————. 2005. *Divided We Govern: Party Control, Lawmaking, and Investigations, 1946–2002.* 2nd edition. New Haven: Yale University Press.

O'Keefe, Ed, and Jenna Johnson. 2013. "No Filibuster Deal, but Senators Agree They Should Meet More Often." *Washington Post,* July 15. Retrieved July 31, 2013, from http://www.washingtonpost.com/blogs/post-politics/wp/2013/07/15/no-filibuster-deal-but-senators-agree-they-should-meet-more-often/.

Poole, Keith T., and Howard Rosenthal. 1997. *Congress: A Political-Economic History of Roll Call Voting.* New York: Oxford University Press.

————. 2013. "NOMINATE and Related Data." *Voteview.com,* Department of Political Science, University of Georgia. Retrieved August 8, 2013, from http://voteview.com/downloads.asp.

Riker, William. 1962. *The Theory of Political Coalitions.* New Haven: Yale University Press.

Rosenthal, Cindy Simon. 1998. *When Women Lead: Integrative Leadership in State Legislatures.* New York: Oxford University Press.

Sellers, Patrick. 2010. *Cycles of Spin: Strategic Communication in the U.S. Congress.* New York: Cambridge University Press.

Sinclair, Barbara. 2006. *Party Wars: Polarization and the Politics of National Policy Making.* Norman: University of Oklahoma Press.

————. 2012. *Unorthodox Lawmaking: New Legislative Processes in the U.S. Congress.* 4th edition. Washington, DC: CQ Press.

Smith, Steven S. 2007. *Party Influence in Congress.* New York: Cambridge University Press.

Sorauf, Frank J. 1992. *Inside Campaign Finance: Myths and Realities.* New Haven: Yale University Press.

Volden, Craig, and Alan E. Wiseman. 2009. "Legislative Effectiveness in Congress." Typescript. Ohio State University.

Volden, Craig, Alan E. Wiseman, and Dana E. Wittmer. 2013. "When Are Women More Effective Lawmakers than Men?" *American Journal of Political Science* 57(2): 326–341.

Wawro, Gregory. 2000. *Legislative Entrepreneurship in the House.* Ann Arbor: University of Michigan Press.

Waxman, Henry, with Joshua Green. 2009. *The Waxman Report: How Congress Really Works.* New York: Twelve.

Yglesias, Matthew. 2011. "Eric Cantor Takes Bargaining Positions out of Context, Poisoning the Atmosphere of Future Negotiations." *Think Progress.* Retrieved July 31, 2013, from http://thinkprogress.org/yglesias/2011/07/12/267092/eric-cantor-takes-bargaining-positions-out-of-context-poisoning-the-atmosphere-of-future-negotiat-ions/.

19

Helping Congress Negotiate

*Jane Mansbridge**

Several important underlying causes of our current polarization in Congress will persist for the foreseeable future. The framers bequeathed us a set of democratic institutions that separate powers more than in almost any other modern industrial democracy, generating veto powers by each of two houses of Congress and a president. We have added an electoral system, based on plurality votes in single-member districts, that gives great power to the individual legislator, making coordination even harder. We eschew systems of compulsory voting that would bring moderate voters into the elections. We pick our candidates through primary elections constructed and timed to bring out the most extreme portion of the electorate. Through the constitutional rulings of our highest court, we have deprived ourselves of the capacity to block out-of-district and out-of-state money aimed at small but close elections at the primary level. Changes to any of these features of the current constitutional system are politically hard to imagine. If we add to this long-standing constitutional and institutional system the current causes of polarization, including two parties that, since the Southern realignment, have become ideologically far more internally consistent and since 1980 have become far more competitive in their potential control of the presidency and Congress, we have a recipe for deadlock.[1]

---

* This chapter draws from the APSA Presidential Task Force on Negotiating Agreement in Politics (Mansbridge and Martin 2013), and particularly on the work of the U.S. working group chaired by Nolan McCarty, the European working group chaired by Cathie Jo Martin, and the normative working group chaired by Mark Warren. The opinions and weight given different explanations are my own.

[1] See Barber and McCarty (2013) for a careful review of the causes of polarization, including the strong probable cause of rising inequality, whose trajectory eerily maps that of polarization as it declined from its earlier height at the turn of the twentieth century to the 1950s, bottomed out from 1950 to 1980, and rose again from 1980 to its current point, which is even higher than at the turn of the previous century (Figure 2 in Bonica, McCarty, Poole, and Rosenthal 2013).

If polarization is the "new normal," we must adopt institutions designed for enemies, not friends. Negotiation is such an institution. Negotiation does not require the parties to put aside their enmity to reach for common ground. To the contrary, even enemies can negotiate as long as both can benefit from a deal. In many cases one or both parties in Congress will benefit from stalemate rather than a deal, in which case negotiation is not the answer. But we know from 50 years of work in the field of negotiation in business and international relations that often parties will walk away from a deal that would benefit all sides because either they are not cool-headedly letting their interests dictate their actions or they are unskilled in looking for ways to "expand the pie" by exploiting differences in value between the parties. Or both.

The citizens and the press in our democracy do not typically demand "Negotiation now!" or "Better negotiation!" Even political science has rarely studied negotiation in depth in Congress or the state legislatures. The great theorists of democracy – Aristotle, Locke, Madison – never mentioned negotiation, and neither have more modern theorists. Negotiation has been thought appropriate for warring parties, but not a critical piece of democracy. This neglect has been costly.

Taking the need for negotiation seriously can help us deal with the polarization that at this point in our country's history we are likely to continue to face. Taking negotiation seriously will, however, require a major reassessment of certain democratic values. We will need to rethink, for example, the desirability of transparency, contested elections, and short terms in office. If we want to make the job of the legislator as negotiator easier, we must look again at these popular proposals in light of the way they impede negotiation.

PUTTING NEGOTIATION AT THE CORE

Putting negotiation conceptually at the core of the legislative process will require taking an institutional perspective on the past 50 years of work on negotiation, which has proceeded from an individual perspective. The existing work in business schools, law schools, and policy schools on how to become a good individual negotiator has produced many insights, including two basic steps forward: defining *successful negotiation* and identifying the *human errors* that most frequently prevent that success.

A *successful negotiation* has two characteristics:

1. When a *zone of possible agreement* exists on any issue in the negotiation, the parties recognize that this zone exists and actually *make* the agreement.

2. When the various parties to the agreement value different outcomes differently and *differential trades* can be made in which parties gain on items of relatively high value to them and lose on items of relatively low value to them, the parties *discover* these differences and use them effectively in making the trades.

Two major sets of *human errors* produce failure to reach agreement when a zone of possible agreement exists or differential trades can create value:

1. *Self-serving bias*: This preconscious cognitive bias makes human beings process facts and interpretations differentially to favor the interpretations that benefit them. Self-serving bias colors our perception of facts as well as our concepts of justice and the common good. Self-serving bias propels us toward optimism: seeing things more favorably to ourselves or our group than the reality warrants. More than half of survey respondents, for example, rate themselves in the top 50% in driving, ethics, managerial prowess, productivity, health, and other desirable traits and skills. Entering a negotiation with a self-serving bias, the parties are likely to overestimate how much they can win from the other side. They may walk away from a deal when they do not get what they expect, even when a real zone of possible agreement exists and settling for less would be in their interest.

2. *Fixed-pie bias*: This bias leads each of the parties to assume that "their gain is our loss." It keeps them from seeing the ways they can "expand the pie" by enlarging the negotiation to include more issues on which the two sides place different values, so that each can gain on the items it considers of highest value. Entering a negotiation with a fixed-pie bias, the parties often fail to ask questions and probe for side issues or for deeper interests that may underlie the others' stated positions.

Studies in the laboratory and in the field have demonstrated that these biases often impede successful negotiation. So too can other cognitive biases, such as the availability heuristic (leading parties to focus on an anchor negotiating point) and loss aversion (leading parties to count losses more heavily than gains), as well as other psychological factors such as anger (leading parties to ignore good offers in the heat of passion), all of which collectively we can think of as forms of "negotiation myopia" (Foster, Mansbridge, and Martin 2013).

In Congress, as in business and international relations, many factors can reduce negotiation myopia. Almost any institution that promotes clear seeing will facilitate negotiation. To reduce both self-serving bias and fixed-pie bias, features of institutions that let each party get to know the perspectives of the opposite side make it more likely both that they will close a deal that benefits all of the negotiating parties and will discover ways of "expanding the pie" for all by bringing in other issues. In one telling study, which sprinkled the description of each side's situation with clues to peripheral issues that could provide high value to one at low cost to the other, the simple instructions before the negotiation to "take the perspective" of the others in the negotiation, to "try to understand what [the others] are thinking, what their interests and purposes are . . . [and] to imagine what you would be thinking in that role" increased from 39% to 76% the percentage of buyer/seller pairs in that study who were able to conclude a deal (Galinsky et al. 2008).

Institutions can either reinforce or reduce human error. As we begin to see negotiation as central to the legislative process, we can consciously design institutions to make the predictable sources of human error in negotiation less, rather than more, likely. The northern European countries, whose electoral systems create multiple political parties that then must continually negotiate with one another, have developed several such institutional features. They provide spaces of privacy, promote repeated interaction among the negotiators, and generate many issues from which side payments can be drawn (Martin 2013). Privacy and repeated interaction are particularly critical. In the experience of many seasoned negotiators in Congress and elsewhere, repeated, private, informal, and free-ranging discussions with the opposing parties can reduce quite dramatically the most common forms of bias, letting each party see more clearly what is to its own and the others' advantage. When individuals from the different parties have known and worked with one another for a long time, such informal discussions are especially likely to allow each of them to unearth the needs, interests, and reasons behind the others' positions, making it far easier to see what goods to introduce into the negotiation to meet those needs.

As we begin to design and implement institutions to reduce human error in negotiation, we must therefore rethink several democratic assumptions. These include the presumed positive value of transparency and contested elections, as well as the negative valence attached to side payments. In every case, our current assumptions derive from a suspicion of the motives and actions of representatives. Changing those assumptions is appropriate only when constituents can actually with good warrant trust their representatives. In political representation, as in many features of the economy and society, warranted trust is the grease of an efficient system. Constituents' loss of trust in their own representatives exacerbates the harms of polarization by making it harder for those representatives to explain the results of negotiation to their constituents and thus harder for them to negotiate in Congress itself, even as enemy to enemy.

RETHINKING ASSUMPTIONS[2]

Transparency: A More Negotiation-Friendly Approach

Negotiation benefits from privacy. Yet democrats today cannot have too much of transparency. As the unity of the post–World War II era faded and citizens became more distrusting of government, demands for greater transparency skyrocketed. Between 1980 and 2004, the frequency of the word "transparency" in books in English more than tripled.[3] Transparency destroys privacy, however, and privacy is critical to negotiation.

Privacy allows opposing parties to explore possible zones of agreement delicately and gradually, beyond the reach of the public media, which may take words out of context, misinterpret "feelers" as "give-aways," and lead constituents to reject parts of an eventual package before the package itself is complete. Privacy allows parties to recognize in an informal setting that their own interpretations of the facts and the justice of a situation are not universal and that persons of goodwill can hold different interpretations. Privacy allows informal rambling into seemingly irrelevant fields and disclosing vulnerabilities that may then present opportunities for high-value/low-cost additions to the negotiation. Privacy can thus greatly decrease both self-serving and fixed-pie bias.

The representatives themselves recognize the importance of privacy. In 1982, for example, U.S. senators singled out "most often" as a reason for the decline in political self-sacrifice the new rule opening committee meetings to the public (Ehrenhalt 1982).

Recognizing the importance of negotiation requires, then, that we make privacy in legislation more legitimate. In the ASPA Presidential Task Force on Negotiating Agreement in Politics, a group of normative theorists addressed this problem. They concluded that privacy can be normatively legitimate in a democracy to the degree that the level of corruption in the system is low, citizens have reason to trust their representatives, and the following other conditions hold:

- Citizens have the opportunity to deliberate beforehand about the reasons for closed-door negotiation.

---

[2] This section summarizes the argument in Warren and Mansbridge et al. (2013).
[3] See calculations in Google Ngram for the percentage by year of a given word in a sample of all the books in English (http://books.google.com/ngrams).

- The relevant interests are represented fairly and effectively in the negotiation.
- The negotiators are transparent subsequently in giving their rationales for the decision, providing enough information and reasoning that citizens can engage in informed debate and judgment (Warren and Mansbridge et al. 2013).

To the degree that negotiation is important and these conditions hold, citizens should not demand *transparency in process,* opening to the public the process of reaching those decisions, but instead *transparency in rationale,* making the reasons for decisions public (Mansbridge 2009). Transparency in rationale must also be accompanied by sufficient publicity for the citizens to be sufficiently informed to make good subsequent decisions (Lindstedt and Naurin 2010).

Contested Elections: A More Negotiation-Friendly Approach

Negotiation benefits from long-standing relationships. Yet in popular reform movements and in political science it is almost an article of faith that elections should be contested. Critics often consider long incumbencies an unquestioned indicator of the lack of democracy. Certain quantitative indexes of democracy use lack of turnover in legislative seats as a measure of low levels of democracy. For negotiation, however, long incumbencies are good. They generate the long-standing, repeated relationships that are critical to successful negotiation. The "great negotiators" in Congress have all been members of the institution for years. Human beings build relationships over time, learning whom they can trust and for what, what parts of what issues are most important to others and why, and how others see both facts and conceptions of the common good.

Recognizing the importance of negotiation thus requires legitimating long incumbencies. On this problem, the normative theorists in the APSA Presidential Task Force concluded that long incumbencies can be normatively legitimate in a democracy to the degree, again, that the level of corruption in the system is low, citizens have reason to trust their representatives, and the following other conditions hold:

- The representative by and large promotes policies and a larger political direction that the majority of constituents approve.
- The majority (and even to a lesser degree the minority) of constituents are relatively satisfied with the representative.

- Satisfaction with the representative is not the result of ignorance or manipulation.
- The existing media and interest group systems are healthy, present alternative policies, and can publicize departures from citizen preferences or interests.
- The internal party system is vital, self-policing, and continually infused with new activists and new ideas.
- The citizens are active in other forms of politics and therefore able to inform themselves easily and take action to remove the incumbent when he or she no longer represents their interests adequately (Warren and Mansbridge et al. 2013).

When negotiation is taken into account, the goals of democracy may be better met by long incumbencies than by conditions that promote high turnover in representatives.

Side Payments: A More Negotiation-Friendly Approach

Negotiation benefits from side payments, which are made possible when parties bring many issues to the table and make trades on issues that are of high value some and low cost to others. Only by expanding the number of issues addressed can parties whose stances otherwise would not produce a zone of possible agreement devise packages that will benefit everyone. Such expansion also allows greater joint gains from the negotiation as a whole. Negotiation theorists often call this process "logrolling." Yet in politics, logrolling has a bad name – and for good reason. In politics, the side payments in logrolling often direct public spending to a limited number of individuals or entities, creating costs to the taxpayer without sufficient legislative scrutiny to ascertain that these expenses promote the public good. The normative theorists in the APSA Presidential Task Force thus concluded that side payments can be normatively legitimate in a democracy to the degree that, in addition to the now familiar overall requirements that the level of corruption in the system be low and that citizens have reason to trust their representatives, the following conditions hold:

- The side payments are transparent.
- The rationale of the benefit provided by the side payment is transparent and justifiable to those affected (e.g., taxpayers) who were not involved in the trade.
- The side payments are required to negotiate an agreement.

- The side payments are elements of a fair compromise or a trade on high/low values that is good for both parties.[4]
- The side payments survive cost-benefit scrutiny on the allocation itself; that is, there must be an overall benefit to the collectivity served as measured against the cost of providing that benefit (Warren and Mansbridge et al. 2013).[5]

Congress already has a great advantage in negotiation in being able to bring in many issues at a time to make logrolling possible (Binder and Lee 2013). As a public, however, we have been hampered in not having criteria with which to distinguish between legitimate and nonlegitimate side payments.

CONSTITUENTS, TRUST, AND THE "SECOND-LEVEL GAME"

The success of negotiations depends not only on the conditions that facilitate or impede the negotiation itself but also, when one person is negotiating on behalf of others, on the quality of relations between the agent negotiating and the principals for whom that agent is acting. Congressional negotiations require success both in the "first-level game" of the negotiation, where privacy, repeated interaction, and the capacity to access side payments greatly improve the chances for success, and in the "second-level game" (Putnam 1998) between agents and principals – that is, between the elected representatives and their constituents. Success on this level is greatly facilitated by warranted trust between those representatives and constituents.

In the United States today, two hard-to-surmount impediments stand in the way of this negotiation-facilitating trust: the reality of evolving perceptions and the way we think about representation.

The reality is that in the United States, trust in the government in Washington "to do what is right" has been declining dramatically since the first time it was measured in 1958. To a far lesser degree, approval of the way one's own representative is "handling his or her job" has also been declining slightly since this question was first measured in 1977.[6] We have no measures at all of trust in one's own representative among the people who voted for that representative, let alone any such measures over time. Yet as many as 61%

---

[4] Warren and Mansbridge et al. (2013), building on the existing nomenclature in negotiation theory, give the name of "partially integrative" solutions to such trades.

[5] I thank the breakout group at the Hewlett conference for this point.

[6] See www.gallup.com/poll/5392/trust-government.aspx and www.gallup.com/poll/162362/ame-ricans-down-congress-own-representative.aspx, conducted May 2–7, 2013, retrieved June 10, 2014.

of "likely voters" report, in response to a relatively loaded question, that they think it at least "somewhat likely" that their "own representative in Congress has sold their vote for either cash or a campaign contribution."[7] These beliefs could certainly undermine one's trust in one's representative.

The way we think about political representation also has its flaws. The current reigning model of representation, both among the public and among political scientists, is based implicitly or explicitly on distrust and the consequent need for sanctions. In this model, politicians are motivated primarily by the desire to win election and reelection. Their ties to the voters derive from the voters being able to exercise the sanction of voting them out of office. The representatives do what the voters want them to do for fear that if they act otherwise the voters will not reelect them. This *sanction model* of political representation dominates current public discourse. It has also become the dominant model in political science since 1974.[8]

Before the 1970s in political science, analyses of political representation typically complemented the sanction model with another model of representation, the *selection model*. In this model, politicians are motivated intrinsically. Voters use reputational signals of intrinsic motivation to choose representatives whose objectives they judge most closely aligned with their own.[9] Although any case of actual representation combines both models, the selection model seems to conform better both to the way many representatives see their jobs and to the kinds of representatives most voters want. It is not a Burkean "trustee" model, because in the selection model voters often choose representatives they perceive as "like" themselves, not people whom they think know better than they do what is good for them. They choose a representative they think will pursue a consistent direction, as if directed, like a ship, by an internal gyroscope. They "de-select" that representative when for one reason or another the representative's goals begin to differ from their own (Mansbridge 2003, 2009, 2011).

For obvious reasons, legislative negotiation behind closed doors works best with legislators primarily of the selection-model "gyroscope" type. The contrasting model, based on sanctions, requires that the voters or their proxies in the media be able to monitor the representative closely. In a selection

---

[7] See   www.rasmussenreports.com/public_content/politics/mood_of_america/congressional_performance for a survey of 1,000 "likely voters" conducted May 19–20, 2014, retrieved June 10, 2014.

[8] Two books published that year, Mayhew (1974) and Fiorina (1974), had some influence on this trend.

[9] This is the path of "Representative Attitude" in Miller and Stokes's (1963) two-path "diamond model" of representative-constituency congruence; it is also what Gosnell (1948) calls "unconscious" representation, in contrast to the "conscious" representation produced by the threat of sanction (for analysis, see Mansbridge 2009).

model voters can expect their representatives to hold the commitments for which the voter originally selected them throughout the representatives' lives, even behind closed doors. The representatives' established reputations for commitment and consistency also make it easier for them to explain to their constituencies the unexpected and sometimes unwanted outcomes of a negotiation (as President Nixon was able to do relatively successfully on China).

A selection model of representation can be normatively legitimate in a democracy whenever citizens have good reason to trust their representatives. In the Congress of the United States today, the degree to which representatives are driven by internal personal commitments congruent with those of a majority of their constituents may be quite high. The chances of illegal corruption are also quite low, a few well-publicized cases to the contrary notwithstanding. In contrast, the chances of "dependence corruption," deriving from the dependence of a representative on legal sources such as campaign contributions, may be relatively high (Lessig 2011). These campaign contributions may well influence a representative's vote. Although legal, such dependence corruption poses a significant problem for the "second-level game" in which representatives must convince their constituents that the outcomes of a negotiation were in fact the best they could get. Dependence corruption based on greatly unequal campaign contributions occurs in a larger field tainted by past Congresses with greater illegal corruption, by a few relatively recent instances of illegal corruption in Congress, and by a greater amount of illegal corruption in state legislatures and administrations. The consequence is considerable distrust among constituents even of the representatives they voted for, let alone the representatives they voted against.

Although polarization causes some distrust of government and distrust of government causes some polarization, the two factors of polarization and distrust of the representatives one voted for are analytically distinct. If polarization is here to stay and representatives must in the future negotiate with one another in this context, it is even more imperative that the polity adopt some set of reforms to bring dependence corruption under control. Many reasons have rightly been given for such reforms, but those reasons have not yet included prominently the way reducing dependence corruption would, by increasing constituent trust, increase the capacity of our elected representatives to negotiate successfully.

CONCLUSION

The current deadlock in the United States derives from structural features that are unlikely to change. Any feasible changes must therefore come at the margins of a structure intentionally rife with veto points and a current polarization of political parties that stems in great part from nontransient causes. Whenever one party fails to hold the presidency and a majority in both houses of Congress, negotiation becomes crucial in crafting legislation. Citizens, journalists, and political scientists facing our current problems in this political structure must therefore begin to address the question of how to improve the prospects for political negotiation in Washington.

Recognizing the importance of negotiation in legislation highlights the institutional rules of collective political engagement that past experience shows us promote successful negotiation. To negotiate successfully, our representatives need closed-door interactions, repeated interactions, and the side payments that can be achieved by bringing more issues into the negotiation. Because currently many normative assumptions stand in the way of redesigning congressional institutions to facilitate these kinds of interactions, we need to rethink those assumptions.

Recognizing the importance of negotiation in legislation also underlines a neglected feature of campaign finance reform – its capacity to strengthen the ties of trust between representatives and the constituents to whom they report, in order to make it more likely that the representatives will be able to explain the results of a negotiation to the constituents in ways the constituents will accept.

Legislative stalemate has relatively few costs when the status quo is relatively acceptable. In conditions of "drift," however, where a situation worsens in the absence of intervention, stalemate can be costly (Burns 1963; Hacker and Pierson 2010; Mansbridge 2012). Budget deficits, economic inequality, and climate change – on all of these issues, failing to take legislative action lets changes for the worse continue unopposed. In the United States, where neither the constitutional structure nor party polarization is likely to change dramatically, our best hopes for productive legislation lie in helping Congress negotiate better. This task requires revising some fundamental assumptions, changing institutions at the margin, and enhancing trust through campaign finance reform. Many of these changes will come about only when the public begins to recognize the importance of negotiation in democratic politics.

References

Barber, Michael, and Nolan McCarty. 2013. "Causes and Consequences of Polarization." In *Negotiating Agreement in Politics*, eds. Jane Mansbridge and Cathie Jo Martin. Washington, DC: American Political Science Association: 19–53.

Binder, Sarah, and Frances Lee. 2013. "Making Deals in Congress." In *Negotiating Agreement in Politics*, eds. Jane Mansbridge and Cathie Jo Martin. Washington, DC: American Political Science Association: 54–72.

Bonica, Adam, Nolan McCarty, Keith T. Poole, and Howard Rosenthal. 2013. "Why Hasn't Democracy Slowed Rising Inequality?" *Journal of Economic Perspectives* 27(3): 103–124.

Burns, James McGregor. 1963. *The Deadlock of Democracy*. Englewood Cliffs: Prentice-Hall.

Ehrenhalt, Alan. 1982. "Special Report: The Individualist Senate." *Congressional Quarterly Weekly* 40(September 4): 2175–2182.

Fiorina, Morris. 1974. *Representatives, Roll Calls, and Constituencies*. Lexington: Lexington Books.

Foster, Chase, Jane Mansbridge, and Cathie Jo Martin. 2013. "Negotiation Myopia." In *Negotiating Agreement in Politics*, eds. Jane Mansbridge and Cathie Jo Martin. Washington, DC: American Political Science Association: 73–85.

Galinsky, Adam D., William W. Maddux, Debra Gilin, and Judith B. White. 2008. "Why It Pays to Get Inside the Head of Your Opponent." *Psychological Science* 19(4): 378–388.

Gosnell, Harold F. 1948. *Democracy: The Threshold of Freedom*. New York: Ronald Press Co.

Hacker, Jacob S., and Paul Pierson. 2010. *Winner-Take-All Politics*. New York: Simon and Schuster.

Lessig, Lawrence. 2011. *Republic Lost: How Money Corrupts Congress – and a Plan to Stop It*. New York: Twelve.

Lindstedt, Catharina, and Daniel Naurin. 2010. "Transparency Is Not Enough: Making Transparency Effective in Reducing Corruption." *International Political Science Review* 31(3): 301–322.

Mansbridge, Jane. 2003. "Rethinking Representation." *American Political Science Review* 97(4): 515–527.

———. 2009. "A 'Selection Model' of Political Representation." *Journal of Political Philosophy* 17(4): 369–398.

———. 2011. "Clarifying Political Representation." *American Political Science Review* 105(3): 621–630.

———. 2012. "On the Importance of Getting Things Done." APSA James Madison Lecture. *P.S.: Political Science and Politics* 45(1): 1–8.

———. 2014. "A Contingency Theory of Accountability." In *Oxford Handbook of Public Accountability*, eds. Robert Goodin and Thomas Schillemans. Oxford: Oxford University Press.

Mansbridge, Jane, and Cathie Jo Martin, eds. 2013. *Negotiating Agreement in Politics*. Washington, DC: American Political Science Association.

Martin, Cathy Jo. 2013. "Conditions for Successful Negotiation: Lessons from Europe." In *Negotiating Agreement in Politics*, eds. Jane Mansbridge and Cathie Jo Martin. Washington, DC: American Political Science Association: 121–143.

Mayhew, David R. 1974. *Congress: The Electoral Connection*. New Haven: Yale University Press.

Miller, Warren E. and Donald E. Stokes. 1963. "Constituency Influence in Congress." *American Political Science Review* 51(1): 45–56.

Putnam, Robert D. 1988. "Diplomacy and Domestic Politics: The Logic of Two-Level Games." *International Organization* 42(3): 427–460.

Warren, Mark E., and Jane Mansbridge, with André Bächtiger, Maxwell A. Cameron, Simone Chambers, John Ferejohn, Alan Jacobs, Jack Knight, Daniel Naurin, Melissa Schwartzberg, Yael Tamir, Dennis Thompson, and Melissa Williams. 2013. "Deliberative Negotiation." In *Negotiating Agreement in Politics*, eds. Jane Mansbridge and Cathie Jo Martin. Washington, DC: American Political Science Association: 86–120.

20

Staying Private

George C. Edwards III

The challenges of governing have rarely been greater. The distance between the parties in Congress and between identifiers with the parties among the public is the greatest in a century. The public accords Congress the lowest approval ratings in modern history, but activists allow its members little leeway to compromise. The inability of Congress and the president to resolve critical problems results in constant crises in financing the government; endless debate over immigration, health care, environmental protection, and other crucial issues; and a failure to plan effectively for the future.

GOING PUBLIC

Modern presidents invest heavily in leading the public in the hope of leveraging public support to win backing in Congress (Edwards 1983, 2004; Kernell 2007). They adopt this strategy for governing at least partly in an attempt to create political capital to overcome the impediments to achieving their policy goals. Highly polarized politics only increases the difficulty of hurdling those obstacles. Nevertheless, there is overwhelming evidence that presidents, even "great communicators," rarely move the public in their direction. Indeed, the public often moves *against* the position the president favors (Edwards 2004, 2007, 2009, 2012).

Presidents not only fail to create opportunities for change by going public but their efforts at persuading the public also may increase public polarization and thus decrease their chances of success in governing. When political leaders take their cases directly to the public, they have to accommodate the limited attention spans of the public and the availability of space on television. Cable television does not offer the president more opportunities to speak directly to the nation. Cable stations are no more eager than the traditional networks to give up to the White House expensive time slots for which they receive no compensation. Moreover, the audiences for cable news programs are small. The internet does offer the president the opportunity to stream videos to viewers, but true believers, those already supporting the president, make up most of the audience for those videos.

As a result, the president and his opponents often reduce choices to stark black-and-white terms. When leaders frame issues in such terms, they typically frustrate rather than facilitate coalition building. It is difficult to compromise on such positions, which hardens negotiating positions as both sides posture as much to mobilize an intense minority of supporters as to convince the other side.

Governing by campaigning is anti-deliberative. Campaigning focuses on persuasion, mobilization, competition, conflict, and short-term victory. Campaigns are waged in either/or terms. Conversely, governing involves deliberation, cooperation, negotiation, and compromise over an extended period. Campaigns prosecute a cause among adversaries rather than deliberate courses of action among collaborators. Campaign communications are designed to win rather than to educate or learn. Thus, the incentives for leaders are to stay on message rather than to engage with opponents and to frame issues rather than inform their audience about anything in detail (Brady and Fiorina 2000; Heclo 2000; Ornstein and Mann 2000).

In the permanent campaign, political leaders do not look for ways to insulate controversial or difficult policy decisions from their vulnerability to demagoguery and oversimplification. Campaigning requires projecting self-assurance rather than admitting ignorance or uncertainty about complex issues; it calls for counterattacking and switching the subject rather than struggling with tough questions. It is better to have a campaign issue for the next election than deal with that issue by governing. Thus, the more campaigning infiltrates into governing, the more we should expect the values of a campaign perspective to dominate over values of deliberation.

Governing by campaigning too often revolves around destroying enemies rather than producing legislative products broadly acceptable to the electorate. The tendencies are for civility to lose out to conflict, compromise to deadlock, deliberation to sound bites, and legislative product to campaign issues. Moreover, frightening people about the evils of the opposition is often the most effective of raising the funds necessary to run a permanent campaign. Such scare tactics encourage ideologically charged and harsh attacks on opponents while discouraging the comity necessary for building coalitions.

When presidents launch aggressive public promotions for their policies and themselves, they invite opponents to challenge them. Business and professional associations use paid advertising, orchestrate events to attract press coverage, and finance think tanks to offer analyses that can serve as sources for reporters and editorial writers seeking to "balance" the administration's case (Smith 2000). Public campaigns to propel health reform into law by Bill Clinton and Barack Obama, for instance, provoked wide-ranging and expensive counter-mobilizations by business associations, the insurance industry, and others threatened by reform (West and Loomis 1999; Jacobs and Shapiro 2000; Jacobs and Skocpol 2012). The effect was to trigger motivated reasoning and thus activate existing conservative attitudes and partisan beliefs among Republicans, which helped produce and reinforce sharp partisan differences in support for the Affordable Care Act (Jacobs and Mettler 2011; Strickland, Taber, and Lodge 2011).

The president and opposition elites provide cues to members of the public predisposed to support them that serve to short-circuit their reasoning processes, trigger motivated reasoning, and thus shape how they process information, including largely ignoring arguments from the opposition (see Druckman, Peterson, and Slothuus 2013).

Partisan identification is a primary anchor of political behavior (Green, Palmquist, and Schickler 2002) and the basis for much motivated reasoning. Partisan leanings significantly influence perceptions of conditions and policies, as well as their interpretations and responses to politics. Even the most basic facts are often in contention between adherents of the parties. Individuals interpret a policy, ranging from war to the budget deficit, in light of existing opinions concerning the policy's sponsor (Druckman and Bolsen 2011). Thus, "when partisan elites debate an issue and the news media cover it, partisan predispositions are activated in the minds of citizens and subsequently constrain their policy preferences" (Dancey and Goren 2010, 686). In times of highly polarized politics, the incentive to be loyal to one's own group and to maximize differences with the outgroup is likely be especially strong (Smith, Terry, Crosier, and Duck 2005; Nicholson 2012).

It is not surprising that party cues influence opinion (Bullock 2011) and that polarized environments decrease the impact of substantive information, intensify the impact of party endorsements on opinions, and, ironically, stimulate greater confidence in those – less substantively grounded – opinions. Under conditions of high polarization, when presented with opposing frames, regardless of their strength, partisans' opinions move only in the direction of the frame endorsed by their party (Druckman, Peterson, and Slothuus 2013).[1] Moreover, when individuals engage in strong partisan-motivated reasoning, they develop increased confidence in their opinions. Thus, they are

---

[1] Party endorsements, particularly under conditions of polarization, do not appear to simply serve as cues people follow. Instead, cues seem to shape how the public views arguments put forth by different sides.

less likely to consider alternative positions and more likely to take action based on their opinions, such as attempting to persuade others (Visser, Bizer, and Krosnick 2006).

The recent debate over immigration reform is instructive regarding the prospects for backlash against the president. Republican antipathy for President Obama is so great that he has had to avoid proposing his own immigration bill (Lizza 2013, 48–49; Wilson and Goldfarb 2013; see also Woodward 2012, 255–256; Shear 2013), because doing so makes it more difficult for Republican members of Congress to support reform. Because Republicans in Congress come from solidly Republican states or districts, it is easier for them to support an immigration bill that also happens to be supported by Obama and the Democratic leadership than to back a bill so popularly identified with the other side. As President Obama said of Republicans, "their base thinks that compromise with me is somehow a betrayal" (News Conference by the President 2013).

A "YIELDING AND ACCOMMODATING SPIRIT"

The framers created a deliberative democracy that requires and encourages reflection and refinement of the public's views through an elaborate decision-making process. Those opposed to change need only win at one point in the policy-making process – say in obtaining a presidential veto – whereas those who favor change must win every battle along the way. To win all these battles usually requires the support of a sizable majority of the country, not just a simple majority of 51%. As a result, the Madisonian system calls for moderation and compromise.

The principal mechanism for overcoming the purposefully inefficient form of government established by the Constitution is the extra-constitutional institution of political parties. Representatives and senators of the president's party are almost always the nucleus of coalitions supporting the president's programs. Thus, parties help overcome the fractures of shared powers. Yet, unless one party controls both the presidency and Congress and has very large majorities in both houses of Congress, little is likely to be accomplished without compromise.

When parties are broad, there is potential for compromise because there will be some ideological overlap among members of the two parties. When the parties are unified and polarized, however, they exacerbate conflict and immobilize the system. Critical issues such as immigration, taxation, and budgeting go unresolved.

We expect political parties in a parliamentary system to take clear stands and vigorously oppose each other. Such a system usually works because the

executive comes from the legislature and can generally rely on a supportive majority to govern. Partisan polarization has given the United States
parliamentary-style political parties operating in a system of shared powers, virtually guaranteeing gridlock. Moreover, minorities that want to stop
change are likely to win, raising troubling questions about the nature of our
democracy.

For the system to work, then, requires a favorable orientation toward compromise. Recalling the events of the Philadelphia Constitutional Convention,
James Madison observed that "the minds of the members were changing"
throughout the convention, in part due to a "yielding and accommodating
spirit" that prevailed among the delegates (Farrand 1966, 578–579). This spirit
is at risk when people sort themselves into enclaves in which their views are
constantly and stridently reaffirmed.

How, then, can the president encourage an "accommodating spirit" among
opposition members of Congress?

STAYING PRIVATE

In the absence of favorable party configurations in Congress, and lacking the
ability to use public opinion to pressure legislators, presidents should consider
an alternative strategy to going public. At the core of this strategy is quiet
negotiations – the opposite of going public, or what I term "staying private."

It is no secret that negotiations are best done in private. James Madison
remembered that, in writing the Constitution,

> It was ... best for the convention for forming the Constitution to sit with
> closed doors, because opinions were so various and at first so crude that
> it was necessary they should be long debated before any uniform system
> of opinion could be formed. Meantime the minds of the members were
> changing.... Had the members committed themselves publicly at first, they
> would have afterwards supposed consistency required them to maintain their
> ground, whereas by secret discussion no man felt himself obliged to retain his
> opinions any longer than he was satisfied of their propriety and truth, and was
> open to the force of argument. Mr. Madison thinks no Constitution would
> ever have been adopted by the convention if the debates had been public
> (Farrand 1966, 578–579).

The same principles of successful negotiation hold more than two centuries
later. Examples of the White House and Congress strategically engaging in
quiet negotiations to produce important legislation include the Clean Air Act
Amendments of 1990, the budget agreement of 1990, and the No Child Left
Behind Act of 2001. Polarization, of course, is even greater now than it was

during the Bush presidencies, which should encourage the president to be all the more open to alternative strategies for governing.

The Balanced Budget Act of 1997 provides an especially telling illustration. The residue of first-term budget battles – and of the ensuing fall 1996 elections, in which Democrats tarred Republicans as Medicare killers – was a deep bitterness that seemed likely to poison the relationship indefinitely between the Clinton White House and Congress. Yet within a few months both sides reached an historic agreement on achieving a balanced budget within five years.

There was a dramatic shift from the rancorous partisan warfare that had dominated the consideration of the budget in the 104th Congress. Low-keyed, good-faith negotiations began shortly after the president submitted his FY 1998 budget, and senior White House officials held a series of private meetings with members of Congress. Unlike the political posturing in late 1995 and early 1996, *neither side focused on moving the negotiations into the public arena.*

Staying private made it easier for both sides to compromise, and they each gained from doing so. For Republicans, the budget agreement capped a balanced-budget and tax-cutting drive that had consumed them since they had taken over Congress in 1995. They won tax and spending cuts, a balanced budget in five years, and a plan to keep Medicare solvent for another decade. Thus, although they did not achieve a radical overhaul of entitlement programs, they did make substantial progress toward their core goals.

For Clinton, the budget agreement represented perhaps his greatest legislative triumph. He left the bargaining table with much of what he wanted, including an increased scope for the child tax credit, a new children's health initiative, restoration of welfare benefits for disabled legal immigrants, increased spending for food stamps, and a host of other incremental increases in social spending.

These compromises did not satisfy everyone, of course. Clinton had to walk a fine line between compromising with Republicans and maintaining the support of Democratic liberals, who did not like budgetary constraints and did not want to hand the Republicans a positive accomplishment. Some Democrats were upset that they were not included in the negotiating process. Similarly, Republican leaders had to deal with die-hard conservatives, who did not want to compromise at all with the president.

The decision of President Clinton and the Republican congressional leaders to seize on the opportunity provided by the surging economy and the groundwork laid by the budgets of 1990 and 1993 and to quietly negotiate and compromise, letting everyone claim victory, made the budget agreement possible. In addition, the success of these executive-legislative negotiations paved the way for additional talks of a similar nature on Social Security and Medicare that may have ultimately proved fruitful if it were not for the confounding influence of the impeachment inquiry in 1998.

Why would the White House attempt to stay private in the face of inflammatory provocations from the opposition? There are two good reasons. First, going public does not work. Second, if elites can make deals, the public is likely to reward them for doing so. Although the polarization we see in Washington has its roots in local elections and constituency politics (Jacobson 2013), the public is less polarized than its elected representatives (Abramowitz 2010; Fiorina 2011). Moreover, it wants elected officials to compromise, as we saw in the Gallup (October 14–15), Pew (October 3–6), and CBS News (October 1–2) polls taken around the time of the 2013 government shutdown.

"Staying private" will not change the electoral incentives to defeat opponents. Nor will it narrow the ideological differences between the parties or produce unified government. However, staying private *is* likely to contribute to reducing gridlock, incivility, and public cynicism and thus deserves a more prominent role in the president's strategic arsenal.

CAVEATS

The White House will not unilaterally disarm in the face of virulent criticism. Presidents will sometimes conclude that they must go public just to maintain the status quo. Maintaining preexisting support or activating those predisposed to back him can be crucial to a president's success. Consolidating core backers may require reassuring them as to his fundamental principles, strengthening their resolve to persist in a political battle, or encouraging them to become more active on behalf of a candidacy or policy proposal. When offered competing views, people are likely to respond according to their predispositions, so the White House will act to reinforce the predispositions of its supporters.

Nevertheless, promotion of policies and reaction to criticism can take a wide range of forms. It is possible to assert values and policies without incendiary rhetoric, and it is not necessary to begin negotiations with the other party by excoriating its elected officials in a cross-national speaking tour.

An additional complication to staying private is the willingness of both parties to make policy and to compromise to do it. Some members of Congress have adopted the approach to policy making of relentless confrontation (Theriault 2008, 2013). In addition, Republicans' preferred position is often to do nothing. Moreover, Republicans in public, especially activist Tea Party Republicans, are much less likely than Democrats or independents to support compromise on policy issues according to polling data (Pew Research Center poll, January 9–13, 2013; Gallup, September 5–8, 2013); see Rapoport, Dost, Lovell, and Stone (2013). We experienced a taste of this inflexibility during a Republican presidential primary debate in Ames, Iowa, on August 11, 2011, when every candidate rejected the notion of a budget deal that would include tax increases even if accompanied by spending cuts 10 times as large.

When the default position of failure to negotiate is unacceptable, as in the fiscal cliff issue at the end of 2012, the parties are likely to negotiate (see Edwards 2013). If the president offers the other party something it likes, as in George W. Bush's funding of community clinics and programs to combat AIDS in Africa, the opposition may well offer its support. Not always, however.

A president's willingness to make policy concessions to the opposition party will not alter the fact that the intense competition over control of the presidency and Congress has increased the incentives to engage in partisan warfare. The differences between the parties and the cohesion within them on floor votes are typically greater when the president takes a stand on issues. When the president adopts a position, members of his party have a stake in his success, whereas opposition party members have a stake in the president losing. Moreover, both parties take cues from the president that help define their policy views, especially when the lines of party cleavage are not clearly at stake nor already well established (Lee 2009, 2013; see also Mann and Ornstein 2012).

Further complicating the process of compromise is the lack of trust between the parties, a product of highly confrontational polarized politics. For years, officials on both sides of the aisle have known that one way to make a dent in the long-term problem of financing Social Security is adjusting the way we measure increases in the cost of living. Within hours of the president's supporting such an adjustment in his budget, some Republicans, including the chair of the House Republican Campaign Committee, were claiming he wanted to balance the budget on the backs of seniors – the Democrat's worst nightmare.

CONCLUSION

The incapacity to govern in the face of an urgent need to do so is a problem that deserves our attention. Staying private will not solve all the problems resulting from our polarized politics. In some instances, however, it can increase the chances of bridging the polarization gap and reaching essential compromises on public policy.

References

Abramowitz, Alan I. 2010. *The Disappearing Center*. New Haven: Yale University Press.

Brady, David, and Morris Fiorina. 2000. "Congress in the Era of the Permanent Campaign." In *The Permanent Campaign and Its Future*, eds. Norman Ornstein and Thomas Mann. Washington, DC: American Enterprise Institute and Brookings Institution: 134–161.

Bullock, John G. 2011. "Elite Influence on Public Opinion in an Informed Electorate." *American Political Science Review* 105(3): 496–515.

Dancey, Logan, and Paul Goren. 2010. "Party Identification, Issue Attitudes, and the Dynamics of Political Debate." *American Journal of Political Science* 54(3): 686–699.

Druckman, James N., and Toby Bolsen. 2011. "Framing, Motivated Reasoning, and Opinions about Emergent Technologies." *Journal of Communication* 61(4): 659–668.

Druckman, James N., Erik Peterson, and Rune Slothuus. 2013. "How Elite Partisan Polarization Affects Public Opinion Formation." *American Political Science Review* 107 (February 2013): 57–79.

Edwards III, George C. 1983. *The Public Presidency*. New York: St. Martin's.

———. 2004. *On Deaf Ears: The Limits of the Bully Pulpit*. New Haven: Yale University Press.

———. 2007. *Governing by Campaigning: The Politics of the Bush Presidency*. 2nd edition. New York: Longman.

———. 2009. *The Strategic President: Persuasion and Opportunity in Presidential Leadership*. Princeton: Princeton University Press.

———. 2012. *Overreach: Leadership in the Obama Presidency*. Princeton: Princeton University Press.

———. 2013. "Persuasion Is Not Power." Presented at the Annual Meeting of the American Political Science Association, Chicago.

Farrand, Max, ed. 1966. "CCCLXVII, Jared Sparks: Journal, April 19, 1830." In *The Records of the Federal Convention of 1787*, vol. III, rev. ed. New Haven: Yale University Press: 578–579.

Fiorina, Morris P., with Samuel J. Abrams and Jeremy C. Pope. 2011. *Culture Wars? The Myth of Polarized America*. 3rd edition. New York: Pearson Longman.

Green, Donald P., Bradley Palmquist, and Eric Schickler. 2002. *Partisan Hearts and Minds*. New Haven: Yale University Press.

Heclo, Hugh. 2000. "Campaigning and Governing: A Conspectus." In *The Permanent Campaign and Its Future*, eds. Norman Ornstein and Thomas Mann. Washington, DC: American Enterprise Institute and Brookings Institution: 1–37.

Jacobs, Lawrence R., and Suzanne Mettler. 2011. "Why Public Opinion Changes: The Implications for Health and Health Policy." *Journal of Health Policy, Politics and Law* 36(6): 917–933.

Jacobs, Lawrence R., and Robert Y. Shapiro. 2000. *Politicians Don't Pander: Political Manipulation and the Loss of Democratic Responsiveness*. Chicago: University of Chicago Press.

Jacobs, Lawrence R., and Theda Skocpol. 2012. *Health Care Reform and American Politics*, rev. ed. New York: Oxford University Press.

Jacobson, Gary C. 2013. "Partisan Polarization in American Politics: A Background Paper." *Presidential Studies Quarterly* 43(4): 688–708.

Kernell, Samuel. 2007. *Going Public: New Strategies of Presidential Leadership*. 4th edition. Washington, DC: CQ Press.

Lee, Frances E. 2009. *Beyond Ideology: Politics, Principles, and Partisanship in the U.S. Senate*. Chicago: University of Chicago Press.

———. 2013. "Presidents and Party Teams: The Politics of Debt Limits and Executive Oversight, 2001–2013." *Presidential Studies Quarterly* 43(4): 775–791.

Lizza, Ryan. 2013. "Getting to Maybe: Inside the Gang of Eight's Immigration Deal." *New Yorker*, June 24.

Mann, Thomas E., and Norman J. Ornstein. 2012. *It's Even Worse than It Looks*. New York: Basic Books.

News Conference by the President. 2013. White House, April 30. Retrieved from www.whitehouse.gov/the-press-office/2013/04/30/news-conference-president.

Nicholson, Stephen P. 2012. "Polarizing Cues." *American Journal of Political Science* 56(4): 52–66.

Ornstein, Norman J., and Thomas E. Mann. 2000. "Conclusion: The Permanent Campaign and the Future of American Democracy." In *The Permanent Campaign and Its Future*, eds. Norman Ornstein and Thomas Mann. Washington, DC: American Enterprise Institute and Brookings Institution: 291–334.

Rapoport, Ronald B., Meredith Dost, Ani-Rae Lovell, and Walter J. Stone. 2013. "Republican Factionalism and Tea Party Activists." Presented at the Annual Meeting of the Midwest Political Science Association, Chicago.

Shear, Michael D. 2013. "Difficult Spot for Obama on Immigration Push." *New York Times*, July 11.

Smith, Joanne R., Deborah J. Terry, Timothy R. Crosier, and Julie M. Duck. 2005. "The Importance of the Relevance of the Issue to the Group in Voting Intentions." *Basic and Applied Social Psychology* 27(2): 163–170.

Smith, Mark. 2000. *American Business and Political Power: Public Opinion, Elections, and Democracy*. Chicago: University of Chicago Press.

Strickland, April A., Charles S. Taber, and Milton Lodge. 2011. "Motivated Reasoning and Public Opinion." *Journal of Health Politics, Policy and Law* 36(6): 935–944.

Theriault, Sean M. 2008. *Party Polarization in Congress*. New York: Cambridge University Press.

———. 2013. *The Gingrich Senators: The Roots of Partisan Warfare in Congress*. New York: Oxford University Press.

Visser, Penny S., George Y. Bizer, and Jon A. Krosnick. 2006. "Exploring the Latent Structure of Strength-Related Attitude Attributes." In *Advances in Experimental Social Psychology* 38, ed. Mark P. Zanna. San Diego: Academic Press: 1–67.

West, Darrel, and Burdett Loomis. 1999. *The Sound of Money: How Political Interests Get What They Want*. New York: W. W. Norton.

Wilson, Scott, and Zachary A. Goldfarb. 2013. "With Domestic Legacy in Lawmakers' Hands, Obama Considers His Options." *New York Times*, April 13.

Woodward, Bob. 2012. *The Price of Politics*. New York: Simon & Schuster.

Index

CPSIA information can be obtained
at www.ICGtesting.com
Printed in the USA
LVHW051936040719
623089LV00016B/336/P

9 781107 451919